An Introduction to

Criminal Justice

CHARLES D. EDELSTEIN

Director of Judicial Administration Program
University of Southern California, Los Angeles

ROBERT J. WICKS

Clinical Senior Instructor
College of Allied Health Professions
Hahnemann Medical College
Philadelphia, Pennsylvania

GREGG DIVISON/McGRAW-HILL BOOK COMPANY

New York
St. Louis
Dallas
San Francisco
Auckland
Bogotá

Düsseldorf
Johannesburg
London
Madrid
Mexico
Montreal
New Delhi
Panama

Paris
São Paulo
Singapore
Sydney
Tokyo
Toronto

Library of Congress Cataloging in Publication Data

Edelstein, Charles D
  An introduction to criminal justice.

  Bibliography: p. 245.
  Includes index.
  1. Criminal justice, Administration of—United
States. I. Wicks, Robert J., joint author.
II. Title.
HV9471.E33   364'.973   76-47635
ISBN 0-07-018980-3

The case studies in this book were prepared by *James Edward Keogh.*

The cover illustration was photographed by *Tracy A. Glasner.*
The photograph on page 8 was supplied by *The Granger Collection.*
The photographs on pages 184, 190, 195, 199, 200, 211, and 225 were
supplied by the *New York City Department of Corrections.*

An Introduction to Criminal Justice

1 2 3 4 5 6 7 8 9 0 DODO 7 8 3 2 1 0 9 8 7 6

The editors for this book were *Susan H. Munger* and *Susan L.
Schwartz,* the designer was *Tracy A. Glasner,* the art supervisor was *George T. Resch,* and the production supervisor
was *Regina R. Malone.* It was set in Garamond by *Holmes
Composition Service.*

contents

foreword

The American criminal justice system has long been subject to criticism. Wicks and Edelstein use this volume to identify and urge correction of deficiencies in the system in a unique manner: They address the critical issue of standards for improving the system. The authors do not attempt to provide all the answers; they do, however, identify many of the significant questions.

It is clear that the phenomena of crime have generated a number of myths. We "know" many things which may not be true at all. For example, we "know" that the crime rate is rising, that the middle class is most often victimized, and that correctional efforts at rehabilitation are failures. This text challenges some of our "knowledge"—data are provided to substantiate or refute that which we "know."

Crime and the agencies that administer justice do not exist apart from society. Neither do these agencies operate independently from one another despite autonomous budgets. It is essential that the justice system be understood as a system and that it be seen as a social control mechanism of the society that created and sustains it. The system orientation, which sequentially deals with law enforcement, the judicial process, and corrections, enriches and contributes to the reader's understanding of criminal justice.

A dozen years have passed since the President's Commission on Law Enforcement and Administration of Justice published *The Challenge of Crime in a Free Society.* During these years a variety of texts and anthologies on crime and criminal justice have been published, and they are of distinctly uneven quality. This volume is superior for it was designed carefully and introduces a broad range of topics in appropriate order, as well as providing a selected bibliography as a resource for those readers who seek to study particular subject matter in greater depth.

This volume is not merely lists of data. Rather, it contains articulate and reasoned judgments about the data, translated into theoretical and policy issues. Readers will note the dilemmas inherent in the American criminal justice system. They will be pressed to agree or disagree with varying positions from both philosophical and operational perspectives. The volume will challenge; it will also reward.

Robert M. Carter
Professor of Public Administration
University of Southern California

preface

An Introduction to Criminal Justice is a beginning-level text that gives students an overview of the American system of criminal justice. We have described in separate parts each of the subsystems—law enforcement, the courts, and the correctional system—and we have also attempted to provide an overall conceptual framework which will encouarge students to take a greater interest in how the system works. We have avoided an extremely detailed description of the structure and procedures of the system for two reasons: structure and procedures change from year to year, and they vary from state to state. The instructor should feel free to supplement the course with materials that meet his or her individual needs and requirements.

There are several unique features to this introductory text which we would like to point out. We take a critical stance by asking pertinent questions on the effectiveness of the criminal justice system and by discussing specific problems and issues. End-of-chapter discussion questions are included to further encourage students to actively participate in the course. Another feature of the book is the inclusion of the case studies, which serve to illustrate with realistic examples how the criminal justice system actually works on a day-to-day basis. And lastly, rather than taking a strictly procedural approach, we have talked about some of the sociological, psychological, and historical forces that influence our criminal justice systems.

The glossary is a handy reference tool, and the reports and excerpts from primary sources at the end of the book provide material for people who wish to investigate further the roots of the American system of justice.

Our system of criminal justice is neither perfect nor totally indefensible. It represents the efforts of many dedicated men and women to do their best to realize the ideals upon which the United States was founded. To these good people, many of whom have been our teachers on the job and in the classroom, we dedicate this volume.

Charles D. Edelstein
Robert J. Wicks

part 1

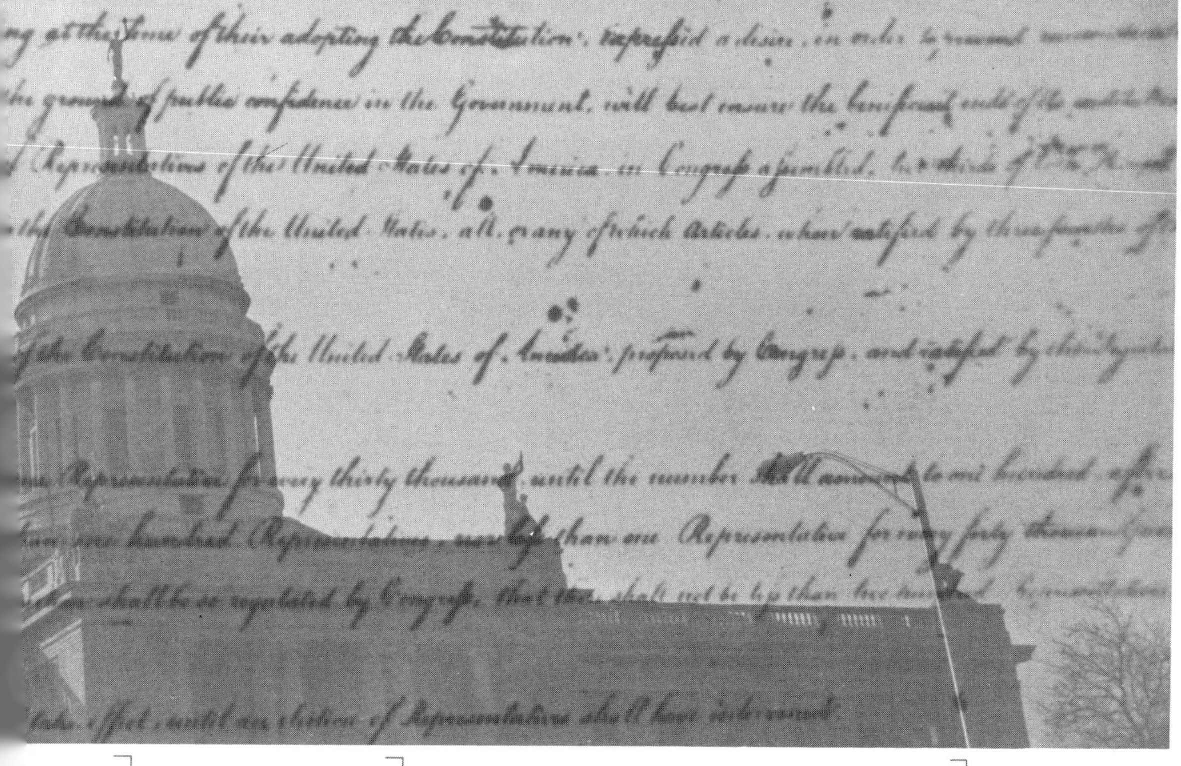

background

Our criminal justice system did not spring upon us fully formed. It has been developing continuously and is still doing so. The next several pages examine this development, with special emphasis on law enforcement and corrections.

COLONIAL CRIMINAL JUSTICE—TO 1784

The first colonists came to America bringing with them the system of justice they had known in England. However, they had to adapt it to fit the harsh environment of the New World. They also had to adjust it to the small settlements which were struggling to survive, often against tremendous odds. Early American justice was essentially rough justice. Jamestown, Virginia, for example, had a code of conduct, called Dale's Law, that made the theft of food a capital crime. This was necessary because of the tragic effect the theft of food could have during the severe winters.

Colonial American justice had strong religious overtones. Some Puritan communities blended civil and religious rules of conduct. They came up with laws against gossiping, blasphemy, and lateness to church. Punishment was harsh and public. Stocks, ducking stools, and pillories were common sights in colonial communities.

For more than a century criminal justice was largely a community effort. Citizens volunteered when protection was needed and elders served as judges. In 1631 in Boston the first formal night watch was formed. Boston was a growing town full of individuals who had come to the New World to find religious liberty and the freedom to work. The job of guarding became the responsibility of its inhabitants.

The character and development of criminal justice differed in various parts of the colonies. Unlike Boston, many Southern communities were founded by members of the English aristocracy. The responsibilities of government and the dispensation of justice fell to this socially elite group.

Despite differences between one locale and another, one fact was true almost everywhere in the thirteen original states. Criminal justice was an informal system. There was nothing like the scope of the

Criminal Justice in American History

innumerable casebooks and procedures that we are accustomed to today. This informality carried our young country through the Revolutionary war. Then followed a period that was shaken with other kinds of social and political change.

THE POST-REVOLUTIONARY PERIOD—1785 TO 1829

The Revolution had left America in a state of economic upheaval. Many well-to-to and well-educated British loyalists left the country. They took away a stabilizing influence from communities badly in need of order and social control. Public officials soon discovered that volunteer citizen guards could not keep up with the challenges of the post-Revolutionary period.

Boston continued to be a leader in law enforcement reform. In 1785 it appointed the country's first detectives. In 1801 it became the first city to pass a law requiring a permanent, paid night watch. The young federal government, too, took note of the growing need for an effective system of justice. It appointed the first federal police officer, a U.S. marshal, in 1789. In that year, too, Congress created the Supreme Court, which fourteen years later would decide the case of *Marbury v. Madison (1803)*. This was to establish the principle of judicial review, a concept which was to ensure the Supreme Court's own dominance. (*Judicial review* is the right of the Court to determine whether a legislative or executive action violates the Constitution. It gives the Court the right to nullify an action that does.) With Boston leading the rest of the country, there were now formal law enforcement agencies. Still, the officers usually dressed in civilian clothes, were unarmed, and were residents of the neighborhoods they policed. While they may not have been loved by the citizenry, they were not disliked or feared, either. By and large they were viewed as people doing an essential social job, and they themselves found it congenial work.

Changes were taking place, too, in the field of corrections. Ducking stools and stocks of the colonial period remained, but efforts were made to find more civilized forms of punishment. While more humane methods were the goal, the result was no less cruel and no more effective.

In 1787 confinement replaced public punishment as the principal means of treating wrongdoers. In Philadelphia the Quakers established the Walnut Street Jail and the Philadelphia Society for Alleviating the Miseries of Public Prisons. These led to what was later called the *Pennsylvania system*, a program of pure solitary confinement where prisoners would do nothing but reflect on their wrongdoing and repent.

The idea of solitary confinement was slow to die, although it consistently broke the spirits of those imprisoned. In the 1820s the Western Penitentiary (Pittsburgh) and the Eastern Penitentiary (Cherry Hill) were both built for solitary confinement. However, eventually a program with a religious orientation began to replace workless isolation in Pennsylvania. This program called for eight to ten hours of handicraft a day.

In 1819 an alternative to the Pennsylvania system was developed at the New York State prison at Auburn. The governing principle there was the *congregate method*. This system of control allowed prisoners to work together. However, it required them to maintain total silence, and they were confined to small, separate cells at night.

Auburn's administrator was the infamous warden Elam Lynds, who saw to it that discipline was maintained by administering periodic floggings. Iron control was practiced at all times. Prisoners marched to and from their cells in lockstep. This was a slow shuffle performed with each man's hand on the shoulder of the man in front. The building consisted of tiers of cell blocks all facing inward, thus eliminating both light and fresh air. It was to become the architectural model for many other prisons.

During this post-Revolutionary period groups of citizens with special interests became active in criminal justice. Most were concerned with stamping out sin; they applied pressure for more laws regulating public morals and more vigorous law enforcement. In Boston the New England Watch and Ward Society was formed. People in Baltimore established the Society for the Suppression of Vice and the Society for Promoting Observance of the Lord's Day. In New York a group was formed to protect the city from the evils of sporting events on Sunday. There was a religious flavor to virtually all efforts at social reform. The harshest measures were declared good for the soul.

Through all these assaults on wickedness there ran a thread of condemnation of alcohol. Prohibitionists crusaded with missionary zeal, and although it was to be some time before they had their way, attempts to outlaw alcohol frequently occurred.

THE GROWTH OF URBANISM—1830 TO 1865

A colorful variety of groups agitated for reforms of various sorts, but social reforms rarely stem from good intentions. Rather, they happen as the result of crises. During this period growing cities were faced with growing crime. Clearly, the traditional methods of law enforcement were not equal to control the increasing crime problem.

In the 1820s London experienced unparalleled lawlessness, although hanging was the punishment for over one hundred categories of crime. A new approach was needed, and in 1829 the Home Secretary, Sir Robert Peel, was able to provide it. That year Parliament passed the Metropolitan Police Act. London's police force, dubbed "Bobbies" in Peel's honor, came into being.

This force, which was to serve as the model for American forces, established these principles:

1. The police must be stable, efficient, and organized along military lines.
2. The police must be under government control.
3. The absence of crime will best prove the efficiency of the police.
4. The distribution of crime news is essential.
5. The deployment of police strength both by time and area is essential.
6. No quality is more indispensable to a policeman than a perfect command of temper; a quiet, determined manner has more effect than violent action.
7. Good appearance commands respect.
8. The securing and training of proper persons is at the root of efficiency.
9. Public security demands that every police officer be given a number.
10. Police headquarters should be centrally located and easily accessible to the people.
11. Policemen should be hired on a probationary basis.
12. Police records are necessary to the correct distribution of police strength.[1]

It was some time before Peel's reforms took firm hold in America, but changes were on the way. Again, Boston led the way. In 1838 its night watch was supplemented by a day shift. In the middle of the nineteenth century, that city had as its marshal one of the country's first great police administrators, Francis Tukey. New York followed in 1844, becoming the first American city to adopt Peel's basic organizational principles. It replaced its night watch with a unified municipal police force that worked around the clock.

1. A. C. Germann, Frank D. Day, and Robert R. J. Gallati, *Introduction to Law Enforcement and Criminal Justice* (Springfield, Ill.: Charles C. Thomas, Publisher, 1970), 54.

Different cities tried to meet the problems of sudden growth in different ways. In 1833, Philadelphia was still without formal police. During that year it received from Stephen Gerard a large sum to create a "competent police." Gerard had some definite views about what that meant. He specified that the twenty-four-man force was to be assigned to four districts. Each district was to be run by a superior officer, and night shift officers were to patrol in pairs.

Although the new police force was a success, it was disbanded within two years when Gerard's money ran out. City officials eventually resurrected the Philadelphia Police Department when it became clear that it was a necessity.

Boston, and indeed the whole field of corrections, also benefited from the generosity of a Boston citizen. In 1841 John Augustus, a shoemaker, decided to post bond for a man charged with drunkenness. He took on the responsibility for seeing that the accused returned to court for sentencing. Spurred on by the faith Augustus had shown in him, the defendant vowed to change his ways. He so impressed the judge on his return to court that the usual jail sentence was suspended. That was the start of a career for Augustus in helping other defendants. It also marked the beginning of the probation system in this country.

While this element of humanity was being injected into the courts, the Auburn system had become the dominant approach to corrections. Prisoners in their striped uniforms were forbidden to talk. They were given meager amounts of food and were brutally disciplined for even the most minor infractions of the rules. Isolation in the "hole"—solitary confinement—was frequently used, together with physical punishment. Prisons and their inmates were out of both the sight and the minds of the great majority of the people.

THE POST-CIVIL WAR PERIOD—1866 TO 1899

By the time the Civil War ended, America was rapidly moving toward industrialism. City streets were crowded, for immigrants were arriving in great numbers. The criminal justice system was hard pressed to meet the challenge. Police forces were organized along Peel's lines. Officers for the first time wore distinguished blue uniforms, which were inspired by the clothing of the Union soldiers.

This period saw a fundamental change in American values. The country was being transformed from an agricultural nation to a heavily industrialized, urban society. In this society immigrant groups became powerful political forces. State governments, however, continued to be dominated by rural legislators. The laws which were passed often reflected agrarian, Anglo-Saxon Protestant values.

Since many cities had Irish Catholic and immigrant leadership, conflict was inevitable. Many state laws were underenforced or altogether ignored in urban areas.

Before the Civil War, politics had largely involved well-educated citizens who viewed service to their communities as an obligation. During what Mark Twain sardonically called "this Gilded Age," all that changed. The new immigrant element burst on the political scene, transforming politics from a part-time obligation to a full-time profession. The political "machine" was born, and with it came both social benefits (jobs) and social evils (graft).

The machines controlled the city governments, including the police and the courts. Payrolls were padded and payoffs were collected from contractors. The citizens didn't mind though. "Padded payrolls were better than no payrolls," they said. The graft was "white graft"—from contractors—never the "dirty graft" of bribes from lawbreakers. Immigrants had just fled from places where they had been victims of the grossest discrimination. They saw this as concern for their welfare, and they considered it a great boon. And so the system prospered.

In 1870 a change came about that was to have far-reaching effects in the field of corrections. Out of a convention of prison administrators that year grew the *reformatory concept.* This concept stressed work, a relaxation of discipline, more civilized prison design, improved sanitary facilities, and training programs. The country's first reformatory was built in Elmira, New York, in 1876, and its distinguished superintendent was Zebulon Brockway.

THE PROGRESSIVE ERA—1900 TO 1918

When the twentieth century opened, social and political reformers, appalled at the corruption triggered by industrialism, moved to end the evils. The Progressive Movement took a close look at the exploitation of children who were being used as a cheap source of labor. Child labor laws were passed, and the juvenile court, a distinctly American institution, was established in 1900.

In the past, responsibility for law enforcement had rested chiefly with the local communities. But the invention of the automobile, coupled with labor unrest, prompted state governments to form their own police agencies. These agencies would enforce traffic regulations and break strikes. Labor violence was largely responsible for ending the friendliness that had existed between the police and the public.

The police in many jurisdictions were becoming farther removed in their operations from the communities they served. However,

The Sandusky, Ohio, police force in 1909 was all male and all white. In this respect, Sandusky was typical of most American communities.

some agencies were actually improving their relationships with the public. One was the Berkeley, California, Police Department under Chief August Vollmer. Chief Vollmer was to become one of America's foremost police administrators. Fortunately this has been a recurring phenomenon in law enforcement. Regardless how dismal the state of the art may appear, individuals of stature come along. They demonstrate what law enforcement can be with sound, imaginative leadership.

Trouble, however, lay ahead. In 1919 the Volstead Act was passed. Prohibition had arrived, and with it came organized crime and widespread erosion of respect for the law.

PROHIBITION, THE DEPRESSION, AND WORLD WAR II—1919 TO 1945

Prohibition, or, more precisely, the public's flaunted violation of it, involved rampant corruption. During this period, the difference between "white" and "dirty" graft was blurred and eventually erased. Americans had been deprived of a commodity for which they were willing to pay. Small hoodlum groups rushed to provide it. One such group, the Mafia, grew, prospered, diversified, and began to make its mark on the nation. Police officers, prosecutors, and judges cheerfully conspired to thwart Prohibition. Meanwhile, those who tried to enforce the law found themselves put out of office.

Although corruption was widespread during Prohibition, two administrators appeared who were to mold superior agencies. J. Edgar Hoover was appointed director of the Federal Bureau of Investigation. He proved the worth of well-educated, carefully selected people to a police agency. In 1928 Orlando Winfield Wilson began his eleven years of innovative leadership as Chief of the Wichita Police Department. Wilson earned it the title "West Point of Law Enforcement." Both these men eventually became targets of harsh criticism for failing to keep up with progress in the administration of criminal justice. The fact remains, however, that when each began his work, he was well ahead of everyone else in the field.

During the Depression, gangsterism was at its height. Names like John Dillinger, Pretty Boy Floyd, Baby Face Nelson, Bonnie Parker, and Clyde Barrow became household words. Armed robbery, especially in the Midwest, was common. When local law enforcement authorities seemed powerless to cope with these desperadoes, the federal government moved to fill the void. Federal laws against bank robbery and kidnapping, among others, were passed. When federal laws were broken, the FBI was authorized to act. Armed and eager, it embarked on a campaign of crime-busting which was to make it legendary.

This period saw both good and bad for the administration of criminal justice. Under the leadership of Sanford Bates, the Federal Bureau of Prisons led the way to what was called the "new penology." Alcatraz, built in 1934, was the symbol of this concept. Citizens in the grip of the Depression had little patience with rehabilitation, so prisons became dumping grounds for the unwanted.

However, massive public works programs were started during the Depression. The construction of new jails, courthouses, police stations, and prisons reached unprecedented proportions. Jobs in police work and corrections became attractive to educated people who would not have wanted them in more prosperous times.

SINCE WORLD WAR II—1946 TO THE PRESENT

After the Second World War there was a massive effort to educate the returning veterans. Enrollment in colleges, universities, and junior colleges mushroomed. Educational opportunities for students interested in careers with criminal justice agencies opened up. By and large this was a good thing, but it led to interagency jealousy and competitiveness. A misunderstanding of the larger role of the criminal justice system was widespread within the field.

Furthermore, the professional development of personnel ranged from dismal to superior, depending on level of government and region of the country. For example, law enforcement education in the Southeast and New England lagged behind that in California. At Berkeley, O. W. Wilson was appointed Dean of the School of Criminology at the University of California. It could be said that in this event the foundation of sound criminal justice education in America was laid.

There were promise and potential within the system in the 1950s. Still, it took the shattering riots and rocketing rise in crime of the early 1960s to bring the needed change. These events moved the government to supply the resources necessary to change direction. The rate of crime rose 120 percent in the 1960s. Political assassinations, race riots, and student unrest became all too common. People asked why nothing was being done about all this. What had become of law and order?

Government commissions took criminal justice agencies to task for failing to come to grips with the realities of crime and violence. The police were charged with being unprofessional. They had ignored the basics of public administration. They were grinding along in a perfunctory way, unable to fulfill the expectations of their communities. Court calendars were clogged with cases. Plea bargaining— the arrangement for the accused to plead guilty to a lesser charge and so escape trial—was widespread and uncontrolled. Many judges lacked minimum qualifications. Rehabilitation was the primary goal of corrections, but recidivism, or repetition of crimes by exoffenders, was rampant. The prisons were overflowing, and financial support for penal reform was lacking.

Various groups, notably the President's Commission on Law Enforcement and Criminal Justice, 1967, made recommendations. Out of these came two related developments. First, the Law Enforcement Assistance Administration (LEAA) was created. Second, unprecedented educational opportunities for education in the field of criminal justice were provided. LEAA, an arm of the Department of Justice, began giving millions of dollars to criminal justice agencies which wanted to improve the quality of their service. The Law Enforcement Education Program (LEEP) gave large sums to colleges and universities for criminal justice programs. These new educational programs increased fivefold in five years. They helped bring about a new, integrated approach to the study of the criminal justice system. At last it had begun to be viewed as a single entity made up of interdependent parts.

Summarizing, then, we see that the development of a philosophy of criminal justice has been haphazard, uneven, fragmented. It was interspersed with scandals and corruption and it was interrupted by the intrusion of partisan political influences. But progress is being made. The various subsystems are talking to each other. Although the criminal justice system has much room for improvement, it has come a long way.

QUESTIONS

1. What historical trends can you identify in policing practices? What do you think the trends will be in the future?
2. Answer the same questions as in number 1 above for the correctional system.
3. Do you see any connections between your answers to number 1 and number 2?

Our democratic method of governing ourselves is based on the concept of separate but equal branches of government. The three major divisions, of course, are the legislative, the executive, and the judicial. Each division is independent of but at the same time related to the others. What one branch does may very well affect the operation of one or both of the others. This concept of independent but interrelated segments of government extends throughout its structure. We will consider what that means in terms of the criminal justice system.

First we should define what a system is. The word "system" is applied to a wide variety of things. We speak of the ignition system in a car; the heating system in a house; the railway system in a state; and so on. "System" usually implies a "structure" through which is funneled a process of some sort.

You turn the key on the dashboard of your car. A number of things happen in different parts of the automobile; these result in the motor's starting. That is, the motor starts if all parts of the ignition system are working properly. So there is a further implication in the word "system": the various parts are related to one another. The functioning of one part affects the system's overall efficiency. A good mechanic does not blindly make an adjustment to one part of a car's ignition system. He or she considers the impact the change will have on the rest of that system and working of the whole car. The individual worker may be a specialist in ignition systems and do only one kind of work. Still, that person must know how the process fits into the car's complete operation. It is essentially the same with any system, whether mechanical or social. In social systems it is often very difficult to foresee the overall impact of an adjustment to one part. It is just as difficult to diagnose which part is out of order if the system is not functioning properly.

A system, then, is a structure of interrelated parts through which a process is funneled. Besides the criminal justice system, our government involves many other systems, including the economic, the educational, and the social. Each one of these is related to the others just

Criminal Justice as a System

as the various systems in a car are related. If one suffers a malfunction, the effectiveness of the whole is hurt.

STRUCTURE AND FUNCTION

At this point we leave the analogy with automobiles to concentrate on the criminal justice system itself. We can outline its elements: law enforcement, the judicial branch, and corrections. Each one of these elements is a unit of the overall criminal justice system. At the same time, each one can be considered a system in its own right. Figure 2-1 demonstrates how the criminal justice system fits into the total social system. It also shows the four subsystems of which the social system is composed.

After seeing how the criminal justice system fits into the total system, we should take a look at how it functions. The structure is there to permit a process to take place. So, from the functional point of view, the criminal justice system looks like Figure 2-2.

There is a fourth element, the legislative, with an inactive role in the day-to-day operation of the criminal justice system. The legislative function—a key one—is a sometime thing compared with the round-the-clock nature of the other three elements.

A helpful way to analyze a social agency, institution, or system is to study

1. Its actual and intended products
2. Its processes that produce the actual product
3. The people who work within it
4. The people and groups who influence those who work within it
5. Its structure

In later chapters some agencies within each subsystem of the criminal justice system will be examined in greater detail. We will concentrate on selected states. In the next few pages each of the subsystems of our criminal justice system will be briefly examined.

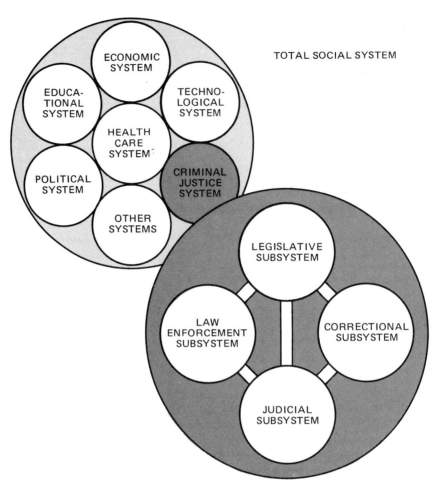

Figure 2-1 The criminal justice system as a part of the total social system.

Legislative Subsystem

The legislative subsystem is not shown on most charts depicting the criminal justice system. Yet the legislative arena is of great importance in the criminal justice system of any state. Legislatures produce many laws that affect the other subsystems within the criminal justice system. They produce the laws that tell us what behavior is forbidden and provide penalties for engaging in prohibited behavior. The existence of a law gives the law enforcement subsystem the authority to apprehend the law violator. Without a specific law prohibiting the behavior, the police cannot legally act. These laws enable the courts to decide guilt or innocence, and the correctional subsys-

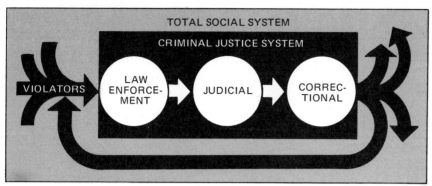

Figure 2-2 The flow of violators through the criminal justice system.

tem to punish or attempt to rehabilitate people. So the functioning of our judicial system all begins with the products of the legislature.

Figure 2-3 presents a very simplified view of a very complex process. The legislative process formally begins with a legislator preparing a proposed law, often called a "bill." A typical bill describes the behavior to be prohibited and the penalty for engaging in such behavior.

After the bill is introduced into the legislature, it is usually sent to a committee. Committees specialize in the consideration of particular kinds of law. In the case of most criminal legislation, the committee on criminal law will consider the bill. Hearings may be held. During these hearings, individuals and groups interested in the bill may give their views. The committee staff may review the bill and make suggestions to committee members. Eventually the committee takes a vote and the bill is accepted or rejected. There are processes

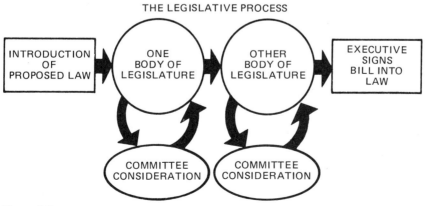

Figure 2-3

that permit consideration of the bill by the legislative body, as a whole despite a negative vote of the committee. Generally, however, a negative vote ends the action for that legislative session. If the committee approves the bill, the legislature itself will consider it and, after some debate, will accept or reject it. Most state legislatures consist of two separate bodies. The smaller one is often called the "Senate," and the larger one is usually called the "House of Representatives" (as in the United States Congress) or the "assembly."

If passed by the legislature, the bill goes to the head of state. The governor (or, for the federal government, the President) may sign the bill or do nothing. In either of these two cases, the law becomes fully effective. The governor (or President) may also veto the bill. After a veto, the legislature can reconsider the law if it wants. If a specified percentage of legislators disagree with a veto, they can override it.

Legislators in the United States are elected by popular vote. The tendency is for legislators to be lawyers or business people. Legislative staffs are usually small compared with the big agencies of the executive branch. It is not unusual for a medium-size city police department to employ more people than the whole legislature of a state. The legislative staff often consists of lawyers, experts on various subjects, public relations personnel, and clerks.

Law Enforcement Subsystem

In Part 3 of this book the process and goals of the law enforcement subsystem are described. Basically, the law enforcement process has these desired goals: to keep the peace, to prevent crime, to apprehend the law violator, and to provide some social services on an emergency basis. Without the law enforcement subsystem, the rest of the criminal justice system cannot perform its functions. Without activity by the police, the courts can do little to exercise power in criminal cases. With but few exceptions, if police don't apprehend violators, there will be no court processing. Legislatures can enact thousands of laws, but if the police fail to act, the law can be violated with impunity.

Despite police patrols and other crime prevention activities, crimes are committed. When a crime is reported by a citizen or discovered by the police, the investigatory phase begins. The investigation may be limited to interviewing the victim or it may call into play detectives and crime laboratory experts. (See Figure 2-4.)

Law enforcement officers these days often have had some college education. They are selected and hired by police departments that seek entrants with a broader range of abilities than in the past. Police

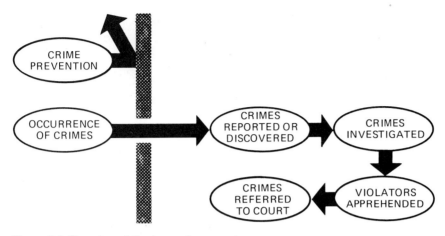

Figure 2-4 Overview of the law enforcement process.

officers are often the sons and daughters of lower middle-class and middle-class parents.

The metropolitan, or city, police department is one of our few social institutions that is open for business twenty-four hours a day, seven days a week. It has radio-equipped cars that cruise the streets, and it is staffed with trained people. At some time we all need police services—the victim of theft, the stranded motorist, the husband and wife in domestic combat. The variety of police activities boggles the mind.

Judicial Subsystem

Part 4 of this text describes the judicial subsystem. Basically, this subsystem determines which of those people apprehended by the police will be processed by the system. Figure 2-5 illustrates this point. The object of its processing is to determine guilt or innocence and to impose or refrain from imposing a penalty. In addition, the courts in our country limit the exercise of power by law enforcement, corrections, and legislative subsystems.

The prosecutor is the person who determines whether an alleged violator will be processed by the judicial subsystem. See Figure 2-5. (An "alleged violator" is a person whom the police have arrested.) To do this, the prosecutor examines the amount and quality of the proof of guilt and the severity of the violation. This is part of the *screening* process.

If the prosecutor feels prosecution is appropriate, formal charges are filed. This act sets the stage for *adjudication*, which now includes many steps prior to the trial. It also includes the trial itself. These

Figure 2-5 Overview of the judicial subsystem's process.

steps are set forth in Part 4 of this book. In the trial process a judge or jury hears the facts, applies the law, and determines guilt or innocence.

The *disposition* of the case answers the question, "What should be done with this person who has been proven guilty?" The options include incarceration, fine, and some restrictions short of actual incarceration (probation).

Judges are either elected by the voters or appointed by a combination of the legislature and the governor. Judges and lawyers have a legal education and frequently come from the middle and upper-middle classes.

The judicial subsystem may be influenced by the news media. It is also affected by its interactions with the law enforcement and correctional subsystems. Witnesses, the accused, jurors, and citizen groups all have an impact upon the processes of our courts.

Correctional Subsystems

In Part 5 of this book, this most recent addition to the criminal justice system is explored. Corrections seeks to rehabilitate the offender so that he or she will not violate the law again. By punishing the offender, it is hoped that other individuals will be deterred from violating the law for even the first time.

There are two basic options in the corrections subsystem, probation and prison. Both involve some restrictions on one's freedom. While on *probation*, the violator may have to report changes of address and work status to the probation officer. He or she may also have to submit to vocational or psychological therapy programs. If the violator is incarcerated, these rehabilitation programs may take place within prison walls.

Prisons are usually classified according to the degree of freedom they permit, ranging from minimum to maximum security. In some situations, the violator may begin serving time in a maximum-security prison and later be placed in a minimum-security institution.

After serving part of the term behind bars, the violator may be placed on *parole*. Parole is much like probation except that it takes

Case Study:
PRETRIAL RELEASE

On October 5, 1976 two police officers in Rockville, New Jersey, were cruising through the community. Recently, several sections of the town had been the targets of burglaries. The officers knew that burglars were difficult to catch. If the police were unable to catch the burglar in the act, there was little if anything the department could do. Therefore, both officers realized they must keep a careful watch.

About ten P.M. in the evening, one of the officers noticed a man standing in the doorway of an unlit house. Having parked the patrol car for a few minutes, the officers kept the suspect under surveillance. Obviously something unusual was happening, and the officers decided to call for a back-up car. They then approached the suspect.

Just as the back-up unit was arriving, the suspect became aware of the two uniformed men walking toward him. Before the officers could identify themselves, the suspect ran around the side of the house and across the back lawns of neighboring houses.

The officers followed quickly. However, even with the back-up patrol, the police were unable to catch the suspect. Procedures had been followed to the letter and nothing the officers could have done would have improved the outcome. Returning to patrol, the officers in both units decided they would continue to check the neighborhood closely.

Just a few hours later, their plan paid off. It appeared that their original burglary suspect was not only inexperienced but also quite stupid. He returned to his position of a few hours before and this time attempted to break into the house. This time the officers were able to make the arrest just as the home owner returned.

The legal process began. During the next two hours, the suspect was booked—fingerprints, photo, and a check with the National Crime Information Network. Then he was sent off to jail to await a hearing. Because of public pressure and a recent court order, the judge had recently decided to hold night court. This enabled anyone arrested to have bail set almost as soon as booking had been completed. Unfortunately, when the officers and the suspect stood before the judge, the only available pertinent information was that the alleged burglar had not jumped bail before. Previous criminal records would not be available until 9 A.M. the following day.

"Fifteen hundred dollars bail," shouted the judge as he banged the gavel.

The suspect made a few phone calls, found enough money to post bail, and was released. The next day, the resident whose house had almost been burglarized by the suspect stopped the officer to report that he had seen the burglar walking down the street. "What are we paying taxes for?" he shouted at the officer.

How would you responsed if you were the officer?

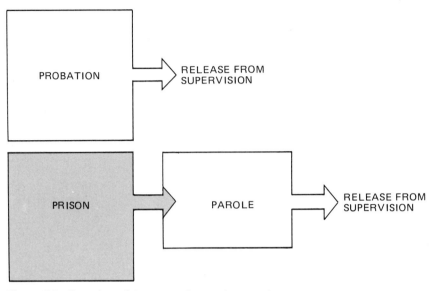

Figure 2-6   Overview of the corrections subsystem's processes.

place after a period of incarceration in the penitentiary. (See Figure 2-6.)

Probation officers are most often college graduates and come from middle-class backgrounds. Prison guards (now called "correctional officers") often have less education and come from the lower-middle and working classes. They are hired by correctional administrators. These administrators typically are appointed by the executive branch of government.

The courts clearly affect the correctional subsystem. Without action by the courts, the correctional system can do very little. The activities of the police, as they relate to probationers and parolees, also affect the workload and functioning of the correctional subsystem.

When the entire criminal justice system is working smoothly, there is a steady flow of action. There is little delay anywhere in the process. No unit should be overburdened, and there should be no bottlenecks along the way. That statement presupposes that each subsystem is in good working order. For that to be true an adequate budget, a good staff, a reasonable caseload, and workable facilities are needed.

However, what happens when one unit in the structure has problems or is out of balance? Assume that the law enforcement subsystem is ticking away nicely and to the satisfaction of public and politicians alike. The judicial unit is also operating smoothly, without a backlog in the calendar and with cases evenly distributed among the judges. The correctional subsystem, however, has run into difficulties. Because of a cutback in funding, there is a shortage of staff in the corrections department. As a result, certain facilities must be closed and the inmates transferred to other prisons. This action leads to overcrowding in the existing facilities. The overcrowding in turn leads to an upsurge in cell-block crime: riots; homosexual rapes; and widespread violence.

In one state the prison system was faced with just such a situation. Its director announced that he was locking the doors of the jails. This was done not only to prevent people from getting out, but also to prevent people from getting in. A situation of this kind cannot exist in a vacuum. It must inevitably be felt by the judicial subsystem. There prosecutors might well respond by dropping charges and judges might react by giving fewer prison sentences.

This judicial reaction will be felt by the law enforcement subsystem. The police, realizing that many arrested are not being sent for trial—are being "let off lightly"—may alter their procedures. At every step in all subsystems, there will be considerable resentment against those forcing the unwanted, undesirable changes.

The chain reaction to the lack of money for corrections will be felt not only in the criminal justice system. It will resound everywhere through reduction in arrests and prosecutions of offenders and through public reaction to the prison disturbances. In this case it might be easy to find the root of the difficulty: a cutback in funds allocated to corrections.

In further examining the theory of interrelationships, it would be useful to study the effect of a less obvious action. We might study in detail a decision made by an obscure unit within a subsystem of the criminal justice system.

A CASE IN POINT

In the following we analyze the far-reaching impact of one apparently minor decision. There will be breakdowns of staff requirements and financial expenditures. These figures have been arranged in Tables 2-1 to 2-5.

The unit we have chosen for our example is the office of the sheriff of High County. High County is a resort section of one of our Southern states with a population of about 1 million people. The sheriff has a staff of 1110, not counting purely administrative and clerical personnel. Of the 1110 people, 1100 are sworn deputies (see Table 2-1). The costs beyond salary that attach to each of the functions performed by the office are analyzed in Table 2-2.

TABLE 2-1   PROFILE OF HIGH COUNTY SHERIFF'S OFFICE

Assignment	Number of officers	Annual arrest rate per deputy	Annual pay rate per deputy
Uniformed patrol deputies	1000	50	$12,000
Homicide-robbery detectives	10	25	15,000
Burglary detectives	20	25	15,000
General-assignment detectives	60	25	15,000
General vice detectives	8	100	15,000
Narcotics enforcement detectives	2	100	15,000
Narcotics laboratory technicians	1	200 (cases)	10,000
General-purpose laboratory technicians	4	200 (cases)	10,000
Property room custodians	5		7,500

TABLE 2-2   SELECTED YEARLY COST FACTORS, HIGH COUNTY SHERIFF'S OFFICE

Assignment	Equipment cost per person	Supervision cost per person	Narcotics purchase costs per person	Fringe benefit costs per person
Burglary	$5000	$3000	$ 0	$3000
Narcotics	6000	3000	2500	3000
Laboratory	5000	2000	0	1000
Property	2000	2000	0	750
Other detectives	5000	3000	0	3000
Uniformed patrol	6000	2500	0	2400

The function of the sheriff's office is a straightforward matter of one, two, three:

1. *In.* Information is received on violations committed.
2. *Processing.* An investigation of the alleged crime is carried out and efforts are made to identify the criminal.
3. *Out.* An arrest is made.

High County shares many of the current problems our society faces: a troubled school system; a high rate of unemployment among the young; and overcrowded or inaccessible recreational facilities. In addition, because of the resort nature of the community, there are some special circumstances. The average age of the population is high, but there are many transients in the fifteen- to twenty-five-year bracket.

The number of drug-related incidents in the county were on the increase. Pressure on the sheriff to deal with the problem was growing. He was coming under attack from press and public alike. It was clear that something would have to be done. A county commission handled the financing of his office. He went to them with a request for more money for additional officers but was turned down.

In this situation there were not many courses of action open to the sheriff short of ignoring the problem. He would have to transfer personnel from other divisions to the narcotics unit. To do this, he took ten detectives each from the burglary and general felony divisions, thereby considerably altering his force's balance. The impact of this decision would be felt throughout the system. In order to see how it could affect each area, we will take them in turn.

Law Enforcement

There might be a dramatic shift in the number of arrests made in the different crime categories. Research reveals that narcotics officers are able to make roughly 100 arrests a year. For detectives in other divisions, the rate is about 25. Therefore, in one year the sheriff's decision could lead to an additional 2000 drug arrests. At the same time there would be a reduction of 500 arrests in the burglary and general felony areas. This is an overall increase of 1500 arrests.

There would be an alteration in the effectiveness of the officers in the now short-handed burglary and general felony divisions. These people would be forced to spread among themselves the workloads normally assumed by the twenty reassigned detectives.

Since drug offenders frequently break other laws, arresting more of these people would cause an overall decline in nondrug crime rates. Or so one might assume. However, increased law enforcement would probably drive up the price of drugs. As a result, heavy users still free would commit more crimes and of a more serious nature to support their habit. In addition, burglars and other criminals who realized that the felony units' efficiency was being stretched would increase their activities.

The impact would also be felt in the crime laboratory. To produce evidence supporting drug abuse charges, new technicians and equipment would be needed for the laboratory work. Furthermore, the great influx of drug offenses would require greater services from the crime laboratory. This would affect its ability to carry on with its work on murder, rape, and other cases.

To handle the increased arrests resulting from the sheriff's decision without impairing the law enforcement units' efficiency will cost $262,250. A projection of the costs is found in Table 2-3.

TABLE 2-3   COST PROJECTION—LAW ENFORCEMENT

EXPENDITURES EACH PERSON

1. 20 narcotics deputies	$ 1,000—equipment 2,500—drug purchased	Total: $ 50,000
2. 10 laboratory analysts	5,000—equipment 2,000—supervision 1,000—fringe benefits 10,000—salary	Total: $180,000
3. 1 property room custodian	2,000—equipment 2,000—supervision 750—fringe benefits 7,500—salary	Total: $ 12,250

TOTAL COST: $262,250

Judicial

The impact on the judicial process will be catastrophic unless new staff is available. Most courts require that offenders be tried within a certain period after arrest. An influx of more than 160 new drug cases each month will jam up the court system within days. With this new burden, it will be difficult to keep the cases flowing. The prosecutor, the public defender, and the judge might have to take steps that would interfere with the administration of justice.

The prosecutor might wish to concentrate on the heavy drug load. To do this she could cut down on the number of other kinds of offenses she wished to bring to trial. Or, in order to dispose of certain cases, she could alter her standards in plea bargaining. (*Plea bargaining* allows the accused to plead guilty to lesser charges rather than stand trial on the original, more serious ones.)

The public defender's office would be swamped with requests to represent those too poor to hire private lawyers. The defender could then alter his standards of the financial test for free legal services.

The judge in turn might strain her own ability to perform her function. She might hear cases late into the night and become too tired to pay proper attention to details. This would increase the chance of a miscarriage of justice. Alternatively, she might simply dismiss a number of cases brought before her in an effort to keep the workload manageable.

Additional costs of the judicial process would be fees paid to private defense lawyers and payments to *bail bonding agents*. (*Bail bonding agents* are those who, for a fee, post bond for a defendant.) The bond permits the defendant to be released pending court ap-

TABLE 2-4   COST PROJECTION—JUDICIAL

EXPENDITURES EACH PERSON

1. Judges $60,000—salary and fringe benefits
  (equivalent to   3,000—supervision
  1½)   2,750—equipment   Total: $65,750
2. Judges' secretary   16,500—salary and fringe benefits
               1,500—equipment   Total: 18,000
3. 4 prosecutors   76,000—salary and fringe benefits
               4,000—equipment
             12,000—supervision   Total: 92,000
4. 2 prosecutors'   20,000—salary and fringe benefits
  secretaries   2,000—equipment
              2,000—supervision   Total: 24,000
5. 4 public defenders 76,000—salary and fringe benefits
               4,000—equipment
             12,000—supervision   Total: 92,000
6. 2 public defenders' 20,000—salary and fringe benefits
  secretaries   2,000—equipment
              2,000—supervision   Total: 24,000
7. Bailiff services   13,500—   Total: 13,500
8. Court clerks (3)   30,000—salary and fringe benefits
               3,000—equipment
             3,000—supervision   Total: 36,000

    Direct court costs: staff and equipment: SUBTOTAL: $365,250.

9. Additional costs for
  a) Private defense lawyers   —$750,000
    for ⅓ of the cases
    brought to court
  b) Private bail bonds   — 75,000
    posted in ⅓ of cases

    All expenditures within Judicial unit: TOTAL: $1,190,250.

pearance. If the defendant fails to appear in court when required, this money is confiscated.) The total projected cost for this subsystem to cope with the new influx of cases is found in Table 2-4. It comes to over 1 million dollars.

Correctional

The effect of the sheriff's decision would be strongly felt in the correctional area. Without adequate prison facilities and additional probation and parole staff, the situation would resemble the one described earlier in this chapter. It would bring additional strains to the system and the community. A breakdown of the projected cost

TABLE 2-5   COST PROJECTION—CORRECTIONAL

100 individuals spending 1 year in prison, 1 year on parole; 1,000 individuals spending 1 year on probation

TOTAL ADDITIONAL EXPENDITURES

1. 5 probation officers and supporting staff	$25,000 each	Total: $125,000
2. Cost of keeping one person in prison for one year	5,000 each	Total: 500,000
3. Cost per year of parole	250 each	Total: 25,000
4. Amortized cost of prison construction: 1 year	50,000	50,000
		TOTAL: $700,000

to the correctional unit to keep it functioning properly can be found in Table 2-5. It amounts to about $700,000.

Now we can add up all the amounts in the tables. The sheriff's decision to respond to the increase in drug offenses by reassigning twenty police officers would cost 2 million dollars. The criminal justice system must bear this staggering burden if it hopes to cope with the additional workload. This figure does not include other necessary costs: the construction cost of new facilities or their maintenance; the cost of persons to investigate offenders' background; the cost of juries, court reporters, interpreters, and court administrators; or the cost of confinement before trial.

The Social System

So far we have examined only the impact on the criminal justice system. Turning to the effect on the total social system, we can consider the group most likely to commit drug offenses. Most of such arrests involve people in the fifteen- to twenty-five-year age group. Although some of them do violate other laws, many of them do not. The impact on this group of citizens of a tenfold increase in police activity is hard to gauge. The invasions of privacy through personal searches and so on leave their mark. That there would be some impact is sure, and we explore some of the possibilities elsewhere in this book.

One effect that would be felt by the community at large would result from the possible increase in nondrug crimes. Take a simple example. Suppose that in one year each of 500 burglars commits 10 crimes, every one of which brings in $100. The total amount lost by the citizens of High County would come to half a million dollars. A side effect could be insurance companies working harder, paying out more in claims, and consequently raising their premiums.

Predicting the precise repercussions of an action is particularly difficult when the total social system is complex, large, and changeable. High County is all of those things. Although it is difficult to be precise about the impact on the community, we can learn some general lessons from this example.

1. The sheriff's action obviously had a profound effect on all the subsystems of the criminal justice system. This was felt in the total social system as well. This fact demonstrates the interrelated nature of the criminal justice structure as we know it.
2. The head of a unit, however obscure in the overall structure, generally can make key decisions without consulting with other heads.
3. The failure of the unit head to consult with others tends to cause fragmentation and confusion. It could even bring about the collapse of the system as a whole. As we have seen, the sheriff's decision could have these results: *(a)* a reduction in police efficiency, *(b)* a breakdown of the court's ability to process cases, and *(c)* overcrowding of the correctional facilities.
4. The actions of the head of one unit within a subsystem could have profound consequences for the total social system. The extra money needed to finance the processing of the increased workload must come from society as a whole. Since tax revenues are limited, fewer resources would be left for other systems such as the educational and the environmental.

POINTS OF VIEW

We turn to a consideration of the various ways in which the criminal justice system can be viewed. If you stand too close to a portrait, you get a great view of the nose but won't see the face. So it is with many who work within the system. The head of a unit may have a tendency to limit his or her world to the boundaries of that unit. There is a tendency to confine the unit's goals within the unit's boundaries.

The heads of different segments of the criminal justice system may well have different measures of success. For the police, it may be the number of arrests. For the prosecutor, it may be the number of convictions. For the defense lawyer, it may be the number of acquittals. Each head shares the same ultimate goal: the reduction of crime. However, by becoming nearsighted and losing peripheral vision, each one can fail to see that larger goal. Each can, therefore, quite unwittingly, contribute to overall failure to reach it.

Certain groups within the criminal justice system have particular ways of regarding it. To some lawyers and police officials, the system consists of a series of decisions. These are made at various points in the processing of an offender from arrest to imprisonment. For the lawyers, the first concern may be the protection of the rights of the accused. It may be to maintain the sanctity of the concept that one is innocent until guilt is proved. And it may be to secure a limitation on the powers of the police.

For the police officials, the main consideration may be the accumulation of proof against a suspect. Or it may be the ultimate solution of the crime and the punishment of the criminal. Although both groups may view the functioning of the system alike, each may feel the other is doing the system harm.

Some who work in social welfare and corrections may view the criminal justice system as an opportunity to improve the offender. They feel that those who violate the law are products of an unbalanced social structure. So they may approach the movement of offenders through the system as an educational process for them. They see prison not as punishment but as a chance to learn new trades as well as to change their world view.

There are others who view our criminal justice system with open disfavor. They point out that other systems in other countries are more efficient. They say this is so because those systems are firmly controlled by their governments. They argue that if one central body controlled all our criminal justice processes, these processes would be far more effective. This is an argument that has been used against the democratic system of government for a very long time.

Certainly crime in Nazi Germany, Communist Russia, or any totalitarian government would be handled more swiftly and efficiently than it is here. But would the process be as just? The question is always the same: Is the gain in efficiency worth the loss in personal liberty?[1] The division of powers that marks our governmental system can lead to situations like our example of High County. But if the sheriff totally controlled the criminal justice system, we might lose some cherished constitutional liberty.

By the same token, it would be a mistake to give complete power over the system to the judicial branch. That could lead to an increase in restrictions on police activity which would hopelessly impair their

1. For a discussion of life under a police state, see Aleksandr Solzhenitsyn's *Gulag Archipelago, 1918–1956* (New York: Harper & Row, 1974).

Case Study:
LAW VIOLATION–RIGHT OR WRONG

Newtown, like many small communities, was facing what appeared to be an increase in crime. Public concern unfortunately was fed not by the reality of the community's problems but by the regional news media, which focused on crime in the urban area neighboring Newtown. When residents returned home at night, television news shows illustrated the many murders, rapes, shootings, and other crimes that took place during the previous night.

After a year or two of this style of reporting, residents of Newtown decided to find out what was causing this ever-increasing crime in their community. Various town groups made crime in Newtown the topic of their meetings. One of the people whom they wanted to question was Newtown's police chief, Tom Rodriquez.

Rumors that flourished throughout the community implied that the police enforced laws only against individuals who were not their friends or did not share their beliefs. A few residents claimed they had facts concerning these occurrences. One pointed to the man who was arrested for trying to break into a house and was walking the streets the following day.

The Newtown PTA organized a community meeting where questions could be posed to the police chief. Chief Rodriquez was not too cheerful about the meeting, but he accepted the invitation to address the group.

A few residents opened the meeting by asking, "What is the crime rate?" The chief gave illustrations of the type of crime found in Newtown and reminded the audience that the news media were reporting crime in the city and not in Newtown. This seemed to quiet most of the group.

Then one of the teachers rose and read from a prepared text: "The police have the task of enforcing the laws and placing behind bars those individuals who are a danger to the community. But in September the police arrested thirty teachers for striking. These teachers were placed behind bars for thirty days. The strike was aimed at preventing an increase in the number of students per class, which would decrease the attention the teacher could give to each student. In October, a man who broke into at least a dozen houses was arrested and then released without spending even a few hours behind bars. Is this justice?"

Other members of the audience applauded and a few shouts could be heard. Chief Rodriquez knew that the statements the teacher had made were true.

How should the police chief respond to the question?

efficiency. Creating some sort of single criminal justice administrator could well distort the system. Then any views which were in conflict with that person's would not be tolerated. The idea of a centrally controlled, efficiently run criminal justice system is attractive. But it could be the first step toward a police state.

SEEKING IMPROVEMENTS

That our criminal justice system is subject to problems does not mean that it is without the hope of improvement. It is not an either-or situation: We do not have to choose between the potential for hopeless inefficiency and the potential for a police state. One example of the efforts at improvement is the creation of the Law Enforcement Assistance Agency within the Justice Department. This agency was set up to dispense advice, equipment, and money to various segments of the criminal justice system. The object was to help improve the system's effectiveness. A prime benefit has been obtained from this new agency. It has led the various heads of units to converse and discuss the best ways to use new resources. It could be argued that communication is better than centralization.

Besides the increased exchange of ideas among workers within the criminal justice system, those wanting to improve it should consider:

1. How do the workings of the various elements within the system affect one another?
2. What are the goals of the various separate elements, and how do they contribute to the overall goals of the system?
3. How are the resources of society as a whole being spent at all levels of the system?
4. Is the criminal justice system succeeding in both protecting individuals' rights and achieving a reduction in the rate of crime?

All these questions involve relating one thing to another. They thereby underline the main point that no one unit of the system stands alone. In viewing only one's own little world, in forgetting effects an action may have on others, any system develops trouble. In human relationships this is called "selfishness"; in administrative circles it is called "taking a narrow view." But whatever it is called, it works against the smooth functioning of any system. As we have seen, all the elements are interrelated.

QUESTIONS

1. What are your goals for the criminal justice system? Do they conflict in any way?
2. What mechanisms should be established to provide for better communication among members of the criminal justice system? Would better communication help the system function more effectively?
3. Given the "facts" about High County, what would have happened if there had been no shift in personnel?
4. If you had been sheriff of High County, what would you have done?
5. How would you redefine the respective roles of the legislative, law enforcement, judicial, and correctional subsystems?
6. Prepare a chart showing the existing system and one showing the system you designed as part of question 5.

part 2

crime

▶ Much ink has been spilled and many shouts exchanged over the word "crime." The subject appears as a major concern in almost every public opinion poll, political speech, and daily newspaper. The incidence of crime, its causes, and its control dominate much of what we read and hear. Not much time is given to a consideration of what it is exactly that we are all talking about.

On one level there are some reasonably straightforward answers. There are legal definitions of crime and there is a criminal justice system which deals with those who commit criminal acts. Yet, on a deeper level, there are no easy answers. Crime is many things, and the machinery created to deal with it is controlled by human beings and is therefore fallible. We will explore some aspects of this complex area to gain a broader understanding of crime and justice in our society. First we should take a look at crime in the basic framework of the system.

In its simplest, legalistic terms, a *crime* is defined as a punishable act of omission or commission violating a law. As we have said, crime is much more than that. For practical purposes, however, a label must be given to the kind of action society has decided is unacceptable.

DEFINITIONS OF CRIME

To begin at the beginning, what is a crime? To a considerable degree, it depends on whom you are talking to, and even the experts do not agree. Some sociologists will tell you that a crime is an act that violates certain group standards. Others consider it to be any act that is injurious to society. Richard Quinney calls "crime" "a definition of human conduct that is created by authorized agents in a politically organized society."[1]

Among lawyers a similar lack of unanimity exists. However, many definitions of crime in current legal writing contain the follow-

1. Morris and Hawkins, *The Honest Politician's Guide to Crime Control* (Chicago: The University of Chicago Press, 1970).

 chapter 3

Crime and Criminals

ing elements: (1) an act or failure to act; (2) an act committed by a person with sufficient mental capacity to be held responsible by society; (3) an act done with a criminal intent or by criminal negligence; (4) an act prohibited by law and punishable by fine, imprisonment, or perhaps loss of certain civil rights. It has also been said that a crime is a wrong against the public interest. With authorities so vague, we expect that the ordinary person would have a certain amount of difficulty in defining *crime*.

We each bring our own perspective to the world around us. Depending on our individual backgrounds and experience, we see things in our own way. Furthermore, the same act may well be viewed in sharply differing lights by different people. In a fight between two individuals in which one gets shot, a different report will be given by: (1) the one who fired the gun; (2) the victim; (3) the arresting officer; (4) the immediate witnesses; and (5) the news representatives who report the event. Was it attempted murder or self-defense?

Another problem of definition arises in the vast variety of human behavior that can be considered criminal by some definition. Most crimes never reach the pages of the newspapers. Examples are: shoplifting; drunkenness; speeding; and, of course, family squabbles that end in blows struck. But even those that are reported cover quite a range of human enterprise. The following is just a small sampling of recent headlines: "Major Corporations Charged with Illegal Campaign Contributions"; "Heiress Kidnapped"; "Shot Fired at the President"; and "318 Arrested as Busing Protest Continues."

Classifications of Crime

To bring order to the confusion created by a grab bag of actions labeled "criminal," attempts at classification were made. First, we have classification by *type of crime*. These are: against the person; against property; against morals; and against public order. Second, we have classification by *degree of seriousness:* from misdemeanor to felony.

Felonies are the most serious grade of crime and misdemeanors the least serious. *Infractions* are violations of city and county laws or ordinances. Many authorities do not consider infractions as crimes. In some states, crimes can be classified as felonies depending upon the place of imprisonment. The California Penal Code defines a *felony* as a crime "punishable by death or by imprisonment in the state prison." Under federal law, a felony is any crime "punishable by death or by imprisonment for a term exceeding one year."

The test for a felony depends upon the maximum punishment that can be imposed upon conviction of the crime. It does not depend upon the sentence the judge passes. A few states give the courts discretion to determine whether conviction of a crime is a felony or a misdemeanor. To further confuse matters, the first conviction of certain crimes are *misdemeanors*. If a person is convicted of violation of the same law again, the second conviction stands as a felony.

It makes a difference if the crime is a felony or misdemeanor. Conviction of a felony may involve loss of certain rights, such as the right to hold public office. Or it may bar a person from practicing professions such as law and medicine. The authority of the police to arrest is greater in felony than in misdemeanor cases. In misdemeanor cases, police cannot arrest without a warrant of arrest issued by a judge. The exception is when the officers perceived the commission of crime in their presence.

In felony prosecutions the accused always has the right to jury trial. In some very minor misdemeanors, on the other hand, states are permitted to eliminate jury trials. Until recently, a poor person charged with a misdemeanor had no free lawyer to defend him during the trial. Typical felonies include murder, robbery, rape, and kidnapping. Public drunkenness, petty theft, and vandalism are misdemeanors across the nation.

States are not required to enact uniform laws governing the classification of specific crimes. Our system of government was designed to permit local conditions and needs to dictate state laws. A particular state need not be entirely consistent or rational in its classification scheme. Unfortunately, results can be absurd. For example, it is a misdemeanor in Maryland to use a machine gun to perpetrate a crime of violence. But in the same state it is a felony to break open a hogshead of tobacco.

Still another way of classifying crime is by the degree to which the prohibited behavior is viewed as intrinsically evil. Those crimes that are "by nature" base, vile, and evil are termed *mala in se*, while the rest are merely *mala prohibita*. Examples of the former are rob-

Case Study:
TYPES OF CRIME

Patrol in Dodds, a community of about 30,000 residents, is no different from other suburban towns. Most nights police officers have enough to do to keep alert. Dodds has its drunks, bar fights, and burglaries; however, it rarely has murders or shootings.

Officer Barbara Grassi was on duty during the 4 P.M.-to-midnight shift on October 3, 1976. It was a quiet night as usual. Only a few calls kept her busy. The first was to break up a marital dispute. It was followed later by a minor traffic accident. At 10 P.M., Officer Grassi felt assured that this was of one more uneventful evening patrolling Dodds.

Grassi heard a call from a neighboring community saying that an officer was in pursuit of a blue Ford. Reports indicated the driver might be drunk and headed for Dodds. Grassi called Dodds police headquarters, stating she would try to intercept the suspected car.

Several crashes could be heard along the main thoroughfare. Officer Grassi was just around the corner. The blue Ford had sideswiped five parked cars as it entered the community. Officer Grassi notified headquarters of the incident and gave the direction of the blue Ford. The vehicle had not stopped but continued down the main street. Grassi did notice that the car was swerving from one side of the road to the other.

Within two minutes Officer Grassi was able to pull alongisde the vehicle. She signaled for the driver to stop, but the car continued. By now two other communities had joined the chase and set up a roadblock about a mile down the road.

Before Grassi could react, a pedestrian started to cross the street and was struck by the suspect's auto. Grassi requested dispatch of a back-up unit to assist the injured pedestrian. A few seconds later the suspect's vehicle crashed into the roadblock, finally coming to a halt.

There was much crushed metal, but no one was injured. Officers quickly arrested the suspect and later brought him to the hospital for a blood test. Hospital authorities reported the test showed the suspect's blood contained a high percentage of alcohol—enough to make a normal person lose control.

Officer Grassi was told that the pedestrian who had been hit by the car had died. Since the incidents occurred mostly in Dodds, it was up to Grassi to file the report and press charges against the driver.

If you were Officer Grassi, what charges would you file against the driver?

bery and murder, while violations of fish and game laws are examples of the latter.

Then, too, some behavior is not regulated by the criminal law at all but is governed by the civil law. If a tenant fails to pay the rent on time, the civil law provides a remedy in a civil court process. The landlord can sue the tenant and force the tenant to pay the rent or to move. If you don't like your name, most states provide a procedure for a legal change of name. Often behavior may be subject to both civil and criminal processes. A drunk driver who hits and kills a pedestrian is subject to being prosecuted for a form of murder called "manslaughter." The same driver could be sued in civil court. He or she would be required to pay money for the loss of the deceased's earning potential, hospital bills, and funeral expenses.

The differences between civil and criminal law violations are significant. In criminal law violations, the violator may face possible imprisonment. If he or she is ordered to pay a fine, the money goes to the government. In civil cases the money goes to the injured party. In civil cases both the person causing harm and the injured party must hire and pay for their own lawyers. In criminal cases the prosecutor is paid by the government. Unless the alleged violator can afford a private lawyer, defense counsel is provided for the accused and paid by the government.

Civil lawsuits must be initiated by the injured party or someone who can legally represent the injured party. Generally criminal prosecutions must be initiated by an agent of the government. These prosecutions are brought in the name of the state, i.e., "People of the State of X versus (against) Sam Smith", or "The State of X versus Alain James." In the drunk driving example given above, the pedestrian's spouse who witnessed the crime could initiaite a civil law suit. This would be for whatever loss the spouse suffered as the result of the pedestrian's death. The criminal case would be brought by the police and prosecution, and the surviving spouse would merely be a witness. The spouse could refuse to sue civilly. However, if the prosecution decides to prosecute, the spouse must cooperate and testify in criminal court.

The lesson to be drawn from all of this is that it is important to define one's terminology when talking about "crime." Someone rushes up and tells you that the police have just arrested old Mrs. Jones—that she has committed a crime. You may instantly conjure up a picture of that kindly old lady with a smoking gun in her hand. In reality she was picked up for lighting a cigarette in a movie theater. On the other hand, someone else hearing the same news may picture Mrs. Jones being carted away for illegally smoking. In fact she may have murdered her next-door neighbor.

The Criminal

This brings us to a consideration of: Who is a criminal? To a certain extent, we all are. The list of crimes is very long and covers a very wide field. It is almost impossible not to violate some law sometime. Leaving aside a whole host of sexual offenses, the overwhelming majority of citizens have done things that violate some law: (1) getting drunk (2) driving a car too fast; (3) experimenting with an illegal drug; (4) going home from work with some office supplies belonging to employers.

When we think of criminals, we don't visualize this category of offender; we imagine someone who has done something "serious." Once again, we need to define our terms. The rapist and the person who trespasses to fish are both criminals, but it is advisable to know which is which. By the same token, it is imperative that society as a whole make that sort of distinction. To brand a person a criminal and have that be the end of it is rough justice indeed.

DIVISIONS OF THE CRIMINAL JUSTICE SYSTEM

There are different classifications of behavior, of felony and misdemeanors, *mala in se* and *mala prohibita*. Just so, there are different levels of government that function in our justice system. Figure 3-1 shows government levels having to do with crime that exist in the states of the United States.

City police departments can enforce all laws passed by the city counsels, the county legislative bodies, and the state legislature. The chief of police may be hired by the city and the salary paid by the city from tax revenues. City courts are limited to deciding cases of the violation only of city laws.

Some counties have county courts with the power to decide only county law violations. Other county courts may also try cases involving state law violations. The sheriff's office may be legally allowed to arrest violators of any county or state law wherever these violations happen. This is true even if the violators are caught within a city that has its own police department.

The state court system is most often limited to hearing violations of state law. Yet it too may be empowered to determine if a person has violated a county or city law. Many state courts are created by state constitutions, but the judges' salaries are paid by the county

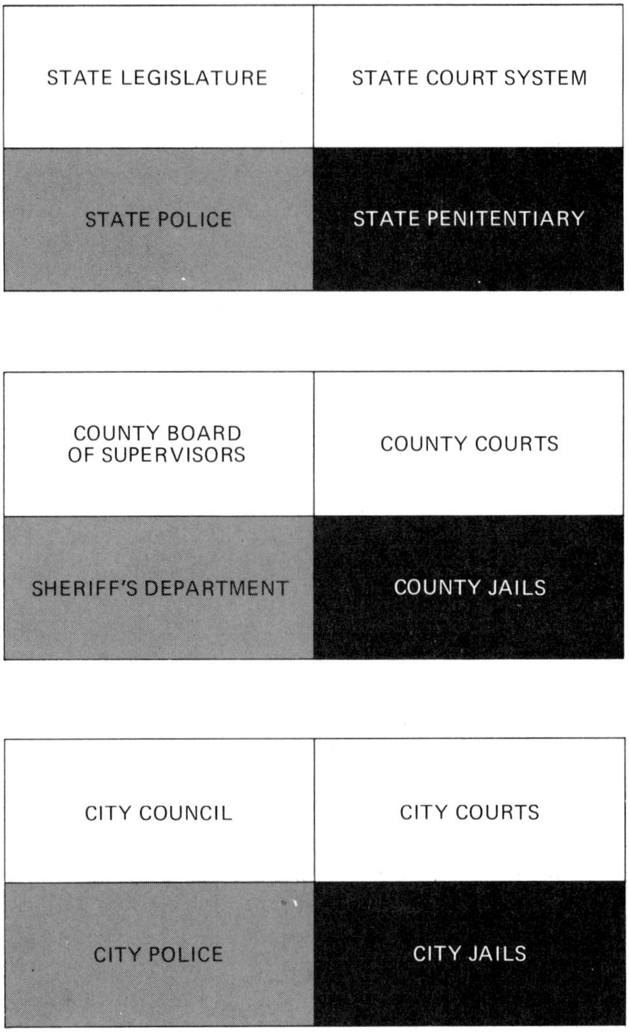

STATE LEGISLATURE	STATE COURT SYSTEM
STATE POLICE	STATE PENITENTIARY

COUNTY BOARD OF SUPERVISORS	COUNTY COURTS
SHERIFF'S DEPARTMENT	COUNTY JAILS

CITY COUNCIL	CITY COURTS
CITY POLICE	CITY JAILS

Figure 3-1 Levels of the criminal justice system.

government. Violators convicted and sentenced as felons are sent to the state penitentiary system for long-term incarceration. Prior to trial they are detained in county or city jails.

Federal laws are passed by the U.S. Congress. Arrests for their violation are made by the FBI or other federal law enforcement agencies. The alleged violators are tried in federal court and, if convicted, are sent to a federal penitentiary. At one time it was possible for the same behavior to violate city, county, state, and federal laws.

Upon conviction in all four courts, the convicted violator could receive four different sentences, to be served in four different institutions.

GOALS OF THE CRIMINAL JUSTICE SYSTEM

It is useful to consider what the purpose of the criminal justice system is and whom it serves. Traditionally the system has had three practical goals: vengeance (or punishment), deterrence, and rehabilitation. The concept of *vengeance* reflects the less noble side of human nature—the desire for revenge. It can be found in the earliest legal code we know, that of Hammurabi of Babylon (1791–1749 B.C.).

In *deterrence* the threat of punishment and seeing punishment given will possibly stop an individual from committing a criminal act. Failing that, the theory goes, experiencing the punishment will deter the offender from repeating the crime.

Rehabilitation is a newer concept, more positive in its approach. If a crime is committed despite the deterrent aspects of the legal system, the offender's behavior can be corrected.

There is a larger purpose of the criminal justice system as well: the *protection of society*. Much speculation of legal philosophers deals with this idea. Their work forms the body of writing which has provided the intellectual foundation for the system. It is important to be familiar with it, and so a few brief excerpts from important works follow. The first is by John Stuart Mill, from his essay *On Liberty*, published in 1859.

The principle is, that the sole end for which mankind are warranted, individually or collectively, in interfering with the liberty of action of any of their members is self protection. That the only purpose for which power can be rightfully exercised over any member of a civilized community against his will, is to prevent harm to others. His own good, either physical or moral, is not sufficient warrant; he cannot be compelled to do or forebear because it would be better for him to do so; because it will make him happier; because in the opinion of others, to do so would be wise or even right.

The next quotation is from *The Honest Politician's Guide to Crime Control*, by Morris and Hawkins.

The prime function of the criminal law is to protect our persons and our property; these purposes are now engulfed in a mass of other distracting, inefficiently performed, legislative duties. When the criminal law invades the spheres of private morality and social welfare, it exceeds its proper limits at the cost of neglecting its primary tasks. This unwarranted extension is expensive, ineffective and criminogenic.[2]

These writers, and many others over the centuries, make two major assumptions. First, the primary purpose of the criminal law and the criminal justice system is the protection of life, limb, and property. Second, these laws and this system actually deter people from acts which threaten life, limb, and property. We will examine this second proposition in a later chapter. In learning about crime and justice in our society, it is worthwhile to take a fresh look at actual accomplishments. It is also profitable to examine what was in the minds of those who created the laws that maintain the system.

The further question of who is served by the criminal justice system also merits another look.

Critics of our legal system, and especially of our criminal law, sometimes charge that the more politically powerful middle and upper class groups are able to define the law in terms that regulate the conduct of the lower classes, that leave them free to act in ways often just as reprehensible. . . . Who is a criminal, and what is a crime are, in this view of the matter, a function of the social stratification system.[3]

The argument made here is that those who make the laws are protecting the status quo, things as they are. It indicates that the balance is tipped toward the conservative middle class, who shy away from innovation and change. This charge has been extended to include not only the legislators, but those at all levels of the criminal justice system. Can anything as cut and dried as the administration of justice be influenced by individuals with personal preferences and prejudices? A look inside the structure of the system may help answer that question.

Personal Discretion

To demonstrate opportunities to exercise personal discretion in every division of the criminal justice system, we will go through four individually.

2.   Ibid.

3.   Alexander B. Smith and Harriet Pollock, *Crime and Justice in a Mass Society* (New York: Xerox Corporation, 1972), 39.

Legislative

Sometimes, in responding to the pressures of particular groups, legislatures will pass laws that strike us as merely quaint. In one agricultural state stealing a hog was a felony, regardless of its value. Stealing a watch of equal worth was only a misdemeanor.

However, other laws reflect deeper issues. Most authorities believe marijuana to be no more, or perhaps even less, harmful than alcohol. Yet the possession of marijuana is still a crime in most states. In not altering their laws, these legislators may be reacting to the wishes of the middle class and the middle-aged. These people support and reelect them, rather than the less politically potent young who want change.

Other examples can be found. Tax laws offer loopholes to the rich; family nonsupport laws can send a father, but not a mother, to jail.

Law Enforcement

At first blush it would seem that police officers have little leeway in the system. In fact, however, they exercise a great deal of discretion, and therefore they help to shape that system. The officer is the one on the spot who must decide whether or not to arrest. As will be discussed in a later chapter, within certain limits this is a personal choice. Whether or not the officer displays good judgment is another matter. In one study it was shown that, after arrest, a middle-class gang rode home in a police car. At the same time a lower-class gang (in the same community) spent a night behind bars after being arrested.

Judicial

Even greater opportunities for individual discretion are seen in the functioning of the judicial system. At every step through the judicial maze, decisions are made by people with minds and viewpoints of their own.

The first decision is whether or not the charges against the accused should be dropped. If it is decided they should not, the question then may be: Should the defendant be allowed to plead guilty to a lesser charge than that in the arrest? (This is *plea bargaining.*) If the accused does stand trial, a judge (or judge and jury) makes a decision as to guilt. Then, should the accused be found guilty, a further decision on the penalty is in order. It is alleged that in some areas of the country members of minority groups are more frequently convicted than others. It is also charged they receive more severe sentences than others charged with the same offense.

The 1972 Supreme Court case *Furman v. Georgia* led briefly to the effective outlawing of the death penalty. The defense claimed that only 50 percent of those convicted of rape were members of minority groups. However, they claimed, some 85 percent of those executed for that crime were from minority groups. Warden Lewis E. Lawes of the prison at Ossining, New York, (popularly known as Sing Sing) put it another way. He said that in all his years as warden he had never seen a rich man die in the electric chair.

Correctional

Discretion within the system extends to the penal field as well. The matter of parole is a case in point. In most states a board of parole meets to decide on whether or not early release should be granted to a prisoner. Although most boards do their best to be fair and objective, the human element can enter and sway one's judgment.

Further, once a prisoner is on parole and under the appropriate officer's supervision, more opportunities for the personal element appear. The parole officer has power to report violations of the most minor kind. This officer can also recommend revocation of parole. Indeed, he or she can close an eye and hope for the best.

All of this is not to say that discretion in the criminal justice system is often abused. But room for personal discretion exists, and sometimes decisions are based on considerations of race, age, sex, or political views. The point can be simply expressed. Although many people violate criminal law, not all pay the listed price, and some are not labeled criminal at all.

SOCIETY AND CRIME

So far we have concerned ourselves with crime and how it is handled. But what of the social aspects of crime? Those who feel the harshness of the criminal justice system most frequently are the young, the poor, and minority groups. The young feel it because of ancient tension between those who value the status quo and those who demand change. The poor feel it because they lack the power to employ those best equipped to fight for them. Minority groups feel it because they arouse prejudices of those with power over them in their journey through the system.

However, there are other social considerations as well. Victims of crime are often thought to be rich or middle-class, white, elderly, and unknown to their assailants. However, the truth is quite otherwise. The typical victim of assault in this country is young,

Case Study:
DISCRETION

Sergeant Kelly of the Ridge Park Police Department seemed to be having one of those days when one call after another proved to be not only unusual but a source of personal failure for him. Kelly was an active policeman. He preferred to work in the radio car rather than sit behind the dispatcher's desk. However, he also had to answer calls just like the rest of the shift.

It was a rainy afternoon with heavy cloudbursts from time to time. One of the bursts caused the roadway to be slick, resulting in an auto accident. Kelly's was the second car to arrive at the accident scene. The two cars in the accident had a few dents, but no one was injured. However, the accident took place on a main thoroughfare, causing traffic to back up. Sergeant Kelly was the unfortunate fellow who had to direct the traffic around the accident. As luck had it, Kelly was minus a raincoat. Sure enough, it began to rain.

After changing clothes, Sergeant Kelly was back on the road, this time answering a call to aid a sick woman. Upon entering the house, Kelly noticed a woman sitting on a chair apparently was having problems breathing. While Kelly administered oxygen, a huge dog rushed from the kitchen and gave Sergeant Kelly a hard time as, in attempting to comfort its owner, it kept pushing the officer to one side.

When the local ambulance corps took control of the situation, Kelly was called to a domestic dispute. Domestic disputes are always tricky, but for an experienced police officer this call should have been routine.

As with the car accident, Kelly's was the first patrol car to arrive. As he pulled up to the curb, Kelly noticed a man and woman who were shouting at each other in fierce tones. He quickly interceded as the back-up unit came to a halt at curbside. According to standard department practice, Kelly started to lead the woman away from the area while the other officer went to talk to the woman's husband. Before these positions could be taken, the man took a swing at Kelly. Fortunately he missed, striking the side of the house and causing himself a slight injury. Quickly the other officer grabbed the man.

The woman, still in an uproar, tried to kick her husband but missed and ended up kicking Sergeant Kelly. Kelly's leg was sore and slightly bleeding. His uniform was also ripped by the woman as she fought for release.

Police brought the couple back into the house quietly. The house was a mess. However, now the couple had apparently made up.

What charges should Sergeant Kelly bring against either person or against both husband and wife? Should he take into account the fact that later that evening the husband, in another outburst, killed the wife?

black, and male. The incidence of burglary appears to be higher in the city ghettos than anywhere else. The majority of personal attacks are by members of one race upon members of the same race. A majority of murder studies have demonstrated killers are more likely to be relatives, friends, or acquaintances than strangers.

Another interesting fact that is not widely appreciated is the extent to which victims invite crime. It has been argued that many victims of assault provoked the action, only to suffer the consequences. Every experienced police officer knows that in domestic disturbances—those which so frequently lead to murder—rarely is the victim totally blameless. On a more commonplace level, laws are passed for our own protection and our police make incessant pleas to us. Yet many of us still leave front doors open and cars unlocked— open invitations to crime.

Indeed, this is in many ways a crime-inviting society. A great deal of crime could be prevented with modest effort, yet that effort is not made. Thirty years ago the storekeeper put his merchandise behind the counter or under glass. Today virtually every kind of retail outlet displays its goods where they can easily be reached—and easily be stolen.

We as a group invite crime in other ways as well. Our modern houses make the burglar's life a happy one. Dimly lit streets make a haven for muggers. Easy access to alcohol ensures an increase in irresponsibility on the road and in personal behavior. Unemployed people may feel that crime is the only way they can survive. The recent 50 percent rate of unemployment among black youths can hardly fail to translate into more crime. The public outcry about crime is deafening. Why we are so tolerant of so much that encourages crime lies beyond the scope of this text. However, it is a factor not to be dismissed.

Another aspect of crime that should not be overlooked is its psychological impact. In the confrontation between society and the hostile individual there lies a drama that attracts most of us. One may side with the offender or the victim, the outlaw or the sheriff. It still provides us with a safe means of releasing certain feelings of our own. Through identifying with the actors, we have a new opportunity to separate the Good Guys from the Bad Guys. And that distinction is not quite as clear-cut today as it was in years past.

SHADES OF GRAY

Today a new element has crept into lawbreaking: social protest. Only relatively recently in this country has much attention been

Case Study:
LETTER OF THE LAW

One of the biggest trials in state history is about to get under way. John Rosen, a former state political leader, is charged with extorting thousands of dollars from contractors doing business with state agencies. For years while his party was in power, Rosen was protected from prosecution, but now the tide had turned.

Under the direction of the chief of the state police, an undercover unit placed itself in a position to be subject to extortion. Rosen made the threat and accepted the bribe and then was arrested. Throughout the pretrial procedures, Rosen's lawyer, the former state attorney general, tried every means in the book to have Rosen freed. However, Rosen had to have his day in court.

The courtroom was packed with spectators and about twenty members of the news media, all waiting to hear the details of the charges. Seated on the bench was Amanda Blake, a judge who had been appointed to the bench by the party Rosen headed. Blake's appointment, unofficially, had required a nod from Rosen before she could don her judicial robes.

Blake refused to make her position known to the parties in the case. She felt assured that the time span between the appointment and the arrest would have erased any memory of the days when she had been seeking the judgeship.

The trial was under way when Judge Blake began to strictly enforce all courtroom procedures open to her discretion. It appeared to all the spectators and the press that the judge was leaning toward a verdict of "not guilty."

Whenever she was permitted to use her discretion in interpreting rules of evidence, she usually favored the defense—her good friend Rosen. Some spectators became upset. Muffled cries from the spectator section caused Judge Blake to order the non-press members to leave the courtroom.

She also imposed a gag order on the news media. A gag order makes it a criminal offense for any member of the press and any part to the case to discuss, print, or broadcast any part of what takes place in the courtroom. Such an order is legal and within the discretion of the presiding judge.

In the press section a young reporter realized what was happening. With the spectators barred from the courtroom and the press prohibited from informing the public about what was taking place, the judge did what she pleased. Judge Blake seemed to be using the law to free her friend, the extortionist. At least, that is what the reporter felt.

Should the reporter print the story? If the reporter prints the story, is he in violation of the law?

focused on this factor. Moreover, from time to time we find ourselves facing the phenomenon of the criminal as hero. Rosa Parks was a lawbreaker. She is the black woman who decided that she was not going to sit in the back of the bus in Montgomery, Alabama, in 1955. Dr. Martin Luther King, Jr., was arrested for protesting against racial segregation. He was sent to the Birmingham jail. More recently the 318 headline makers that we met earlier in this chapter were arrested for protesting school-busing decisions. Whether or not one agrees with the motives of these people, the fact remains that they committed illegal acts.

Clear lines must be drawn defining criminal behavior, or order is impossible. The law classifies acts as black or white. But people are human, and human beings live in a world of shades of gray. Laws must be observed, enforced, and respected; they are what protect our liberty. But it is important to understand the weaknesses of our system as well as to appreciate its strengths. Nothing in life is perfect; but without understanding, improvement is impossible.

QUESTIONS

1. Define *crime*.
2. What is your personal definition of the word *criminal*? Try comparing it with definitions by your friends and classmates.
3. Define your personal goals for the criminal justice system. Once again, compare them with the goals of the system as seen by your friends and classmates.
4. Which division of the criminal justice system—police, courts, corrections—seems to allow the most personal discretion? Is this personal discretion necessary? Is it a good thing?
5. Have you ever committed a crime?

SCENE: 123 Peaceful Lane, Suburbia, U.S.A.; 7 A.M. any week-
day. Wolf, the family watchdog, waits patiently while Mrs. Jones

- Switches off the burglar alarm
- Opens the dead-bolt lock
- Removes the security chain
- Opens the door and takes in the paper

After Wolf runs out, Mrs. Jones closes the self-locking door and
replaces the chain.

On her way to the kitchen, Mrs. Jones passes the telephone with
the police emergency number prominently displayed. She glances at
the newspaper with its headlines of robbery and rape.

At breakfast Mr. and Mrs. Jones and their three children watch
the morning television news. It is heavily laced with accounts of
national and local crime. Then the eldest child walks the others to the
corner and sees them safely onto the school bus. Mr. Jones unlocks
the garage door, wrestles with the antitheft device on the car's steer-
ing column, and drives into town. He makes sure his doors are
locked and the windows are up as he hurries through the ghetto.

Once in the office parking lot, he locks the car and walks briskly
to his office building. There he is greeted by the armed security
guard. A closed-circuit television camera monitors the entrance hall;
in the elevator a security mirror reflects his image from above. At the
morning staff meeting the rising cost of insurance and increasing
customer and employee theft are the principal topics.

Meanwhile, Mrs. Jones prepares to go out, having brought Wolf
in from his morning run. She puts wallet, keys, and can of teargas in
her coat pocket, leaving only less important items in her handbag.
On her way out she checks the device that turns the lights on automatically at dusk. She switches on the burglar alarm and double-locks
the door.

On her return Mrs. Jones opens the garage door by remote
control. As the automatically timed garage light stays on, she unlocks
the connecting kitchen door and secures it behind her.

The Incidence of Crime

At 11:30 that night there is a sudden noise. Wolf barks and growls, Mrs. Jones reaches for the telephone, and Mr. Jones gropes for his .38-caliber revolver.

Exaggerated? Yes. Absurd? No. Because everybody knows the crime rate in America is soaring, right? Wrong. Everybody *thinks* the crime rate in America is soaring. The press tells us it's so. Television news shows us it's so. The neighbors insist that it's so.

Indeed, the argument that there is an epidemic of crime has led to great expenditures. Almost twice as much was spent on the police in 1970 as in 1960. Expenditures for private guards and protective services rose by 75 percent in the same period. In 1970, 3.3 billion dollars was spent on private protection. This is equal to two-thirds of the amount spent by state and federal governments on public protection. It is probably true that crime is on the rise. Still, we should try to find out what facts we have to rely on to support this sort of assumption.

GENERAL SOURCES OF INFORMATION

A main source of information is *word of mouth*. Few of us have not been told, in lurid detail, of a crime that happened to a friend's friend. It is a safe bet that with each retelling the incident grows in horror. This is not to suggest that the crime didn't happen. The trouble with word-of-mouth information is that it is highly selective and not necessarily accurate.

The rape in the nearby park may be one of a hundred rapes during a year in a particular city. But it may have been the only rape in that particular park in twenty years. The constant retelling of the tale of that one incident, however, may lead to a tremendous fear of that park. It can mean a sharp increase in anxiety for personal safety among the inhabitants of the city.

Almost everyone has difficulty dealing rationally with the fear of crime. In the late 1960s, the director of the New York City subway system proudly displayed statistics on subway safety. These proved that passengers were safer on the subway than at home. However, when asked if he would let his family ride the subway at night, he paused and finally said no.

The news media are a second general source of crime information. The editor of *The Christian Science Monitor* once said:

Newspapers are often guilty of excesses in big cases. This is more often true in communities where papers are competing for business with other papers

Case Study:
MISCONCEPTION OF CRIME RATE

Just outside a major Eastern city, the community of Ridge Park was in an election year. Every four years residents selected five commissioners to run the town. In past elections, issues were more concerned with taxes than anything else.

However, this year was something different. The major worry in the minds of Ridge Park residents was the increase of crime in this relatively small community. This deep concern was fed through talk and publicity started by candidates who were out of office. One flyer pointed to the fact that murder had increased 100 percent in one year in Ridge Park.

Murder in Ridge Park was almost unheard of, but the 100 percent figure was accurate. In July a burglar had broken into an apartment. He was startled when two young people who shared the apartment arrived home too early. Instead of permitting the intruder to escape and then calling the police, the tenants apparently tried to make a citizen's arrest. One of them grabbed a knife and yelled, "Halt!" The burglar, only eighteen years old, became nervous and felt he was backed into a corner. A fight ensued which resulted in the death of the two tenants.

Fortunately, one of the neighbors heard the commotion and notified police, who quickly arrested the suspect outside the apartment building. He confessed the crime and described the incident. Later he was sentenced to twenty-five years in prison. The report of the case appeared in all the local newspapers and on the regional radio and television stations.

The previous year a woman had killed her husband in a drunken fight. Before these two incidents, Ridge Park had not had a murder in twenty years.

The five commissioners and the mayor were up in arms over the attacks by their opponents. They felt that crime in the neighboring city was much higher than in Ridge Park, but public opinion apparently was not on their side.

Turning to the police chief, the mayor and commissioners asked for an explanation. The chief agreed that the crime rate had not really increased significantly. He and his officers were receiving almost the same criticism. Apparently both the governing body and the police department needed to inform the public of the situation behind the figures.

If you were the police chief, how would you explain the 100 percent increase in murder? What could have been done to prevent these crimes?

[and] with radio and television stations. . . . Screaming headlines and titillating stories are examples of crass commercialism that sells papers regardless of who is hurt.[1]

The stories that find their way into print are those which the editors and publishers think will sell newspapers. The police or court beat is often the training ground for a young reporter. The hours are long, the environment seamy, and the pay low. For better assignments, more pay, and a by-line, the young newshound would do well to write a "big" crime story. It sells newspapers.

Most television news programs have to cover all the major developments internationally, nationally, and locally in about thirty minutes. Since TV is a visual medium, pictures are important, and certain types of crime coverage often provide interesting film. A shot of the Wall Street brokerage house where a million dollars was embezzled is unlikely to be exciting. But one of the sobbing old lady knocked down when her purse was snatched will probably catch the viewer's eye.

Judging from the number of television detectives and police officers, Americans are getting arrested as often as they engage in sports. It is estimated an American child reaching the age of eighteen will have spent more time watching television than in school. Whether children will try their own hand at crime as a result of this exposure is an open question. Certainly an awareness of crime, and a fear of it, will result from such an intensive exposure to it.

POLICE REPORTING

Roughly 92 percent of all police departments report their crime figures to the FBI, which collects and publishes them. It is important to ask what these statistics mean.

One officer who receives a report of a stolen television set might classify the theft as a *petty larceny*. Another would call it *grand larceny*. To one officer an alleged attack might be an attempted rape but to another, the same alleged attack might be a minor assault. Such human variation results in variation in crime reporting to the FBI and to the public.

To further complicate the situation, the age at which a child legally reaches adulthood varies from state to state. In some states it is fifteen; in others it is seventeen or eighteen. Therefore, a crime

1. Howard James, *Crises in the Courts* (New York: David McKay, 1971), p. 218.

committed by a fifteen-year-old in one state would be an unreported juvenile offense. In another it would be reported as a felony. As if that were not sufficiently confusing, states occasionally change their definitions of legal adulthood. This leads to variations in their crime reporting from one year to the next.

In an another chapter we discuss the effect of shifting police personnel from one area to another. Specifically, we discuss a dramatic rise in reported drug arrests as a result of increased strength in the narcotics unit. A change in concentration of police manpower will be reflected in the crimes reported. For example, a decision to crack down on prostitution in a city makes the place look like the capital of sin. It also leads to charges that vice is soaring in the state.

Police reporting practices vary in a number of ways. Some report the number of suspects arrested; others, the number of crimes for which arrests were made. The confusing thing here is that one offender may have broken several laws in the course of the same incident. In sum, there are no absolute standards for reporting crimes. Police practice varies from place to place and from time to time, and police officers are, after all, human beings.

CRIME STATISTICS

The *Uniform Crime Reports* (UCR), published by the FBI, are the most reliable source of information we have about crime frequency. These reports, published annually, reflect the information gathered by the various police agencies. They have been severely criticized for being incomplete, inaccurate, and biased, and much of this criticism is deserved. However, it should be remembered that for many years they were the only source of such information. Figure 4-1 gives an idea of what determines whether a crime is recorded in official statistics.

Regardless of how accurate statistics about the incidence of crime become, they cannot come close to being completely precise. A report says there were x number of crimes committed in the United States in a given year. This would mean that every crime committed in the country had been counted, and we know this is not so. (See Table 4-1.)

Basically there are eight aspects upon which crime reporting can focus:

1. All crimes committed
2. All crimes reported
3. All crimes discovered by the police

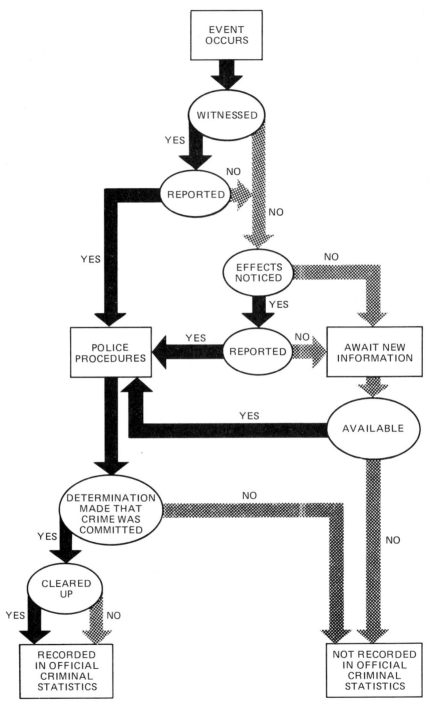

Figure 4-1 How crimes are reported. (SOURCE: M. A. Willmer, *Crime and Information Theory.* Chicago: Aldine, 1970, p. 2.)

TABLE 4-1   COMPARISON OF SURVEY AND UCR RATES,[1] SHOWING THAT THE AMOUNT OF CRIME IN THE U.S. IS SEVERAL TIMES THAT REPORTED IN THE UCR

CRIMES	NORC[2] SURVEY 1965–1966	UCR RATES FOR INDIVIDUALS, 1965	UCR RATES FOR INDIVIDUALS AND ORGANIZATIONS, 1965
Willful homicide	3.0	5.1	5.1
Forcible rape	42.5	11.6	11.6
Robbery	94.0	61.4	61.4
Aggravated assault	218.3	106.6	106.6
Burglary	949.1	299.6	605.3
Larceny ($50 and over)	606.5	267.4	398.3
Motor vehicle theft	206.2	226.0	251.0
Total violence	353.8	184.7	184.7
Total property	1761.8	793.0	1249.6

[1]Per 100,000 population
[2]NORC is the National Opinion Research Center of the University of Chicago.
SOURCE: The President's Commission on Law Enforcement and Administration of Justice, 1968.

4.   All crimes investigated by the police
5.   All arrests
6.   All filings of formal charges against suspects
7.   All convictions
8.   All prison sentences given

Starting with number 1 and ending with number 8, the figures become in'creasingly accurate. Those giving the number of people in jail are the most reliable while the number of crimes committed is the least accurate. Figure 4-2 estimates the statistics that would derive from 100 crimes committed in the United States. Out of 100 crimes said to have been committed there were 10 arrests. From these, 8 suspects were charged, 6 were convicted, and 1 was imprisoned. (Remember that these figures are guesses.) This imbalance comes from the difficulties that are a part of crime reporting. Let's take a closer look at some of them.

Crimes Discovered

Not every crime is discovered. In the business world many crimes go undetected. For example, industries handling perishables have a relatively high rate of spoilage. There is often no way for the owners to know if some of that spoilage is really theft. Also, inventories, especially in businesses handling large numbers of small, inexpensive items, are rarely 100 percent accurate. Unaccountable losses could be the work of thieves. In banks and other large cor-

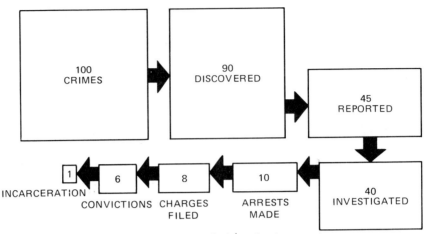

Figure 4-2 Fallout rate from the commission of crimes through incarceration.

porations, embezzlement and fraud may not be discovered for years, if ever.

Another type of crime that often goes undiscovered is so-called "victimless" crime. Drug abusers, gamblers, and some types of sex offenders do not report their violations. In these cases there is no injured party to report them. The actions are crimes nonetheless.

Crimes Reported

The crimes that are reported with the greatest frequency appear to be those for which the victim carries insurance. Many insurance policies require that a burglary be reported to the police before payment is made for a loss. Most automobiles are insured, and the rate of reporting in automobile theft cases is high. It would be fair to conclude that there is a relationship between insurance coverage and crime reporting. In light of this idea, we must remember that insurance coverage is selective; for example, there is no rape insurance.

Despite the obligation of a citizen to report a crime, victims and witnesses often fail to do so. (See Table 4-2.) This state of affairs appears to stem from a variety of attitudes:

1. A feeling that the police are ineffective in recovering property and catching offenders. Although this view appears to cut across social, economic, and racial lines, it is most widespread in the inner cities. The idea persists that the police don't bother much about ghetto crime.
2. Fear of the police by members of some minorities and by the poor. Some criminologists hold that although this fear was common in the past, it is breaking down. However, there are no facts to confirm or deny this view.

TABLE 4-2   VICTIMS' MOST IMPORTANT REASON FOR NOT NOTIFYING THE POLICE, IN PERCENTAGES

		REASONS FOR NOT NOTIFYING POLICE				
CRIMES	PERCENT OF CASES IN WHICH POLICE NOT NOTIFIED	FELT IT WAS PRIVATE MATTER OR DID NOT WANT TO HARM OFFENDER	POLICE COULD NOT BE EFFECTIVE OR WOULD NOT WANT TO BE BOTHERED	DID NOT WANT TO TAKE TIME	TOO CONFUSED OR DID NOT KNOW HOW TO REPORT	FEAR OF REPRISAL
Robbery	35	27	45	9	18	0
Aggravated assault	35	50	25	4	8	13
Simple assault	54	50	35	4	4	7
Burglary	42	30	63	4	2	2
Larceny ($50 and over)	40	23	62	7	7	0
Larceny (under $50)	63	31	58	7	3	*
Auto theft	11	20[1]	60[1]	0[1]	0[1]	20[1]
Malicious mischief	62	23	68	5	2	2
Consumer fraud	90	50	40	0	10	0
Other fraud (bad checks, swindling, etc.)	74	41	35	16	8	0
Sex offenses (other than forcible rape)	49	40	50	0	5	5
Family crimes (desertion, nonsupport, etc.)	50	65	17	10	0	7

*Less than 0.5%

[1]There were only 5 instances in which auto theft was not reported.

SOURCE: The President's Commission on Law Enforcement and Administration of Justice, 1968.

3. A sense among some minority groups of racial and ethnic solidarity, combined with a distrust of the police. Once again, the existence of this factor cannot be proved.
4. Fear that the criminal will return and take revenge. The fact that police protection for witnesses can rarely be provided contributes to this fear.
5. A desire not to get involved. The most notorious of such incidents was the case of Kitty Genovese. This young girl was stabbed to death in New York in full view of many witnesses while screaming for help. No one came to her aid or called the police.

However, it is not only the public which complicates the gathering of accurate crime figures. The *Uniform Crime Reports* themselves are not without blame. They received the criticism that only gross numbers of offenses were reported and not rates of occurrence per 100,000 people. As a result of such criticism the UCR changed its reporting methods. It started recording both figures—the gross number of offenses, and the number per 100,000 of the population. The trouble was that the basic population figures from which UCR worked were changed only once every ten years. This was after the official census had been taken. It is unrealistic to suppose a large community would keep a stable population year after year in this mobile society. Furthermore, resort areas have peak seasons when their populations may be swollen by as much as 50 percent thanks to tourists. Some of these tourists are breaking the law. Comparison of the error rates in Table 4-3 illustrates the problem with this method.

TABLE 4-3   THE PROBLEM OF BASING YEARLY CRIME STATISTICS ON TEN-YEARLY CENSUSES

	1961
Number of violations	100
Census population	1,000,000
Rate per 100,000	10
Actual population	1,000,000
Rate per 100,000	10
Error rate	0
	1969
Number of violations	200
Census population	1,000,000
Rate per 100,000	20
Actual population	2,000,000
Rate per 100,000	10
Error rate	100
	1971
Number of violations	200
Census population	2,000,000
Rate per 100,000	10
Actual population	2,000,000
Rate per 100,000	10
Error rate	0

HOW FAIR ARE THE FIGURES?

We have looked at our main sources of information; word of mouth, the media, police reporting, and crime statistics. None of them is fully accurate. But another question to consider is: How fair are they?

Case Study:
UNREPORTED CRIME

Having accurate records of crime in any community depends upon many factors. Calling the police is the first step. The follow-up investigation will enable the officer who is sent out to define the nature of the alleged crime. However, this inquiry is influenced by the police officer conducting the investigation. The officer may or may not believe the complainant. Then the desk officer who must complete the paper work can alter the original determination of the investigating officer.

Many individuals can affect the accuracy of the data. Police officers realize that a person who wants to collect insurance could break his or her own car window and then call the police to report items that have allegedly been stolen. The crime, according to police records, could range from simple vandalism to burglary.

The police chief in the town of Columbia was completing the year-end police report for the community. From all indications, things looked good for the department. Although some crime rates had not decreased, there were no increases. The chief prepared a summary of the year, claiming that better police management, coupled with more help from residents, was a major factor in presenting a reasonable record for the period.

Newspapers reported that while other neighboring towns showed an increase in crime, Columbia had an unusually good crime rate. Residents in general, upon hearing the news, felt more secure, although the chief warned that this condition could change.

A few residents, on the other hand, were pleased by the report but had some reservations. They had been hearing rumors of burglaries in the area. People would talk about a neighbor's missing a few hundred dollars after finding the front door open when returning home. One resident informally kept track of those friends in town who were burglarized. Her figures were much higher than those in the police report. In fact, her figures were higher than the figures reported for the previous three years.

This resident believed that the low reported rate was created by the chief to make the department look good. There had been reports of community departments keeping improper reports to make the crime rate look low. Doing this was easy, since the department was the only organization gathering the data.

For the most part, as long as the department report seemed to indicate that the community was pretty safe, residents would not complain. Life would go on as if the report never existed. However, a public outcry would occur if the report showed a marked increase in crime.

What possible explanations are there for this situation? How would the police department have an idea of the number of unreported crimes? Why might a victim not report a crime?

We have seen examples of bias in media reporting of crime. That is, material selected to be printed or broadcast has been slanted to favor the paper's or program's success. This same sort of process goes on in the statistical field. After all, just as policemen are human beings, so are statisticians and those who issue reports for organizations.

Bias in the UCR

An example of this can be seen in the "Careers in Crime" section of the UCR. This was an attempt to establish the rate of rearrest for those released by the federal law enforcement system. The conclusion was that 65 percent of all offenders were rearrested within six years.

That figure, however, includes people who were found not guilty or who had their cases dismissed. People who have been acquitted of a crime cannot be classified as offenders. By the same token, if people have not even been tried, they are presumed innocent. Every citizen has a right to this presumption, which protects a person from being called an offender.

In a further point, the report gave data on those found not guilty or whose cases were dismissed. It said that 92 percent of these were rearrested for other crimes within six years. The problem here is in the sample studied. The total number in the not-guilty and case-dismissed category was 4974. Among these the FBI selected a group of only 1190 for their follow-up study. This particular group included a high proportion of people charged with narcotics offenses, auto theft, and other crimes. These offenders are known to have high rates of recidivism (relapse into the previous condition, that is, habitual lawbreaking). The 92 percent figure which the Bureau reported was based on the behavior of this selected group.

It has been suggested that the *Uniform Crime Reports'* figures were gathered and presented with a specific intent. This was to place the blame for the rise in crime on judges who are "soft on crime." As Ernest Friesen, former Director of the Administrative Office of the Courts of the United States, said, "What you count, counts."

Police Bias

There has been much investigation of racial bias among police. Several authorities have found among police definite racial prejudice against certain minorities. Some newer studies attempt to soften the picture. They say that police officers as a group reflect no more racial prejudice than others of similar socioeconomic background. That appears to mean that a prejudiced society produces a police force of similar prejudices.

As we note elsewhere, the police exercise considerable discretion, and the power to arrest includes the power not to arrest. We can assume, therefore, that their use of the power to arrest reflects the current racial bias of the society. Does the high arrest rate among some minorities reflect racial or socioeconomic prejudice on the part of the police? In fairness it must be pointed out that this is hard to determine. There is also the possibility that some groups simply commit more crimes.

Court Bias

Courts tend to reflect the attitudes of society as a whole. Sentencing studies clearly demonstrate that blacks receive more and longer prison sentences than whites for the same crimes.

The President's Commission on Law Enforcement and Administration of Justice said: "The offender at the end of the road in prison is likely to be a member of the lowest social and economic groups in the country, poorly educated and unemployed, unmarried, reared in a broken home and to have a prior criminal record."

GATHERING ACCURATE STATISTICS

The picture so far is of a frightened society which believes itself helpless before a surge of criminal activity. But this society is frightened without any real knowledge of the facts. (Figure 4-3 illustrates the difference between the public perception of crime rates and the official statistics.) Is the crime rate rising? If so, by how much? Which crimes are on the rise? Who is committing them? Where? Are there really more crimes being committed, or just more being reported? Does the rising arrest rate reflect more crime or better police work?

To know anything, one has to have facts, and, in this case, sets of facts spanning a period of several years. Further, the facts must be exactly comparable—that is, gathered identically in the same place for the same length of time. It's no good comparing convictions for robbery in 1975 with arrests for robbery in 1976. One cannot compare arrests in the first three months of 1975 with arrests in the last three months of 1976.

Accurate crime statistics could present a true picture of the amount, location, and rate of change in crime. With this information, it would be possible for administrators to make wise decisions. This covers about everything from the assignment of police patrols to the installation of high-intensity lighting on the streets. Effective crime prevention depends on accurate information.

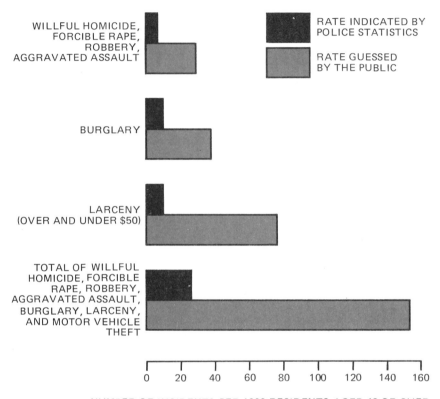

ESTIMATED RATES OF CERTAIN CRIMES
IN THREE WASHINGTON, D.C., PRECINCTS

NUMBER OF INCIDENTS PER 1000 RESIDENTS AGED 18 OR OVER

Figure 4-3

Informed decisions could also be made about complex questions. Is the continued use of police dogs justified in spite of the damage they might do to police-community relations? Is stopping and questioning on mere suspicion worth the damage it may do to a citizen's right to freedom of movement?

Figuring out how to get accurate crime statistics is difficult. However, there does seem to be one area of promise—the sample survey. A *sample survey* studies a randomly selected group that is representative of a larger population. It can provide accurate data about the incidence of crime in a particular area if three conditions are met:

1. The area and the size of population should be small.

2. The sample must be truly representative of the total population being surveyed.
3. The information must be collected fairly and objectively.

The problem with a limited survey is that the results may be valid *only* for the population being surveyed. The next step, then, would seem to be to do the same study in many different locations and compare the results. No doubt the results would vary in several particulars, but trends and patterns might be seen to be developing.

What can be learned from this sample survey approach? Examples are these conclusions drawn from a comparison between the Dayton–San Jose Study[2] and information from other surveys.

1. Homicides and assaults are more likely to happen in the inner city than in suburbs or rural areas.
2. The criminal is likely to be known to the victim but not related by blood.
3. Robbery generally occurs in public places, such as streets and parking lots.
4. Small commercial establishments seem to bear the brunt of business robberies.
5. Both robbery and burglary are more likely to happen at night than in the daytime.
6. Larceny is the most frequent crime involving a victim.
7. Two-thirds of all thefts take place either in homes or at outdoor public places.
8. The victim of crime is more likely to be young than old, male rather than female.
9. While more whites than blacks are victims of crime, the *percentage* of blacks who are victims is significantly higher.
10. The large majority of crimes are committed by a member of one race against someone of the same race. However, there is a trend toward interracial crime.

This is an age in love with "hard facts," and the computer is king. But facts are gathered by fallible people and computers are programmed by human beings. The results of the most elaborate electronic studies are compiled by men and women. Newspaper reporters and television news writers suffer from the weaknesses of human nature. Similarly, the local police chief, the state director of public safety, and the head of the FBI are all human beings. All are therefore less than perfect.

2. *Crimes and Victims—A Report on the Dayton–San Jose Pilot Survey on Victimization* (Washington: U.S. Department of Justice, 1974).

However, we recognize that we need objective, standardized information about crime in order to protect ourselves from it. We can work to get that information. Living in a fortress in suburbia won't lower the crime rate. Nor will slanting the news or loading the figures in a crime report. Crime is our enemy, but so is our own inclination to see only what we want to see.

QUESTIONS

1. Do you think there is more or less crime now than in the past (look back ten years, fifty years, one hundred years)? How do you know?
2. Why do you think gory crime newspaper stories may help sell more newspapers?
3. Have you been the victim of a crime? Did you report the crime? Why or why not?
4. Ask you friends and classmates question number 3 above. How do their answers compare with yours?

Throughout history people have been fascinated by the phenomenon of crime. As they have watched as others have broken the barriers of acceptable behavior, they have asked: Why? Why do some people do these things? And they have received different answers at different periods. It was the work of the devil; Witchcraft; Reaction to a broken home; The fault of society.

Ever since we moved into the era of scientific method, there have been countless efforts to study crime and criminals. It has been a search for the final answer to the question: What causes crime? We will take a brief look at some of these efforts, past and present.

Most research into the crime-causation riddle falls into one of two broad schools of thought: the Classical and the Positivist. Recently a third school, the Interactionist, has developed. It is important to examine these schools because of their influence on social programs and on methods of correction.

CLASSICAL SCHOOL

Probably the most significant base of Western civilization is Christian philosophy. For a long time religion was a part of everyone's everyday life. One of the basic beliefs of early Christian faith was that human beings had free will; they had the choice to do right or wrong. Naturally, the first organized school of crime thought was based on an old idea: A criminal act is a deliberate act of immorality.

It was assumed that offenders had chosen to do wrong. It followed that they should be punished for it. At the same time, they should be made to see the error of their ways. In 1767 the Italian Cesare Beccaria wrote *An Essay on Crimes and Punishments*. In it he set out a theory of crime which held that society must help the morally weak to resist crime. Because of this work Beccaria has been called the father of the Classical School.

In essence Beccaria devised a system of pinning a price tag on a crime: Each criminal act carried a certain punishment with it. The idea behind this plan was that someone contemplating a crime would stop and think. If it was known that being caught would result in a

chapter 5

Theories of Crime Causation

certain punishment, the offender would desist. The emphasis, then, was on the *free will* of the offender. This approach to deterring crime is still in use today. It can be seen in the system of requiring mandatory sentences for certain offenses.

Prisons were built to keep the criminal from further temptation as well as to protect innocent people. As we noted in Chapter 2, the treatment in prisons in the eighteenth and nineteenth centuries usually involved isolation and hard work. Exposure to readings from the Scriptures and visits from "model citizens" who encouraged prisoners to reform were also used.

This program may seem outdated. Yet today more than in past decades there is a widespread move to deal more and more sternly with offenders. Lip service is often paid to "treatment" and "rehabilitation." Still the cry for more law and order often boils down to a call for stiffer sentences.

POSITIVIST SCHOOL

As those concerned with crime problems turned away from the crime and considered the criminal, a new approach was developed. Those who concentrated on the criminal in their search for an explanation of the existence of crime were called Positivists. However, that is a catchall name covering many different theories of crime causation.

Physiological

As the traditional view that a criminal is simply a person who has chosen to be bad was rejected, another theory grew up. This was that some people are born criminals—because of their physical makeup, they cannot help turning to crime.

The most famous of those holding this view was Cesare Lombroso (1836–1909), whose book *Crime, Its Causes and Remedies* was influential. In it Lombroso put forward his view that some men were born to be criminals. It was an accident of birth and could not be helped. Further, he held that such "criminal types" could be identified by certain physical features he called "stigmata."

Lombroso used a highly scientific method in his researches and studied the bodily structure of 5907 criminals. He concluded that a combination of certain physical features were sure signs of a born criminal. Some of these were the shape of the forehead, the length of the lower jaw, and certain abnormalities of the teeth.

This view was widely popular for some time until it was finally discredited by further scientific studies. The echo of it lingers on in comments like: "He has beady little eyes and looks like a killer." By and large, however, interest in inborn criminal characteristics lagged for some fifty years after Lombroso's death in 1909.

In the 1960s research was being done on the basic building blocks of the human body, the chromosomes. The normal male chromosome is described in scientific language as being composed of 46 XY. However, it was discovered that occasionally an abnormality in these male chromosomes takes the form of an extra Y element. The formula is written 47 XYY.

An effort was made to discover how frequently this abnormality occurred and what its effect was on the person. Early and incomplete reports turned up a possible connection between this abnormality and violent and aggressive behavior. These reports were seized on by those who felt that perhaps here was the long-sought answer to what causes crime.

After more work on the subject, however, enthusiasm for the XYY chromosome as the cause of crime in men died out. Like Lombroso's theory of "criminal types," a belief that the body alone held the answer to crime appeared to be doomed.

Psychological

Various groups of psychiatrists and psychologists have produced theories of crime causation based on the mind of the offender. Following the pioneering work of Sigmund Freud, some hold that the springs of criminal behavior lie deep in the unconscious mind. With effort and time, they feel, criminal behavior can be traced to painful events or relationships hidden in childhood.

On a more superficial level are those who trace the offender's actions to other things. They suggest a lack of self-respect, which leads to hostile feelings toward others. Some of the current approaches to treatment on this middle level of awareness include: (1) reality therapy; (2) guided group interaction; (3) therapeutic communities; and (4) transactional analysis.

Still other psychologists do not examine the depths of the mind at all. They believe the most effective way to deal with criminal behavior is to come to grips with the behavior itself. The Behaviorists leave aside the whole concept of crime as a symptom of a disordered personality. Instead, they attempt to substitute acceptable behavior for the unacceptable.

Behaviorists working with a criminal will look at the surrounding circumstances and try to spot which elements encourage unacceptable behavior. They will then try to replace those reinforcers with ones suggesting good behavior.

Sociological

Emile Durkheim wrote on criminology in the late nineteenth and early twentieth centuries. On the basis of his work, a number of sociologists developed theories concerning the roots of crime. These broadened the focus to include not only the offender but the society in which he or she lived.

From this angle crime came to be seen as something unavoidable. A look was taken at the different environments that made up society. The conclusion was that a change in the environment would lead to a change in behavior. It was reasoned: If disadvantaged people could have the same opportunity for success and status as more fortunate people, they wouldn't use crime.

The deepest effect of these sociological theories of crime causation was to shift the blame from the offender to society. Reformers went to work with a will upon projects for slum clearance, foster home programs, and equal job opportunities. But in all the activity an important point made by Durkheim had been lost: Crime was not restricted to a single group; it afflicted the whole of society.

Another problem which the Classical and the Positivist schools avoided was the unequal treatment delivered by the criminal justice system. It was not until recently that criminologists have begun to concern themselves with this question.

Interactionist School

A number of studies have been done recently in this country and abroad. On the basis of this work Eugene Doleschal and Nora Klapmuts put forward a new theory which they call "Interactionist." Two of the most significant findings they present are the following:

1. A person is labeled a criminal, not because of committing a crime, but because of being arrested and convicted. Many people commit crimes; not all are caught and labeled.
2. No single socioeconomic class is responsible for committing a majority of criminal offenses. Rather, members of certain racial and economic groups are selected for arrest. They are more likely to be prosecuted and they receive comparatively harsh punishments.

The implications of these findings about the actual rather than the theoretical workings of the criminal justice system are far-reaching.

Any approach to crime that concentrates on the characteristics of the convicted criminal, the "causes" of his behavior, or his treatment aimed at preventing further convictions is likely to be unproductive. If the population of officially labeled criminals is as unrepresentative of the crime problem as these studies indicate, a very large portion of criminological literature is leading up a dead-end street.[1]

The Interactionists followed Durkheim's lead in accepting that criminal behavior is inevitable in all segments of society. They question why certain acts have come to be called criminal. They also delve into how the laws governing those acts are actually enforced. In essence they are shifting the focus from both the offender and the environment as the lone causes of crime. They point the finger at a system which singles out certain groups for vigorous law enforcement while treating others leniently.

The target of the Interactionists is unequal treatment before the law. They point out injustices: An elected government official convicted of bribery and tax evasion in the hundreds of thousands of dollars is spared prison. Meanwhile a shoplifter making off with $80 worth of goods goes to jail. Crime, they contend, is not the property of one class of people; it must be vigorously confronted wherever it appears.

None of these theories answers the basic question: Why do some people commit crimes? Indeed, we may never know the answer. But by continuing to search, we may at least find better ways of discouraging crime and effectively treating criminals. We may improve our criminal justice system, approaching the ideal of justice tempered with mercy and wisdom.

QUESTIONS

1. Is it better to view crime as a symptom, a label, or an end result?
2. Considering the rise in crime, which criminological school of thought makes the most sense today? Why?
3. What implications does the idea that society is at fault with respect to the rise in crime have for correctional reform?
4. Assuming that the criminal justice system discriminates against certain groups, what steps should now be taken to correct the injustices by police agencies, the courts, and corrections units?

1. Eugene Doleschal and Nora Klapmuts, "Toward a New Criminology," *Crime and Delinquency Literature,* 5 (4), 1973, p. 616.

part 3

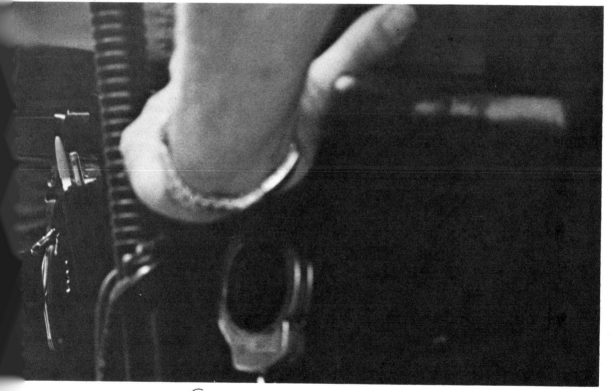

enforcement

Many of the police-related events which have caught the attention of the public have involved federal investigative bureaus. Exploits of the Federal Bureau of Investigation and the Secret Service have been well publicized, both factually and in fiction. Citizens often think the federal government has a greater responsibility for policing the United States than it really does.

In truth, law enforcement is primarily a local responsibility. Of the some 40,000 different police agencies in the United States, about 39,750 are local. There are only 50 federal and 200 or so state police departments. Thus, to say that policing in America is fragmented and decentralized is an understatement. Especially is this evident in light of the fact that the average-sized local department has approximately ten employees. For an idea of how a larger law enforcement agency might be organized, see Figure 6-1.

Every level of government—municipal, county, state, and federal—employs police officers. Many police functions overlap as one segment of government provides law enforcement activities which are duplicated by another. In any given city, routine patrol is carried out by the city department. Yet a dozen or more different agencies will be empowered to enforce certain laws affecting that city's citizens. Moreover, these agencies will operate within the city limits. The result is an often confusing situation in which jurisdictional disputes are common.

Because police decentralization creates such complexity, a survey by level of govenment initiates our discussion of law enforcement organization and administration.

AMERICAN POLICE: CITY, COUNTY, STATE, AND NATION

It would take an entire volume to survey fully the American police enterprise. Law enforcement is so diverse that there simply is no one system of policing. We have city, county, state, and federal agencies. Besides these there are tax districts, port authorities, housing developments, regulatory agencies, and the like, which have police officers. In order to keep this discussion to a reasonable

chapter 6

Organization and Administration of the Police

length, we will examine only municipal, county, state, and federal police.

The Municipal Police

There are some 17,000 municipalities in America, 55 of which are cities with more than 250,000 residents. It is here, in these large cities, where scholars have concentrated their studies. And it is here where some of the greatest challenges are facing law enforcement. The cities' failures in law enforcement are, in many ways, the country's failures.

Big-city police administration affects other police agencies. Programs, practices, and values are copied by departments outside the core cities. When a city has a superior police department, adjacent agencies will profit from its example. Unhappily, a bad city police department often spawns imitators, too. A good example of how a well-run department has wide-ranging influence can be seen in Los Angeles of the 1950s.

In 1950, William H. Parker became chief of police in Los Angeles. He moved to create an agency of which the public and police officers could be proud. Parker had his faults. He was rigid, stubborn, fiercely conservative, and personally abrasive. Nevertheless, he was honest, professional, and willing to innovate. He was strict, but it was a time when strictness was needed. He helped create one of the finest police departments in the country. In so doing he also contributed to police excellence throughout southern California. His legacy, then, was to a region, not merely to a single department. He furnished a blueprint and an example which were used by neighboring police executives. Many of these people were former Los Angeles police commanders who had profited from Parker's instruction.

The ability of large police departments to specialize thrusts them into leadership roles for two reasons. First, most have planning and research units which test new ideas, products, programs, and technology. The results are shared with smaller agencies, which then either implement or discard the innovations. Hence, the large city's

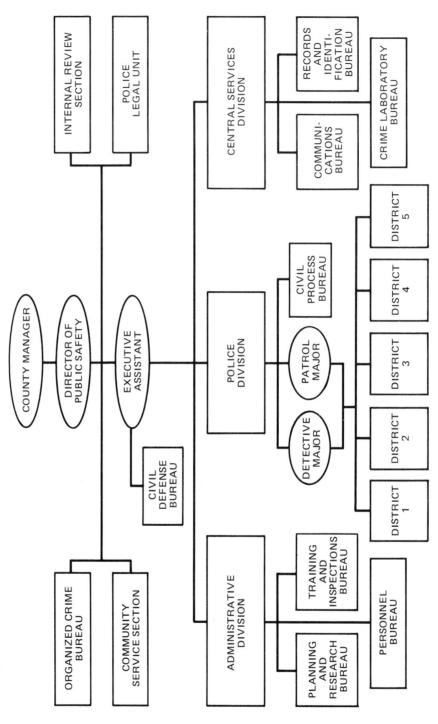

Figure 6-1 A typical large law enforcement agency.

department functions, in a sense, as a research department for those of the smaller cities. Second, specialization allows departmental personnel to seek out the work areas in which they are happiest and most productive. Officers can choose either investigative work or a specific type of detective work, such as homicide, vice, fraud, or auto theft. As a result, some of the most promising young talent seek employment in the cities. There they find the opportunity for specialization and promotion and the work is interesting and challenging.

Metropolitan law enforcement has a history of contrasts. Just as opportunities for excellence are present in urban police departments, so too is the potential for mischief. Some of the most professional services have been provided to the community by such agencies. However, so have some of the grossest forms of malpractice: brutality, graft, corruption, and civil rights abuses.

The organization of municipal police forces is a very important topic by itself. Therefore it will be covered in somewhat greater depth later in this chapter.

County Police

Counties usually employ both police and corrections personnel. Sections of the county which are not within city or town limits—the unincorporated areas—are patrolled by a county police force, usually the sheriff's department. Certain facilities such as county courts and confinement institutions also are in its jurisdiction.

A chief of police is almost always appointed to his position. The sheriff, on the other hand, is usually elected, being one of the few department heads who still are. Because the selection process is political, individuals have, in the past, been elected sheriff without even fulfilling minimal qualifications. As a consequence, sheriffs' departments have often lagged behind municipal agencies in professionalizing their service. This seems to be changing somewhat.

State Police

Every state in the union has a uniformed patrol force which is dispersed throughout the state. Each force is either a *highway patrol* or a *state police* agency. This is not a mere difference in names, but a sharp functional distinction. A highway patrol is concerned almost exclusively with traffic control and enforcement but has limited general police authority. A state police force, on the other hand, engages in a full range of law enforcement activities including criminal investigation.

State uniformed forces are supported by plainclothes investigators who conduct follow-up investigations on cases generated by the patrol force. They are an essential part of a state police agency. In the case of highway patrols, the investigators usually comprise a separate agency. It assists local police departments and enforces state laws relating to gambling, fraud, organized crime, narcotics, and the like.

There are other state law enforcement agencies that perform specialized duties. They have authority for fish and game regulation, alcoholic beverage control, state park patrol, wildlife management, etc.

Federal Police

No fewer than a dozen federal departments have law enforcement units. Even the Department of Transportation has several departments, including the Federal Aviation Administration and the Air Security Program. However, the Department of Justice and the Department of the Treasury have the major burden of federal law enforcement.

The *Justice Department* is headed by the attorney general. Like other department heads, the attorney general is a cabinet member appointed by the President with consent of the Senate. The attorney general is the government's chief legal officer. The Federal Bureau of Investigation, the Drug Enforcement Agency, the Border Patrol, the United States Marshal's Office, etc., are under the attorney general.

The FBI is the federal government's largest, most celebrated, and most powerful police agency. During its early years the bureau was racked with scandal. However, in 1924, when John Edgar Hoover took charge of the beleaguered agency, things began to change. Hoover committed the Bureau to excellence and an ongoing public relations program dramatizing the FBI's accomplishments while ignoring its faults.

Today, the FBI's 7000 agents enforce a wide variety of federal laws. These laws forbid bank robbery, kidnapping, interstate transportation of stolen property, civil rights violations, fraud against the government, and other crimes. The Bureau also operates a massive laboratory and maintains a central fingerprint repository. It sponsors an ongoing training program for local law enforcement officers. It also runs the National Crime Information Center (NCIC), a computerized information bank which shares criminal data with police agencies nationwide.

The Drug Enforcement Agency is responsible for enforcing federal laws controlling narcotics and dangerous drugs. The DEA main-

Case Study:
JURISDICTION

Yardstone, a quiet little town on the West Coast, was patrolled by a twelve-person police force. Even the chief took a shift during the busy periods and vacation time. During a calm summer night, an officer on patrol noticed a normal flow of traffic for the period of the year. Even the local drunks were in their usual positions. All was at ease.

Near midnight, the officer noticed an out-of-state car passing a stop sign. She followed the vehicle for a few blocks while deciding whether to make the driver pull over. Then, with the siren turned on, the officer stopped the vehicle, which contained two males.

Startled, the driver asked the officer what was wrong, as he presented his license and car registration. The officer informed the driver of the stop sign, then returned to her patrol car for a National Crime Information Computer check and a back-up unit. While waiting for the results, the officer noticed that the occupants of the auto were becoming jittery.

By the time the back-up car arrived, the officer knew there was no warrant for arrest from the computer. But when returning the documents, the officer noticed a gun butt protruding from beneath the front seat. With gun drawn, she asked the men to step out of the car.

The chief was called in. Police officers started to make a complete search of the car. When the rear of the back seat was removed, the officers found several cardboard boxes containing interesting material.

One of the boxes held two dozen pistols. On closer examination, it was discovered that the serial numbers had been removed from all the weapons. The guns matched the pistol found under the front seat of the car. It, too, had had the serial number scratched off.

The second box contained a large jar of pills and several large bags of a substance that was later identified as heroin. The driver of the vehicle and his companion were quickly placed under arrest. They were brought to headquarters for further questioning while the search continued.

More illegal material was found in the car trunk under the spare tire. An officer discovered $10,000 in cash, of which $200 was counterfeit. The complete haul and the car were taken to police headquarters and held as evidence.

The chief realized he had an unusual case before him. At least the case was unusual for his town. According to department policy, the desk officer filed the report and contacted other law enforcement agencies who would have an interest in the case.

Whom should the desk officer contact? Why?

tains close contact with other agencies, such as the FBI and the Bureau of Customs, which have related duties. The DEA focuses its attention on large manufacturers, smugglers, distributors, and organized crime.

The Border Patrol is the police arm of the Immigration and Naturalization Service. Primarily a uniformed force, the Border Patrol attempts to stop smuggling and the unlawful entry of aliens into the country.

United States marshals serve as officers of the federal court system. They keep order in the courts, serve legal papers, transport federal prisoners, and oversee the implementation of court orders. Formerly a patronage job, the position of U.S. Marshal now is part of the federal civil service system.

The *Treasury Department* is headed by the Secretary of the Treasury, an officer of cabinet rank. The department has approximately a dozen police agencies. The most important are the Internal Revenue Service, the Secret Service, the Bureau of Customs, and the Executive Protective Service.

The Internal Revenue Service has several sections, including the alcohol, tobacco, and firearms division. This division investigates violations of federal laws concerning the manufacture, sale, importation, and taxation of alcohol, tobacco products, and guns.

The Secret Service has two major responsibilities which have no relationship to one another. The first is the suppression of counterfeiting. The second is protecting the President, Vice-President, past Presidents, Presidential and Vice-Presidential candidates, and their families.

Agents of the Customs Bureau ensure that the government is not cheated of revenue from goods coming into the country. They also attempt to keep illegal commodities such as narcotics from being smuggled across our national borders.

A recently reorganized agency is the Executive Protective Service, a uniformed force. This service protects the White House, buildings where Presidential offices are located, and diplomatic missions in the District of Columbia.

ORGANIZATION OF THE MUNICIPAL POLICE

When most Americans think of the police, they picture municipal police officers. Local police have developed an organizational mode which, in some departments, has not changed much in more than a half-century. This traditional method of organizing agencies receives much criticism from scholars convinced that it is no longer appropriate.

The Traditional Method

Traditionally, the police have been organized in a semimilitary manner. This can be seen in their uniforms, rank structure, personnel policies, and management style. Police uniforms, with few exceptions, are either brown or blue. If they are blue, they usually resemble Civil War uniforms worn by union officers, after which they were modeled. Brown uniforms were modeled after Teddy Roosevelt's Rough Riders, who served in the Spanish-American War.[1]

Rank in law enforcement is similar to that of the army. In large departments, the chief may wear stars like a general. The people who serve beneath the chief in the department will wear insignias of colonels, majors, captains, lieutenants, and sergeants. Furthermore, with each promotion, stripes, bars, epaulets, braid, or brass, and the like, will be added to the uniform. All of these decorations are ceremonial, not functional. These things are supposed to show subordinates that managers are different and somehow special. Saluting is not often seen in law enforcement. However, military courtesies such as using the term "sir" or "ma'am" to address higher-ranking officers are quite common. Also, it is considered bad form for lower-ranking officers to refer to a supervisor by a first name in public.

Most police departments have big rule books designed to govern the behavior of officers, both on duty and off duty. Dozens of pages are often directed at uniforms and the officers' public appearance. Policies relating to hair styles are often precisely spelled out, and male officers' sideburns and mustaches also are often regulated. Most rule books warn against "conduct unbecoming an officer," a catchall section aimed at covering moral issues not covered elsewhere.

Chiefs of police have adopted distinctive management styles. The dominant one is a legacy from O. W. Wilson, scholar, author, and Superintendent of Police in Chicago. He was the most influential force in law enforcement in the past half-century. The Wilson style is set forth in the following description of Wilson by William Bopp, his biographer.

He grounded his philosophy of change on the assumption that the core of police reform was reorganization. A well-organized police department, with up-to-date resources and equipment, administered with a firm hand was, to Wilson, a good police department. Inject massive amounts of education and training, along with an on-going public relations program, into the system of the organization, and the result would be a professional police force. Under-

---

1. William J. Bopp, *Police Personnel Administration* (Boston: Holbrook Press, Inc., 1974).

lying all this was Wilson's premise that line officers must be closely supervised, the subjects of massive policy pronouncements limiting their discretion and consequently threatened with punishment lest they misbehave. Wilson held that policemen, if not closely controlled, would avoid work, engage in extralegal behavior, and would subvert the administration's goals. It is an idea which has been disputed by a great mass of social science research data which indicates that men want to work, they derive a great satisfaction from it, and creative managers will attempt to reconcile agency objectives with those of individuals. Still, Wilson never questioned the idea that officers must be coerced, controlled, directed and threatened before they would exert an effort to achieve the department's objectives. . . . Wilson was an expert at constructing the superstructure on which substantive reform could be built. Unfortunately, O. W. mistook the foundation that he laid as true form.[2]

A Contemporary Method

Severe criticism has been leveled at the traditional method of police organization. Critics feel that: (1) It retards creativity; (2) it fosters a kind of isolationism that leads to corruption; (3) it triggers rank-and-file labor militancy; (4) it results in having the police function like an occupying army in the community rather than like a social service agency; (5) it fails to recognize police officers as people with something valuable to contribute to department decision-making apparatus. Progressive police administrators have tried to end these problems by instituting a different organizational approach.

Contemporary theory holds that there are too many layers of management in many police departments. Having too many levels of authority, according to this theory, leads to poor communication. To combat this problem, decision making is decentralized, allowing commanders, supervisors, and patrol officers to exercise the maximum discretion.

Another target of reformers is the traditional military-type mode of operating a police department. In some localities the old uniforms are replaced by blazer-like jackets. Also, the traditional rank structure may be eliminated through the use of new titles such as "agent." Less emphasis is placed on superficial military courtesies. Team policing (explained in the next chapter) is also coming into vogue.

A form of organizational democracy is, in some departments, replacing authoritarian rule. This is not to say that rules are established by a vote of the employees. Rather, committees are formed to

2. William J. Bopp, *O. W.: A Biography of Orlando W. Wilson* (Port Washington, N. Y.: Kennikat Press, 1976).

Case Study:
TRADITIONAL VERSUS CONTEMPORARY

Officers in the Gairfield Police Department felt as if they were students in a strict private school. The Gairfield police chief believed everyone must follow his policies to the letter. Unfortunately the chief was nearly sixty-five years old and was still living by rules established before World War II. First of all, he did not believe in allowing women on the force. Officers were forbidden to let their hair grow long, and by "long" the chief meant hair touching the officer's collar. Everyone in the department had to be clean shaven and have no sideburns. Hair had to be cut at the top of the ear.

The older police officers did not mind as much as the younger men. The problem was with the new men who wanted to join the force but found it illogical to cater to the old-style police image.

Policy was so strictly followed that before the officers could begin a shift, they would have to line up in the ready room and be inspected by either the chief or the captain. Following inspection each officer would be required to salute the superior in command of the shift. Then, in line, they would march out to the patrol cars. Even the older officers felt this was going a little too far, but they also knew there was nothing they could do except comply.

After two years of the chief's management of the department, most of the younger men had had enough. Their attitudes on almost everything seem to counter to the chief's, making their job more difficult. The Patrolmen's Association started discussions with the elected officials on a new contract. One of the points in the new document was the management of the department.

Fortunately for the officers, members of the governing body held an open mind. They realize that what was policy forty years ago would need alteration in today's society. On the other hand, the commissioners knew that management of a police department was unlike that of a business, since the police are a paramilitary organization.

Because of the conflict, the commissioners decided the best way to reach a decision was to invite both parties to a meeting. Each party would be allowed to present its side of the issue. The only ground rule for the discussions prevented the chief from taking any action against the men because of their participation in the talks. The chief agreed.

If you were on the negotiations committee and were asked to present the views of your men at the meeting, what arguments would you plan to voice? What arguments would you expect from the chief? What decision could result from this meeting?

encourage officers to express their ideas on policy matters to management. Furthermore, a type of in-house due process, including a police officers' bill of rights, has been instituted in some places. These innovations aim to ease the harsh working environment which characterizes municipal law enforcement.

THE POLICE MISSION

The social control role of the police in our society is a terribly complex phenomenon. It is complicated by constitutional restrictions on police powers and by conflicting cries by many people for "law and order." The police officer must attempt to deal with crime and to balance the rights of the accused with the need for civil order. This complicated mission of the police is described by the International City Management Association as involving the following main duties:

1. *Preventing criminality.*   The police take a constructive role in seeking to reduce the causes of crime. They work in sectors of the community where criminal tendencies are bred.
2. *Repressing crime.*   This activity involves making routine patrols plus continually trying to eliminate or reduce hazards as the principal means of reducing opportunities for criminal actions.
3. *Apprehending offenders.*   Quick apprehension is viewed as the means to discourage would-be offenders. It has a deterrent quality. Additionally, apprehension enables society to punish offenders, remove them from society (and thus lessen the prospect of repetition), and try to rehabilitate them.
4. *Recovering property.*   When the police recover stolen property, they help to reduce the monetary cost of crime and to restrain people who, though not active criminals, might benefit from it.
5. *Regulating noncriminal conduct.*   Many police activities are only incidentally concerned with criminal behavior. For example, the police enforce traffic laws and sanitary codes. They aim at securing public compliance with the regulations by educating citizens and issuing oral or written means of securing compliance.
6. *Performing miscellaneous services.*   The miscellaneous services that the police perform are rescue operations, licensing, supervising elections, staffing courts with administrative and security personnel, and even chauffeuring public officials.[3]

3.   International City Management Association, *Municipal Police Administration,* 6th ed. (Washington, D.C.: ICMA, 1969). 3–4.

Case Study:
EQUALITY OF LAWS

Increasing financial costs of operating the city caused the police department to cut back their personnel by almost 30 percent. The civil service job was once thought of as safe from layoffs. Many government workers felt that if the government laid off workers, the country would be going under. Nevertheless, layoffs occurred.

The people who lost their jobs had a major problem facing them and their families. Commander Rapinsky, the head of one precinct, came under pressure. With 30 percent of his force cut back and crime increasing, it was almost impossible for him to keep the lid on the criminal element. The commander had barely enough police officers to answer the normal flow of calls. He had no idea how his people could conduct investigations.

The commander's fears were justified. Crime of all types had been rising even before the layoffs. Violent crimes were up 47 percent over the previous year. Gambling and other organized crime had increased 65 percent. On top of this, the area under his command was poverty-stricken. Residents charged that the police did not give them the service or protection they would have if they lived on the rich side of town.

Commander Rapinsky knew his public had a point, but he was doing all within his power to assure equal protection to everyone in the community. For some reason, there was more crime in the neighborhoods under his command.

One afternoon the mayor, police chief, and police commanders gathered for a meeting to determine the impact the layoffs had had on the operation of the department. All five commanders pointed to the high crime rate in the various categories even before the reduction in the force. They also illustrated in detail what areas of the department were cut back. These included special community and investigations units.

The mayor brought out other facts. About 48 percent of the city's rentable buildings had been abandoned. In terms of dollars, the city was in the red. If the city were a private corporation, the mayor claimed, it would be in bankruptcy court. In short, according to the city's chief executive, no additional funds could be brought in through taxes. Therefore there could be no increase in the size of the department.

The commanders had to return to the precincts and make some tough management decisions. With the limited number of officers available on any given shift, their efforts would have to be concentrated in a limited area of law enforcement. The force could not handle emergency medical calls, complaints from residents, gambling and numbers running, and narcotics sales. Only one or two areas could be covered.

If you were Commander Rapinsky, what decision would you make? Why?

We have slowly realized that crime is a complex social phenomenon against which law enforcement can have only limited success. So, much recent reform in law enforcement institutions has involved items 5 and 6 (regulation of noncriminal conduct and performance of miscellaneous services). These activities take up most of police officers' time and give them direct contact with people whose support they need.

HIRING AND MANAGING POLICE OFFICERS

The most important resource of any police agency is the human one: the men and women who staff the department. It was not always this way, however. Historically, personnel were the cheapest commodity—hired and fired with little thought of cost, effectiveness, or continuity. Now, things have changed. People, quantitatively and qualitatively, are what decide whether an agency will succeed in its objectives. William J. Bopp, in his book *Police Personnel Administration,* presents the concept of the police officer as a *human resource*. This discussion is based on that presentation.

The key to any police department's administrative scheme is a sound personnel policy. Basically, a personnel policy is a plan for the human resources of the department rather than equipment or physical facilities. The recognized major elements of a personnel plan are:

- Recruitment
- Selection
- Compensation
- Training
- Evaluation
- Promotion
- Discipline
- Labor relations

Recruitment

The federal government has set down rather specific requirements on the recruitment of minority groups. Municipal agencies must widely advertise police openings to ensure that applicants are drawn from a cross section of the community. There are differing pulls involved here. Many police administrators would like to recruit college graduates exclusively. Yet they have often been prohibited from doing so because of a lack of college-educated minority candidates. On the other hand, the rights of the ethnic majority must also be protected. Installing affirmative action programs without practicing reverse discrimination is a challenging assignment.

Selection

Every police department has standards for personnel. Some of the most common requirements relate to height, weight, residence, citizenship, vision, hearing, age, and education. A number of standards have had to be modified because they keep out certain groups. Minimum and maximum age requirements have been extended. Unreasonable height and weight requirements which discriminate against women and some minority groups are being modified. Although each police department has different standards, a typical selection process involves seven steps:

1. Formal application
2. A written examination
3. An interview
4. A physical examination
5. A physical agility test
6. A psychological evaluation
7. An investigation of the applicant's background

A good *application* form asks for information about: (1) the candidate's education, (2) previous employment, (3) credit and personal references, (4) prior residences, (5) arrests, (6) traffic tickets and accidents, (7) medical history, and (8) physical condition. The answers to these questions give investigators background information to check up on. Any intentional lying or evasion on the application is grounds for exclusion from employment.

Entrance tests are usually of the multiple-choice type. They vary in length, generally lasting from one to four hours. They do not measure prior police experience; the objective is to find people who have an aptitude for law enforcement. According to court decisions, they must be reliable and objective.

Applicants who pass the written test are scheduled for an *interview*, often before a panel of three police officers. The interviewers grade each applicant on his or her responses to questions. The examination score and the interview score are then combined for a total grade. A list of eligible candidates is developed based on their grades secured by this means. The remainder of the steps is not usually graded—one simply passes or fails. Failing any of the following steps bars an individual from further consideration.

The purpose of the *physical examination* is to make sure the candidate can withstand the physical demands of police work. It includes x-rays, a blood pressure reading, urinalysis, a blood count, vision and hearing exams, and a general evaluation. Many departments also demand an electrocardiogram.

The *physical agility test* is given to make sure that applicants can handle the physical chores of police officers. Every candidate is expected to show that he or she is strong enough for police work. Push-ups, pull-ups, and swimming are often part of this stage of the selection process.

A good *psychological evaluation* involves two steps: (1) the completion of personality inventory forms or tests, and (2) a personal interview with a clinical psychologist. This step is aimed at keeping out of the police force people who are not emotionally suited for police work. An individual who reacts to minor stress with violence would be a person to keep out of the police department.

A comprehensive *background investigation* is conducted on all applicants by experienced detectives. Furnished with data from application forms, background investigators learn whether the candidate's past suits him or her to police work.

Compensation

Police compensation plans include wages and fringe benefits. Police departments wish to recruit the best people available, so they must offer the same salaries offered by other employers. Fringe benefits must also be competitive. The most common police benefits are: (1) time-and-a-half pay for overtime; (2) uniform allowances; (3) shift differential; (4) longevity compensation; (5) hospitalization; (6) life insurance; (7) disability compensation; (8) sick leave; (9) vacation; and (10) retirement.

Training

Major police departments have ongoing training programs for all members. A number of states require minimum training standards for police recruits. Usually it is up to each agency to provide training beyond the police academy.

A favorite instructional device is roll-call training. This is a small block of time—fifteen to thirty minutes—set aside for training purposes prior to each patrol shift. These brief sessions are among the few times when a significant number of officers are assembled together. They actually add up to more than forty hours of instruction per year.

An adequate departmental training system includes: (1) inside instruction; (2) publication of training bulletins; and (3) use of outside training opportunities offered by universities and management training academies. The International Association of Chiefs of Police is one of several groups which sponsor regional courses on contemporary issues. Some other distinguished police-instruction institutes

Case Study:
POLICE VERSUS THE COURTS

Residents of a community know very little about how a police department and the legal system operate. In fact, some police officers feel that, if it were not for television police drama, residents would come in contact with an officer only when they received a traffic ticket.

The post-arrest and pretrial process is complicated for the police officer and the defendant, let alone members of the general public. This gap in education can cause the police department a great many headaches. Captain Jefferson was confronted with just this situation one evening.

Patrol officers in his department had decided to pull a job action over a pay dispute with the commissioners. The Patrol Officers' Association informally called for rule book operations. This meant many cars would be stopped and checked, holding up traffic for minutes. Any infraction of the law was strictly enforced. Residents were arriving in court not only for parking tickets but also for having dirty license plates, forgetting to sign their licenses, and other minor offenses.

The department was even running short on tickets for the officers to give out. Members of the governing body were obviously under pressure from the voters to curtail such action. Some members of the Patrol Officers' Association felt the pressure was enough to force the issue. However, for Captain Jefferson, still another issue was forced, and he was in line to render an opinion.

Several civic organizations decided to hold a general meeting and invite a member of the department for a question-and-answer session concerning the police force and their actions.

The chief informed the groups that he would be on vacation during that period; but that Captain Jefferson, who was second in command, would be glad to attend. Jefferson was later informed of the meeting.

An angry resident rose from the audience with a handful of tickets. "What's going on here?" he asked. "The real crooks go free hours after they get arrested, but the small taxpayer gets hit with these tickets."

Jefferson realized that the resident had a point. Every day the public hears stories of unresolved crimes and of criminals released from jail who return to a life of crime. Jefferson knew the public blames the police for not doing their job in the first place. Apparently the ticket blitz was just the spark to set off this explosion. Before him this evening were taxpayers who were not only being harrassed but who were paying his salary. Therefore an accurate reply was in order—and fast. Jefferson knew he had no control over the police officers, nor could he make suggestions to reform the judicial system, although members of the audience felt it was a police problem.

What should Captain Jefferson say?

for continuing training are: the Southern Police Institute at the University of Louisville; the University of Georgia's Police Science Division; and the Delinquency Control Institute and the National Sheriffs' Institute, both at the University of Southern California.

Evaluation

In municipal police departments, everyone is evaluated in one way or another. Formal evaluations are usually done annually when supervisors complete special forms rating their subordinates' work during the year. Merit raises are tied to these annual ratings. Also, the forms are kept in personnel folders and referred to when people become eligible for promotion. A below-satisfactory rating may mean the loss of a pay raise. Consistently low evaluations can result in extra training or even disciplinary action.

Promotion

Eligibility for promotion is generally based on *time in grade*. This means that an officer must spend a number of years in one classification before being eligible for a higher one. Some agencies also have educational standards for promotion. For instance, eligibility requirements for a promotion to sergeant might be: (1) to have been a patrol officer for three years; (2) to possess a college degree. This would not mean that an officer meeting these requirements would automatically be promoted. It would mean only that the necessary qualifications were fulfilled for competing for a sergeant's position.

When an individual is eligible for promotion, the next step is a written examination. These examinations are commonly given once a year. Everyone who passes the test is qualified to move on to the next hurdle. This is the interview before a panel usually consisting of police commanders. The candidate is graded on the interview, and this score is combined with that of the written exam. A list of people who can be considered for promotion is then developed and promotions are made from it.

Although police promotional systems vary, the one discussed here is in widespread use.

Discipline

Departmental rule books contain codes of conduct, and police officers are penalized for breaking the rules. Discipline has often been harsh. Now it has become a subject of controversy as police unions focus on what they consider injustices in the system.

The group whose job is to investigate suspected violations of police department rules is usually called the "internal affairs" unit. Internal affairs investigators conduct inquiries into complaints of misconduct against individual officers. These complaints usually come from outside the police force, although they occasionally come from other officers.

While internal affairs procedures vary from agency to agency, we can describe a typical system. When a complaint is lodged with the internal affairs unit, a detective is assigned to investigate. A number is given to the case and all witnesses to the incident are interviewed, including the accused police officer. An accused officer who refuses to submit to the interrogation faces dismissal. After the investigation, one of five findings is attached to the final report:

1. *Not involved.* The accused was not involved in the alleged incident (this can happen when a citizen jots down a wrong badge number).
2. *Unfounded.* The alleged incident did not occur or did not involve police personnel.
3. *Exonerated.* Acts did occur, but they were lawful and proper.
4. *Not sustained.* The investigation failed to uncover sufficient evidence to clearly prove or disprove the allegations.
5. *Sustained.* The investigation disclosed enough evidence to prove the allegation.

If the complaint is sustained, the officer will be disciplined. One of six penalties may be applied: (1) oral reprimand; (2) written reprimand; (3) transfer; (4) suspension without pay; (5) demotion; or (6) dismissal from the department.

Once disciplinary action has been ordered, the officer usually has the right to appeal it to a civil service board. The board investigates and returns one of the following verdicts:

1. The charges are true and they justify the penalty.
2. The charges are true but the penalty is too harsh. A lesser penalty is substituted.
3. The charges are not sustained.

An officer having a verdict against him or her may appeal it to the appellate court having jurisdiction in the area. Many police officers have done this. The result has been a mountain of case law which has often overturned the decisions of civil service boards. It has also established due-process guidelines for police managers to follow in internal disciplinary actions.

Labor Relations

Police unions and employee organizations are now a fact of life in the affairs of most police departments. Some function as powerful special-interest groups engaged in wide-ranging activities aimed at improving the lot of their membership. Their tactics include lobbying, litigation (going to court), collective bargaining, even strikes. Strikes, however, are rare.

Collective bargaining has meant that police administrators now operate with contracts regulating pay, fringe benefits, and working conditions. Decisions that had been up to management are now the subjects of negotiations. Power, then, is less centralized.

Police administration in a department which bargains collectively and is served by an active police employee organization is a challenging undertaking. Police officers are no longer satisfied with the traditional rigid styles of management. Therefore, administrators are being forced to implement a form of organizational democracy. The nature of contemporary law enforcement is changed. So active employee relations programs are becoming an essential part of the personnel plans of most major departments.

QUESTIONS

1. There are many different police agencies. If you could redesign the total law enforcement structure, how would you handle the multiplicity of police agencies? What would your model structure look like? Why?
2. What form of organization do you feel works best? Why?
3. How would you modify the police recruitment and selection processes?
4. If you were a police chief faced with the prospect of your officers forming a union, how would you respond?

Case Study:
RIGHT TO STRIKE

The negotiations between police officers and the governing body in a particular town became hot and heavy. Members of the governing body sought to increase productivity. The officers wanted more money and two patrol officers to a car instead of one. Contract talks continued for more than three months. Both sides stood their ground. The officers felt it was difficult to measure increases in productivity. Their position was: How do you measure the productivity of a police officer?

The commissioners realized this was a problem; however, they had to justify to residents the increases in pay. The mayor pointed to the increasing rate in minor crime without a corresponding increase in the rate of arrests. He charged that the police were lax in performance: "All they do is respond to an incident after it occurs, which does not help."

On the other hand, members of the department had become very leery of stopping cars and trucks and rushing to calls because of the increase in shootings of police officers in the United States. Their attitude was: "Why should I stick my neck out and risk being shot? If I do get shot, no one will take care of my family." They would feel better if there were two police officers assigned to a patrol car, thereby providing a back-up in case of trouble.

Although sympathetic to the situation, the commissioners realized there had not been a shooting of any kind in the community in fifty years. In fact, not a single police officer had ever been fired at in the history of the county. Besides, the department would have to double its personnel to put two people in every patrol car.

Apparently both sides had good arguments and would not bend their positions. After four months passed without a contract, the police officers held a special meeting to decide on a course of action. They were angry—especially after learning that they were the lowest-paid department in the area. They had their families and financial problems to consider.

The head of the police officers' association outlined the situation to the membership and indicated alternatives. Both parties could call in an arbitrator who would decide the terms of the contract. The arbitrator's decision would be binding. They could strike and place pressure on the elected officials. Or they could try for only an increase in pay and not push for two officers to a car.

A member of the group suggested that they take a mail vote on the issue. The membership agreed. Within a day or two ballots were sent to the officers. Four days later the result was known. An overwhelming number wanted to strike. Striking would be a violation of the law, but the officers felt that their problem was important enough to warrant this action.

If you were a member of the department, would you have voted for a strike? Would you expect someone who had voted against the strike to show up for work? How would the community accept the strike?

There is general agreement among scholars and police officers over the role of the police in America. However, the role has many facets. People disagree about which are the most important and which should be given less attention.

For use in this chapter, we will define "role" as what a person is expected to do in a given relationship.

Society's role expectation for a police officer—regardless of his or her personal characteristics—applies to all officers. It represents what "the people" demand of law enforcement workers. Police officers are expected to subordinate their individuality to exhibit the qualities and perform the tasks that the department wants.

SOCIAL CONTROL

As the police go about their work, they perform a wide spectrum of activities. They range from traffic direction to homicide investigation, from routine patrol to vice control. In all their varied tasks, though, one aspect of their role remains the same: Law enforcement officers are agents of social control. *Social control* refers to the machinery and techniques used to standardize behavior and produce order.

Social control produces social order, and social order consists of two factors. One factor is *normative order*, the agreed-upon rules governing behavior. The other is *social organization*, the patterned relations of individuals and groups in society. Social control is a product of social organization because individuals are dependent upon one another for satisfaction. Individuals realize that mutual dependencies also mean mutual cooperation, so they do not offend those on whom they are dependent. Among the aspects of life that contribute to social organization are a person's family, job, and civic group membership. Because of things like these, people are more subject to social control. This is because they depend on other people and others depend on them.

Social control among people is based primarily on custom. It may be either *formal* or *informal*. An example of informal controls are

The Police Role

those that the family uses to regulate the behavior of children. Formal controls are those initiated by government, such as police actions. Effective informal controls will often lessen the need for formal control. The police are agents of formal social control. Their work is made necessary by the failure of the family, the church, and peers to fulfill their roles adequately.

Police officers fulfill their responsibilities by employing methods of persuasive control or coercive control. Each of these is acceptable in selected situations. *Persuasive social control* comes from the police officer with the personality, training, desire, and opportunity to work closely with people. He or she must be the kind of person to whom adults and children will look for help.

Coercive social control relies on force, either actual or threatened. Coercive control is not often really needed. Yet there is some evidence that police officers tend to perceive it as their main instrument of enforcement. Control is most effective when people willingly support the institutions that have been established to protect their community.

THE POLICE CULTURE

As we discussed in the preceding chapter, the police, especially the municipal police, are organized and administered in semimilitary fashion. They are subject to stern disciplinary action and a rigid system of authority. They are forbidden to display conduct unbecoming an officer.

Out of this harsh operating environment, an identifiable police culture has developed. Although there are certainly exceptions, we can describe the typical members of this culture. (1) They are political conservatives who demonstrate authoritarian behavior. (2) They believe in the need for cynicism and physical toughness in their dealings with citizens. (3) They feel isolated from the public and in constant danger. (4) They are sure that they must support their colleagues, even when the colleagues are wrong. Some scholars believe that many of the unproductive elements of the police culture can be lessened. We can do this (1) by moving away from the traditional semimilitary organization and (2) by using instead the organizational models of business and industry.

Styles of Policing

Law enforcement agencies often develop recognizable styles of policing. Most police departments have a characteristic way of responding to social control situations, especially those involving maintenance of order. There are fundamental similarities between all law enforcement agencies. Yet the different value systems in different communities create pressures which make each agency in some way unique. Community values influence police administrators and help to institutionalize a policing system. Sometimes two police departments in the same geographical area react to similar situations in precisely opposite ways. In city A it may be common for an officer to make an arrest at the scene of family disturbances. In city B a police officer may help with the problem and leave without taking anyone into custody. Both officers are basing their decisions not merely on the elements of each case. They are also relying on their experience, professional values, training, and perception of what their department deems appropriate. In effect, then, each police department has assumed a distinct style of policing.

The department's style of policing will not make much difference in situations involving a clear-cut, serious violation of a law. In cases of rape, robbery, and murder, all departments arrest offenders who commit these acts. It is where the response is not so automatic, when discretion may be exercised, that a policing style is assumed.

James Q. Wilson has identified three types of policing styles which municipal police departments exhibit as they perform their duties. These are the *watchman style*, the *legalistic style*, and the *service style*.[1]

Police departments that use the *watchman approach* generally see their primary responsibility as maintaining order. They are permissive regarding minor crimes, choosing either to ignore them completely or to deal with them in nonpunitive ways. Police officers in agencies using watchman style are not pressed to produce measurable units of work, such as traffic summonses. Although issuing traffic tickets is part of police work, it is not a high-priority item. On the other hand, incidents which pose a threat to order are likely to be handled in a brusque way. For instance, mob violence or behavior which might lead to civil unrest will be put down firmly and quickly.

1. James Q. Wilson, *Varieties of Police Behavior* (Cambridge, Mass.: Harvard University Press, 1968).

Case Study:
CRIME PREVENTION

Lincoln, a medium-size community outside a major urban area, was due for a major change in police administration. For years the town had been closely run by politicians while the department was led by a conservative chief who rarely opposed a decision made by the mayor and council. Whatever the governing body felt that the police department should do, he agreed.

But now the old-time politics of Lincoln was over. A new administration was headed by a part-time mayor whose only goal was to operate the community efficiently. Fortunately for the newly elected officials, the police chief was near retirement age and agreed to step aside without any fight with the new government.

The new mayor, Grace Ortiz, felt her town needed a chief with modern ideas who was willing to try and experiment with new concepts. Ortiz realized it was a gamble, but she understood that the conservative approach to law enforcement was not working. Change was the only possible solution, with respect not only to the town government but also to the municipal department heads.

Scott Coda, captain of police in a neighboring community, applied for the police chief position. During the interview, Coda presented several thoughts he had on law enforcement. One of the ideas involved burglary. Coda felt this crime could be reduced throughout the country. His method involved a carefully prepared three-month community relations program.

Mayor Ortiz found Coda's proposal interesting. For once the department would take an active public role in reducing crime. Ortiz felt Coda's views were positive and could bring about solutions. Following conferences with the complete city council and other law enforcement leaders in the area,

Ortiz offered Coda the top spot on Lincoln's police department.

On the job for about three months, Coda decided it was time to begin introducing his public relations program against burglary. He started by writing a flyer about what residents should be alerted to, such as receiving calls and having the other party either hang up or pretend to be selling something. The flyer would also contain basic steps in home security.

The next step was posters to be placed in every store in the community asking people to call the police if they noticed something strange in the neighborhood. Regular and special police were used to lecture on home security and on when the public should call the police. Members of the department would also make security checks upon request of the home owner.

At the next mayor-and-council meeting, the formal plan was presented. The new officials agreed it was worth a try and voted approval. Coda obtained past burglary data for a five-year period. These would be compared with the results of the program.

Do you think this program will reduce the burglary rate? Why do you think this way? Do you have any ideas for a better plan?

Where the *legalistic style* prevails, police officers are trained to respond to situations in terms of the law. They exercise little personal discretion. If someone breaks the law, the violator is arrested. Legalistic police officers see their role as that of neutral arbitrators. They apply the law uniformly wherever and whenever possible, consistently and without interpretation. Their guiding documents are the statute books and local ordinances.

The watchman style and the legalistic style combine to make up the *service style*. Police officers who staff service-oriented agencies are encouraged to exercise discretion. However, written guidelines usually exist which limit them. Arrests are made, but sparingly and as a last resort. Nonpolice agencies are used as resources by police officers, who refer cases to them for follow-up action. So-called "soft" approaches to crime control are given high priority in these types of agencies. Citizen awareness campaigns and burglary prevention programs are examples of the activities in which the agencies will engage. Obviously, emphasis on police discretion and using outside resources requires that officers be well trained, well educated, and carefully selected.

We can compare these three approaches to policing. In the case of a homicide, the three types of organizations will probably react in exactly the same way. However, a car traveling eight miles per hour faster than the law permits may call forth strikingly different responses. The watchman police force might ignore such violations altogether. The legalistic force will most likely issue citations to everyone they can catch doing this. The service force may stop as many violators as it can but give warnings instead of tickets.

Behavioral Requirements

Some years ago, a team of scholars from the University of Chicago conducted an exhaustive survey of Chicago police officers. Out of that study came a list of behavioral requirements for the police. It is the most comprehensive job description ever produced. According to the Chicago study, line police officers must:

- Endure a long period of boredom on routine patrol yet react quickly (almost instantaneously) and effectively to problem situations or to radio orders.
- Know the patrol area and the normal routine of its residents.
- Show street sense, that is, solve problems and exercise effective judgment and imagination in coping with situations. These can include, among other things, (1) a family disturbance, (2) a neighborhood disagreement, (3) a gang fight, (4) a potential suicide, (5) a robbery in progress, (6) an accident, or (7) a disaster.

Case Study:
INTERAGENCY COMMUNICATION

Teenager problems face every community in the country. These youngsters meet with friends. Before anyone realizes it, the group increases to ten or more, and the noise level becomes almost intolerable. Then a call is made to police headquarters and a car is sent to chase the kids down to the park. An hour later, still another call is received from an elderly couple who want to walk through the park but are afraid because a "gang" is present. Again a patrol car disperses the teenagers. The problem is lack of activity and of part-time jobs. The young people are really not troublemakers.

Some teenagers, however, have deep problems and find criminal activity challenging and profitable. John Robertson was one of these kids. At sixteen he was having growing pains and broke a few car windows following an aborted joyride. Robertson was caught and then released after his parents agreed to pay for the damage.

Six months later he was stopped for joyriding. This time his parents could do little. The boy went to juvenile court and was told he would not be able to get a driver's license until he reached his eighteenth birthday. In his state, teenagers were able to drive at seventeen. The judge felt that such a ruling would be more effective punishment than placing Robertson in a juvenile home.

The day after Robertson's seventeenth birthday, police arrested him for breaking into a house and stealing a carton of cigarettes. The owner of the house had arrived home to discover the boy running out the back door. She recognized him from when he had been a cub scout and called the police to report the incident.

If nothing else, Robertson was honest. After a police officer arrived at his house, he admitted that he had committed the crime.

He was brought to court again, and this time the judge, impressed with the teenager's admitting he was guilty, placed him on what amounted to a year's probation.

Almost a year passed after this incident. Everyone felt Robertson was reforming—that the trouble had been just a part of growing up. But one of the detectives, staking out a block on another case, noticed Robertson looking closely at a house. The detective knew all about Robertson and that he was apparently going straight. Robertson stood there for ten minutes and then left, only to return in another ten minutes. The detective realized what was happening. Robertson was planning another break-in.

Several alternatives existed for the detective. He could approach Robertson now and arrest him on a minor charge used for detaining suspects. Or he could wait until Robertson committed the crime. Or he could simply forget about the situation.

If you were the detective, what would you do? Why?

- Make prompt and effective decisions, sometimes in life-and-death situations, and be able to size up a situation quickly and take appropriate action.
- Demonstrate mature judgment, as in deciding whether an arrest is necessary or a warning is sufficient, or in determining whether a situation requires force and, if so, what kind.
- Have the critical awareness to notice signs of out-of-the-ordinary conditions that indicate trouble.
- Use a number of complex psychomotor skills in tasks such as (1) driving a car in normal and emergency situations, (2) firing a gun under extremely varied conditions, (3) defending oneself in a fight, and (4) taking a person into custody with a minimum of force in both routine and emergency situations.
- Give oral reports, write up formal records, and complete official forms.
- Deal effectively with criminals, informers, local business people, residents, school officials, visitors, and others in situations that require various attitudes. These will range from friendliness and persuasion at one extreme to firmness and force at the other.
- Endure verbal and physical abuse from the general public (as when placing a person under arrest or facing constant race prejudice) while using only necessary force to maintain order.
- Look professional and self-assured when dealing with offenders, the public, and the court.
- Question suspected offenders, victims, and witnesses of crime.
- Take charge of the situation at the scene of a crime or accident without unduly alienating participants or bystanders.
- Be flexible enough to work under loose supervision in most day-to-day activities (either alone or as part of a team) and also under the direct supervision of superiors in situations where large numbers of officers are required.
- Tolerate many kinds of stress in situations such as (1) facing a violent mob, (2) waking people in a burning building, (3) chasing a suspect at high speeds, (4) being shot at by him, and (5) assisting a woman giving birth.
- Face bravely situations which may result in serious injury or death.
- Deal objectively with special-interest groups ranging from relatives of offenders to members of the press.
- Maintain integrity—for example, provide impartial law enforcement and refrain from accepting bribes or favors.[2]

CORRUPTION

The history of American law enforcement is full of major scandals. Considering the pressures under which police officers work and

2. Adapted from Jim L. Munro, *Administrative Behavior and Police Organization* (Cincinnati: W. H. Anderson Co., 1974), 15–16.

the temptations to which they are exposed, this is not surprising. Since earliest times, corruption has been a barrier to the evolution of police professionalism.

Twentieth-Century Scandals

Police corruption seems to peak during times when popular activities are prohibited by law but in great demand by citizens. The most dramatic illustration of this point occurred during Prohibition as exposés of police corruption became commonplace. Systematic inquiry into police misconduct was, in fact, born during Prohibition. In 1925, the Cleveland Foundation issued a report containing the passage which appears here.

Police machinery in the United States has not kept pace with modern demands. . . . Clinging to old conditions, bound by old practices which business and industry long ago discarded, employing a personnel poorly adapted to its purpose, it grinds away on its perfunctory task without self-criticism, without imagination, and with little initiative.[3]

The following year, the Illinois Association for Criminal Justice concluded that the fundamental cause of the demoralization of the police "is the corrupt political influence, the departments being dominated and controlled for years by such influence. Until the condition is removed, there is little hope for substantial betterment."[4]

In 1928, a grand jury was convened in Cook County to investigate the Chicago Police Department. It found widespread corruption and reported to citizens that the department was "rotten to the core."

The federal government was not immune from criticism. The National Popular Government League—a committee of attorneys led by Roscoe Pound and Felix Frankfurter—investigated federal agents in the Department of Justice. They discovered that agents had: (1) used corporal punishment on suspected criminals, (2) infiltrated radical political organizations, (3) forced individuals to testify against themselves, and (4) propagandized against racial groups to gain public support for the department's harassment activities.

In 1931, the National Commission on Law Observance and Enforcement (the Wickersham Commission), after two years' study,

3.   Quoted in William J. Bopp and Donald O. Schultz, *A Short History of American Law Enforcement* (Springfield, Ill.: Charles C. Thomas, Publisher, 1972), 99–101.

4.   Ibid.

submitted the most comprehensive report on American criminal justice in history. Among other things, the Wickersham Commission charged that the police (1) made widespread use of third-degree methods (that is, they used physical or psychological force), (2) were generally corrupt, had little or no training, and (3) were inefficient. Its major recommendation was that the police organization should be kept away from the corrupting influence of politics.

Prohibition was followed by the Depression and World War II. Police misconduct during these times of crisis was not nearly so widespread as it had been during Prohibition. The 1950s dawned with prosperity in postwar America. Affluent citizens demanded illegal services—primarily prostitution and gambling—once again leading to ethical problems for the police. In 1950, a Senate Crime Committee, chaired by Senator Estes Kefauver of Tennessee, discovered the Mafia. The Committee uncovered a virtual epidemic of police corruption. Police officials from every part of the country were found to be working with hoodlums to thwart vice laws. Hundreds of police officers were arrested and indicted. Ten years later, history repeated itself.

During the early 1960s, citizens' confidence in law enforcement was once again shattered by a series of scandals. In 1960 eight Chicago police officers were arrested for burglary in the notorious "Summerdale Scandal." Thirty Denver officers were indicted for burglary. Police officers in Buffalo were found to be on the payroll of gamblers. In 1961, the police commissioner in Boston resigned after a television documentary showed police officers frequenting a well-known illegal gambling establishment. In 1964, twenty-two gambling indictments were returned against Indianapolis police officers, all but three of whom were high-ranking officers.

The Knapp Commission

On August 3, 1972, the Commission to Investigate Allegations of Police Corruption in New York City released a report on police malpractice. The investigation and the report which followed it startled the nation. This was not simply because of the type of illegal activity uncovered, but because of its scope. The Commission found widespread corruption. New York police officers were reported to be accepting—indeed, soliciting—payoffs, even from narcotics peddlers.

The Commission divided corrupt officers into two categories: "grass-eaters" and "meat-eaters." *Grass-eaters* were ones who "simply accept the payoffs that the happenstances of police work throw their way." These bribes were small payoffs and presents from people such as cab drivers, traffic violators, and parking lot owners. They were given in return for overlooking slight infractions of the law. *Meat-eaters*, on the other hand, were defined as those who "aggressively misuse their police powers for personal gain." (These were protectors of narcotic dealers and big-time gamblers.) The grass-eaters were many, while meat-eaters were few. Although the meat-eaters received the major share of notoriety, the Knapp Commission held that the grass-eaters really did more damage.

Grass-eaters are the heart of the problem. Their great numbers tend to make corruption "respectable." They also tend to encourage the code of silence that brands anyone who exposes corruption a traitor. . . . The rookie who comes into the department is faced with the situation where it is easier for him to become corrupt than to remain honest.[5]

In terms of police department attitude toward corruption, the Knapp Commission's findings have relevance to the entire law enforcement establishment. The passage from the report that appears below gives the Commission's opinion on how and why corruption grows.

Feelings of isolation and hostility are experienced by policemen not just in New York, but everywhere. To understand these feelings, one must appreciate an important characteristic of any metropolitan police department, namely an extremely intense group loyalty. . . .

Pressures that give rise to this group loyalty include the danger to which policemen are constantly exposed and the hostility they encounter from society at large. . . .

Two principal characteristics emerge from this group loyalty: suspicion and hostility directed at any outside interference with the Department, and an intense desire to be proud of the Department. This mixture of hostility and pride has created what the Commission has found to be the most serious roadblock to a rational attack upon police corruption: stubborn refusal at all levels of the Department to acknowledge that a serious problem exists.

The interaction of stubbornness, hostility and pride has given rise to the so-called "rotten apple" theory. According to this theory, which bordered on official department doctrine, any policeman found to be corrupt must promptly be denounced as a rotten apple in an otherwise clean barrel. It must never be admitted that his individual corruption may be symptomatic of underlying disease.[6]

5. *The Knapp Commission* Report on Police Corruption (New York: George Braziller, 1972), 4.

6. Ibid., 5–6.

Police Corruption as Part of the System

Some social scientists have suggested an alternative to the "rotten-apple" theory of corruption. It formed much of the basis for the Knapp Commission findings and recommendations. This approach holds that police corruption in some communities is so common that a police subculture has developed to protect it. Ellwyn Stoddard made a major study of one police agency. New officers were introduced into a professional life of crime as rookies were oriented to their police duties by veteran officers. According to Stoddard, the rank and file saw graft as a fringe benefit.

Stoddard's findings are supported by Jack Kuykendall. According to Kuykendall:

The initial response of each officer will depend upon departmental orientation and how each situation is classified. Classification is a function of the actual and perceived situational indicators and the personal biases of each officer. Biases result from both personal and organizational factors. Personal factors for consideration include preemployment and existing socioeconomic status, racial and ethnic identification, family and friends. Organizational factors include subgroup identified with, position in the department, and the length of employment as it affects attitudes toward the role. . . . All these factors have the possibility of initiating or reinforcing the personal biases of the police officer and influencing how he classifies and reacts to enforcement contacts.[7]

Kuykendall asserts that police administrators can help combat internal lawlessness by installing certain control mechanisms. He identifies three approaches to internal control: legalistic, nonlegalistic, and dualistic. In the *legalistic* style, proper training, close supervision, and prompt disciplinary action for misconduct are basic. They convey to police officers the message that the department is committed to maintaining integrity. The *nonlegalistic* approach is very permissive; the department lets discipline take care of itself. The *dualistic* style is inconsistent. It is firm on some offenses and permissive on others, without any formal mechanisms of internal control. Kuykendall concludes that agencies using the legalistic approach are least likely to experience institutionalized corruption.

LAW ENFORCEMENT AS A SUBSYSTEM

Thus far, the discussion has centered on police officers' role, the policing styles it produces, and its impact on corruption. We have

7. Jack L. Kuykendall, "Police Deviancy in the Enforcement Role," *Police* (July–August, 1971), 44–49.

used the term *role* in relation to an individual. Whole institutions, however, can also be said to have roles. A major role of a police department is as a subsystem of the criminal justice system.

There is an acute need for police departments to recognize their role as part of the larger system. Such recognition would end the isolation which has characterized them in the past. Isolation has fostered an attitude that has contributed to institutional corruption. Police officers must stop thinking of themselves as the "thin blue line"—the last line of defense protecting citizens from disorder. Then the situation will improve. The police are *not* the only people assigned to protect citizens. Corrections workers and the courts have no less responsibility, although police officers do practice their craft in more dramatic fashion.

Crime prevention and the protection of due process are ties which bind the agents of criminal justice. Law enforcement must see the other two subsystems of the criminal justice system (the courts and corrections) as partners, not adversaries. Police officers and other justice professionals, such as probation officers, have more in common than they have in opposition. They have much to learn from each other, much to share.

POLICE-COMMUNITY RELATIONS

The riots of the 1960s dramatically illustrated that police-community relations were not good. Distrust, hostility, and outright violence directed against police officers convinced police administrators extraordinary programs were needed to heal the wounds. Now many police departments have developed a multiplicity of programs aimed at reaching the people, whose support they desperately need. They are trying to upgrade their standing in the community. Four approaches are used by leading municipal law enforcement agencies to promote good will. They are formal personnel training, internal investigating units, formal police-community relations programs, and persuasive social control.

Formal Training for Personnel

There are three general kinds of police training programs: preservice, in-service, and specialized. *Preservice* training is the instruction given new officers before they assume full police duties. In almost every police academy, a block of time is set aside for community-relations instruction. Its purpose is to teach future officers that they have public relations responsibilities in addition to traditional police authority.

These officers are using televisions to monitor civil disorders. Devices such as closed-circuit TV increase the efficiency of the police, but they also lessen the direct contact between the public and law enforcement personnel that could help improve police-community relations.

In-service programs are refresher training courses conducted on a continuing basis. Their aim is to help officers master subjects they know something about. Community relations instruction has become an essential part of in-service programs.

The purpose of *specialized* training is to keep officers abreast of new concepts. Although community relations is not generally a subject of specialized instruction, it is often an aspect of the main topic. When a technical subject is presented, its implications for community relations is covered. For instance, the department may be training officers in the use of a new tear gas spray. There will be discussion of the effect abuse of the device can have on the department's relationship with the public.

Internal Investigating Units

It is unreasonable to expect that no police encounters with citizens will lead to complaints. So it is only logical that a unit of the department should be assigned to investigate charges against officers. Many agencies have created internal investigating squads, staffed by detectives, to handle complaints against the police by outsiders. The assignment is not popular among police officers, although it is a critical one. Maintaining departmental integrity is also a primary

Case Study:
POLICE IMAGE

Community residents know the police are just a phone call away, but sometimes they do not really understand what the police do. Almost all the residents are television buffs, and police dramas are on for hours every night. In these shows police officers are cheered on and admired for arresting law violators.

In reality there are few if any police officers and police departments that can meet the standards set by television police departments. The routine of daily police work in most towns is a far cry from that of the television police officer.

Residents in the town of Bellview have been complaining about the actions of the police department in fighting criminals. They point to the many cars speeding through the community and the teen-age gangs walking the street. An elderly man stood up at a council meeting and claimed the police were too slow in arriving at his house. He had called around six o'clock to report that a cat was hit by a car and was lying in the street. At the same time police were handling a traffic accident.

The police chief decided that the image of the department was being tarnished. The cause of this problem, as the chief saw it, was that the residents were comparing their own department with the police departments they saw on television.

"Affirmative action is needed," said the chief during a department meeting. All the officers agreed to be more polite and alert, and they promised to dress in full uniform. Furthermore, the officers decided to use extreme restraint when dealing with an incident in public.

While on patrol, one of the officers noticed three men fighting outside a bar. With back-up units on the way, the officer decided to intervene, especially since a crowd had formed. In the struggle that developed, the officer tried to use little if any force in arresting the men. Even when one of the suspects punched the officer in the stomach, the officer did not return the blow but instead pushed the man against a nearby wall.

The back-up units arrived. As other officers were bringing the suspects to the car, one of the suspects reached under his coat. The first officer on the scene noticed a knife in the suspect's belt, took his night stick, and smashed the suspect's hand.

However, to the onlookers who did not see the knife, the incident looked like police brutality. They thought that the police officer began to use undue force as soon as he thought the crowd could no longer see what was going on. Residents became disturbed over the incident and complained to the town council when the chief failed to suspend the officer.

As police chief, what action would you have taken with the officer? How would you handle informing the public of the incident? Could this situation have been prevented? Did the officer handle the situation properly?

function of the unit, as investigations into suspected corruption are given high priority.

In the preceding chapter we discussed the procedures for investigating a complaint against the police. Internal affairs units are expected to be aggressive but fair in their investigations. They must balance the rights of citizens with the rights of accused officers. It is a delicate balance, difficult to maintain.

Formal Police-Community Relations

Many medium- and large-sized police departments have formal police-community relations (P-CR) units. These are staffed full-time by police officers. The units' exclusive job is to carry out programs which will improve the department's rapport with the public.

There is almost always an emphasis on reaching specific groups, usually the press, young people, and minority groups. Furthermore, the department furnishes speakers to civic organizations, schools, and churches.

Officers assigned to the P-CR unit are carefully chosen for: (1) their good appearance, (2) ability to speak well, (3) coolness in the face of provocation, (4) knowledge of department policy, and (5) loyalty to the agency. These officers are, after all, ambassadors to the community.

Unfortunately, many P-CR programs are not sincere attempts to create a bond between citizens and police officers. They are, rather, propaganda units to promote the department's "line." Many community relations officers feel compelled to justify their agency's activities in all cases. They do not meet with citizens to determine how the department can be improved. Too often the role of a P-CR unit is to bring the agency's message to the community, not the reverse.

Another problem associated with P-CR units is the effect they often have on police officers in the field. When a unit is formed, there is a danger of misunderstanding. Line police officers may view the new unit's members as the only ones with community relations responsibilities. After all, that is the way other specialized units work. For example, homicide detectives investigate murders. Vice officers investigate narcotics offenses. Juvenile department detectives handle young offenders. In these three situations line officers have only supporting duties. If this misapprehension occurs with respect to P-CR, uniformed officers will ignore their duty to be attuned to citizen needs. The existence of a special P-CR unit does not relieve uniformed officers of their community obligations. Neither does it mean that the department must speak when it should be listening.

Persuasive Social Control

The police have come under much pressure to decentralize their operations and implement programs of persuasive social control. As government grows in size, citizens are becoming increasingly sensitive to bureaucracies concerned more with paperwork than with people. Accordingly, as police departments have expanded, there has been a corresponding demand that they provide a more personal service. Good agencies have responded positively to community pressure in a variety of ways. They try to prevent trouble and, when it does occur, to keep it at as low a level as possible. In other words, they use *persuasive social control*. The most noteworthy types of persuasive social control programs have been team policing and crisis intervention.

Team policing is a scheme of decentralized geographic districts. Teams are created and staffed by officers who provide full police services for the district's citizens. A command officer is placed in charge of the district and functions more or less as a smalltown chief of police would. Patrol officers, detectives, and specialists work closely together in the district, fostering team spirit and a client-centered outlook. Detectives and uniformed personnel are expected to build a closer working relationship.

Crisis intervention is another method of persuasive social control. It means that officers are trained to use nonpunitive measures to stop trouble wherever possible. For example, a family fight might be ended by a well-known device. One spouse is lured out of the house and then arrested for public drunkenness. This is, at best, a temporary solution. Moreover, state after state has declared that public drunkenness is not a criminal activity, thus making the tactic useless.

The chief strategies of crisis intervention are: negotiation, basic counseling, and referral to social service agencies. They are used in handling domestic disturbances, juvenile fights, racial turmoil, and landlord-tenant disagreements. Even very dangerous situations, as when armed robbers are barricaded in buildings with hostages, are targets of this new concept. Officers trained in negotiations may be sent to talk rather than to shoot.

QUESTIONS

1. Describe the impact of the police culture on the public.
2. What policing styles do you think exist in your community?
3. Given the Chicago study conclusions, design a system for recruiting and selecting prospective police officers.
4. What can be done to reduce police corruption?
5. What kinds of programs might make the police a more valued institution in the eyes of the public? In your eyes?

part 4

MIDDLE   9. LEFT RING   10. LEFT LITTLE

courts

Many of the fundamental principles of our judicial system have their roots in the Judeo-Christian origins of our culture. The concepts of fair-minded judges, clearly defined punishments, and rules governing the witnesses' testimony can be traced to the Old Testament.

But how the truth is to be determined has changed throughout history. Out of trial by combat grew the idea of champions ready to fight on behalf of those less strong. From that ultimately came our adversary system of courtroom justice. Just so, the scribe who recorded judicial proceedings before the birth of Christ is the forefather of today's court reporter.

The direct ancestor of our courts, however, is the English judicial system. It was the idea of that system which our earliest settlers brought to this country with them. That system, and our own adaptation from it, are remarkable creations bearing the mark of a high degree of civilization. Men and women are willing to put their most keenly felt disputes before a third person and then abide by that judge's decision no matter how painful. This is proof of their desire to live in peace together.

But at the same time it puts a heavy responsibility on the judicial system itself. It is the confidence of the citizens in the fairness and honesty of the courts that makes the system work. The rule of law is a peaceable one. Without the willingness of the people to live by it, society would very likely fall into lawlessness. And lawlessness ultimately leads, not to greater freedom, but to a police state.

The standards of those within the judicial system must be of the highest if it is to continue to serve society well. In order better to understand this fundamental structure of our way of life, we will look at the purposes served by the court system. Then we will examine the participants in it.

PURPOSES SERVED BY THE COURTS

We can identify seven purposes served by the courts in the United States:

Personnel, Purposes, and Structure of the Courts

1. To provide a forum for the resolution of disputes
2. To do justice in each case
3. To demonstrate that justice is done in each case
4. To protect the individual from arbitrary government power
5. To give legal and social recognition to changes in status
6. To correct, deter, and punish
7. To maintain the proper distribution of power between the levels and branches of government

Providing a Forum

Conflict seems to be inevitable when people come together. The courtroom provides the setting, and the trial the process, for finding a fair and peaceful resolution. Every citizen has the right to bring his or her case before an impartial judge. It is also each citizen's right to present his or her side of the argument. Doing so has saved a great deal of bloodshed.

Doing Justice

The cornerstone of the British common law system was the doctrine of *stare decisis.* That is the development of basic legal principles out of individual cases and the application of them in similar cases. Each specific case must have those basic legal principles applies to it; when it does, the outcome is legal justice. The court must not be swayed by other concerns; what is at issue is legal right and wrong.

Demonstrating That Justice Is Done

Not only must justice be done, it must be seen that justice is being done. By consistently fair procedures the courts demonstrate their fairness. Such operation shows that the results of a specific case would be the same regardless of the particular parties to it. They make clear that it is a question of issues, not of personalities.

Another aspect of this is the need for consistency in the procedures of a trial. What is required of both the prosecution and the defense is set out in advance. In this way everyone involved will know what is expected of him or her. It would be very disconcerting to have the rules changed in the middle of the game.

Protecting Individuals from the Government

The Constitution has strong safeguards to protect the individual from a tyrannical government. The Bill of Rights specifically sets out the citizens' rights. The Fourteenth Amendment was added after the Civil War. It provides that every citizen of every state has the right to equal protection under the law. It also sets forth that every citizen is entitled to due process of the law.

"Due process of the law" is a vague term. In essence it means that everyone must be treated with fundamental fairness by the courts. Each citizen has the rights of freedom of speech, press, assembly, and religion. He or she also has the right to a fair and impartial trial by a jury of fellow citizens.

It is up to the courts to interpret these rights and others which are written into state constitutions. A large body of basic principles, arrived at through the process of deciding individual cases, exists. These rights are limitations on the power of the government over its citizens. Thus, each time the court rules on the legality of the seizure of evidence, for example, it clarifies a principle. It has defined the limits of the government's power in that area.

A court may rule that a search was illegal because the police officer did not have a valid search warrant. The court is thereby limiting the power of an agent of the government, the police officer. These citizens' rights, however, are not absolute. One cannot yell "Fire" in a crowded theater if there is no fire and then justify it as an expression of free speech. There are limits on one's rights, and it is up to the courts to decide where they are.

There is built-in tension in the judicial system. If there weren't two sides to every argument, there would be no courts. No decision is going to make everyone happy. While protecting the individual's rights, courts often enrage large groups of citizens as well as agents of the government. In the famous *Brown v. The Board of Education of Topeka, Kansas* (1954), the court ordered the racial integration of the schools. The shock waves of that bold decision are still felt today.

Courts must remain independent if they are to protect the rights of the individual. They must be free to make the unpopular decisions when they are the right ones. The judicial system must remain strong and free from all pressures so it can put justice ahead of practical considerations.

Recognizing Changes in Status

More than half the cases dealt with by the courts have to do with such changes in legal status. These refer to divorce, adoption, name

Case Study:
ROLE OF COURTS

It is rare for police officers to be able to attend a family gathering, since they work on shifts. When the time arrived for Patrolman Kotter to have a day off the same day such a gathering was scheduled, he and his family were happy.

Whenever his family gathered, Patrolman Kotter always became the center of attention and the topic was his job. Since the department required every officer to carry his gun while in public—on or off duty—the children in the family would always want to see his gun.

Kotter seemed to enjoy discussing his work and compared it with that of the famous television police officers. After the main meal, he and his brothers and sisters and cousins would group together to discuss the court system and criminals. One of Kotter's cousins claimed the judicial system is really unfair. He claimed that he knew two people where he was employed who had both been ticketed for failing to be licensed drivers. One of the men did have an operator's license but had forgotten to renew it at the end of the year. The other fellow worker had arrived from another country ten years before and had been driving a vehicle without a license since then.

The two men were brought before two different judges, since their offenses occurred in different towns. The one who simply forgot to renew the document received the maximum sentence—a $250 fine—while the newcomer received the minimum—$10 fine and $5 cost of court.

Patrolman Kotter agreed that such things happen, mainly in minor cases when records of sentences are not usually kept and each judge is required to set his own policy. When Kotter brought up the subject of judges, his sister made another charge. She suggested that the judicial system is corrupt, since politicians appoint judges.

Another cousin agreed, claiming that if a lawyer was a good party worker or donated a large sum to the campaign fund drive, he was sure to receive a judgeship if he wanted it. Of course, once on the bench, favors could easily be done without anyone really knowing what was going on.

Kotter's brother stated that if a friend of a top politician was in trouble, it would only take a talk with the right judge to set things straight again. On the other hand, if a defendant does not have connections, his or her chances of receiving equal treatment are almost nil.

Kotter's other relatives weren't sure of this conclusion. They realized that some judges are appointed by elected officials but thought that inferring that judges are therefore corrupt is a little out in left field. They turned to Kotter, the apparent expert in the room, for his views on whether his brother's statement and conclusions were valid.

If you were Kotter, what would you say?

change, and the distribution of property when death occurs (probate). These are seldom adversary proceedings, but rather the legal recognition of a new set of circumstances.

Correcting, Deterring, and Punishing

The power to impose a punishment upon another human being is a heavy responsibility. When it includes authority to condemn someone to death or to life behind bars, it becomes an awesome one. Such decisions are often final and not subject to review by any other body. A judge must measure the punitive effect of a sentence on the offender and its deterrent impact on others. For this he or she needs wisdom and restraint. And a judge needs self-confidence to take the criticism some of his sentencing decisions may provoke.

Maintaining a Balance of Power within the Government

This function of the courts is virtually unique to the American democratic system. Our form of government divides authority between state and federal governments. Also, it separates the powers of the three basic branches. The courts (the judicial branch) are responsible for keeping each level, and each branch, from meddling in the affairs of the others.

This power can and sometimes does result in hostility. President Franklin Roosevelt was unhappy with a number of court decisions which limited the power of the executive branch. He threatened to enlarge the U.S. Supreme Court by adding more judges who, presumably, would see things his way.

This effort to "pack" the Court was defeated. Yet one occasionally sees state legislatures react to unpopular decisions by cutting budgets for the judiciary. However, the federal Constitution and many state constitutions as well recognize the danger of this kind of "revenge." Therefore, clauses have been added which prevent the legislature from reducing a judge's salary while he or she is in office.

PARTICIPANTS IN THE COURT SYSTEM

The principal participants in the judicial system are: (1) trial and appellate court judges; (2) public prosecutors (often district attorneys); (3) public and private defense lawyers; and (4) court clerks and court reporters. In addition, important functions are performed by: (1) pretrial release agencies; (2) the jury commissioner; (3) the jury; (4) the bailiff; and (5) research aides and the clerical staff. (See Figure 8-1.)

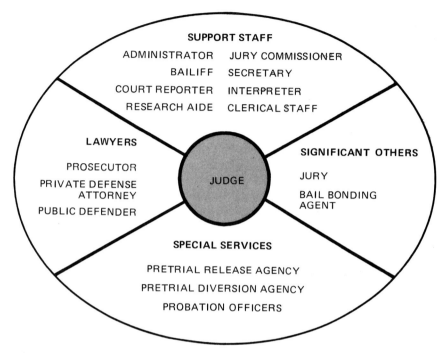

Figure 8-1 Not all courts have all the personnel indicated above. In some jurisdictions support staff and people in the special services area do not work directly under the judge. The lawyers and the significant others are independent agents.

Functions of the Participants

Trial judges are responsible for applying the law in cases brought to court. They may decide factual questions surrounding guilt and innocence if there is no jury. They also may set the amount of bail. Unless these are laid down by statute, they may decide on sentences to be given convicted offenders.

Appellate court judges may review the actions of trial judges to see if any errors of law were made by them.

The *public prosecutor,* or the *district attorney,* represents the government in prosecuting those arrested and charged with an offense. (It will be remembered that only the state can bring a criminal prosecution against a citizen.) Prosecutors screen cases to determine which will come before the courts and which will be dropped. If formal charges are brought, the prosecutor presents the case in court. In order to secure a conviction, the prosecutor must prove guilt beyond a reasonable doubt. Since the defendant is presumed innocent until proved guilty, it is up to the prosecutor to prove it.

Defense counsel represents the accused and tries to establish clear innocence in the minds of the judge or jury. If not that, then at least they must suggest the reasonable doubt which will lead to a verdict of not guilty.

Both the prosecutor and the defense lawyer are considered officers of the court. They have a special responsibility to bear in mind the overriding goal of the proper administration of justice. Thus they represent the court at the same time that they represent their clients.

The *clerk of the court* is the official record keeper. It is his or her responsibility to see that records are kept. Also, the records must accurately reflect the actions of the court in the handling of each case.

The *court reporter* keeps a word-for-word record of the proceedings of the court. Accuracy is of the greatest importance, since in a legal matter a great deal can hang on a single word.

Pretrial release agencies and *private bail bonding agents* arrange for the release before trial of those charged with an offense. They may also supervise the accused while on release.

The *jury commissioner* provides a pool of people eligible to serve on juries.

The *jury* is composed of up to twelve citizens. When "empaneled," or selected for a certain case, they will decide the issue of guilt or innocence. In a few states the jury also has the power to set sentences.

Research aides assist the judge in researching the law and in the preparation of orders and opinions of the court.

The *bailiff* keeps order in the court and may also take administrative charge of the jury during a trial.

The *clerical staff* provides important recordkeeping and other support services.

How Court Personnel Are Selected

The method of selecting judges varies, but there are basically three ways in which it is done: (1) by appointment, (2) by election, and (3) by the Missouri plan. *Appointment* is the method used by the federal system and in most of the Northeastern states. In general, the chief executive chooses a candidate, who is then either accepted or rejected by the legislature. In the federal system such an appointment is for life. Under many state systems the judge stands for election after completing one term.

Election of judges by the voters of the state is favored in most of the South and West of the country.

Case Study:
DISCRETION IN PROSECUTION

In a few months the department expected to have an opening in the detective bureau. The position, like any high-level position in the department, would go to the senior patrol officer who had a good arrest and overall performance record. Superiors looked for those officers who not only arrested the average minor criminal (such as a drunk driver or a driver of a hit-and-run vehicle) but who also took time to develop a case. One of the most important concerns within the department was conviction.

Officer Davidson, a senior member of the patrol force, had had her eyes on a detective shield for some time, but her routine work rarely gave her the opportunity for making interesting arrests. Most of her peers were in the same situation. Therefore if she could make just one good arrest, she might have that new badge.

Davidson heard rumors about a bookie operation being run in a glass store in town. She wasn't sure that the rumors were true but decided to do a little work on her own time, out of uniform. The officer went to almost every candy store and diner in the area, hoping to start up a conversation about racing and the problems of getting to the track daily. Davidson hoped someone would give her a number to call to solve the problem.

After a month she was lucky. A bartender slipped her a number to call. She played the game to the letter—made a phone call to the bookie and placed a bet.

Davidson went into the glass store the following day, claiming that her car had broken down, and asked to use the phone. She was surprised to learn that the only phone in the store was a pay phone on the wall. There was no phone number listed on the dial. She called home and, during the call, told the owner of the glass store that some-one would be calling back. Naturally, she asked for the number of the phone. The owner gave the number—the same number Davidson had used earlier to place a bet.

While Davidson waited for the return call, she noticed flash paper near the ashtray on the counter. Nothing was written on the paper. A local newspaper lying nearby was open to the racing section. The officer felt she had all she needed to make the arrest—the paper, newspaper, and the telephone number she had used to make a bet. Davidson proceeded to arrest the store owner for bookmaking.

The case was presented to the town prosecutor for adjudication. A week after the arrest, Officer Davidson was notified in writing that there was not enough evidence to warrant court action. Furthermore, the prosecutor was dismissing the charges. The local judge had also agreed.

Did the prosecutor have the power to do this? Was there any legal reason for him to do this? What should the officer have done before making the arrest?

In the *Missouri plan,* a citizen panel, all lawyers or lawyers and laymen, chooses a small group of the applicants. From these the executive or legislative branch makes the final selection. After a judge has served on the bench for a period of time, an election is held. This is to determine whether he or she is accepted or rejected by the people.

In the federal system public prosecutors are generally appointed by the executive. In state systems some are appointed, but mostly the voters choose them from a field of at least two candidates. Public prosecutors are often opposed in elections. Judges, however, seldom are—for a practical reason. A lawyer who opposes a judge running for reelection may later receive a hostile reception in the courtroom.

Public defenders are chosen in the same way as public prosecutors.

In the past the position of chief clerk was usually an elective office. Now, however, the trend is toward appointment to this post.

Practice for choosing court reporters varies widely. In some states they are hired by the court and work directly for it. In others they are independent agents whose services can be hired by parties to the case or by the court.

With an increase in federal funds for the purpose, the number of state-supported pretrial release agencies has grown. They are operated by the county government, the district attorney's office, or sometimes by the courts themselves. Graduates in social work, sociology and the social sciences frequently staff these agencies. Also, more and more ex-offenders are finding work there as well.

Sometimes a vacancy occurs in an elective office because of death, illness, or resignation. It is then usual for the executive or the legislature to appoint a successor. The appointment is either confirmed or rejected by the people in a special election.

Education and Training of Court Personnel

Since very early times in America, most of our judges have had some form of legal training. In fact, they have had far more training than is the case in other countries. In England, for example, the majority of minor cases are heard by respected community members rather than trained lawyer-judges.

The educational requirements for judgeship in this country vary, starting with reading law with a practicing lawyer. The far more usual ones are a college degree, law school degree, and passing the bar examination. The activities of the American Bar Association and other lawyer groups have virtually driven the nonlawyer judge from the scene.

Of the few judges without formal legal education, most are to be found in the lower courts. These are called "courts of inferior jurisdiction" and have power only over misdemeanors and preliminary hearings in felony cases. Many of these judges work only part-time and are usually found in sparsely settled rural areas.

For public prosecutors and defense lawyers, formal legal training is required—successful completion of law school and passing the bar examination. The legal training hallmark is to understand the case issues well enough to take either side and argue it successfully.

Lawyers are frequently asked, "How can you defend a person you know is guilty?" or, "How can you prosecute when you feel less than sure of the accused's guilt?" The important fact is that every citizen is guaranteed the right to a free and fair trial. The state, through the public prosecutor, has the responsibility to prove the guilt of the accused beyond a reasonable doubt. It is the defense lawyer's duty to put the state to the test of proving that guilt. The lawyers simply present the arguments for their clients (the state on the one hand and the accused on the other). The decision as to guilt or innocence must be left to the judge or jury.

Clerks of the court often start out as deputy clerks of the court. This is a post requiring a high school diploma in most states. They are then trained on the job by the senior clerks. However, community colleges are beginning to offer courses for aspiring clerks of the court.

Great technical skill is required of court reporters since they must capture every word spoken during a trial. Training can take up to two years. It is a demanding job that commands a high salary—occasionally higher than that of the judge.

PROMOTIONS AND REMOVAL FROM OFFICE

For judges, promotion to a higher court comes either through election or by appointment. Removal from office can be achieved in a number of ways, depending on federal or state rules: (1) the action of a group of fellow-judges who form a qualification committee; (2) defeat at an election; (3) the action of the state supreme court; or (4) impeachment proceedings in the legislature. Among the grounds for removal from the bench are incompetence, criminal activity, and violations of judicial codes of ethics.

Civil service administrations more and more frequently determine promotion for public prosecutors and public defenders. Where that is not the case, promotion generally results from a combination of length of service and demonstrated trial ability. In most urban areas assistants to the public prosecutor and public defender are full-time employees. However, in some rural areas these are part-time posts and can present serious problems of conflict of interest. In such a situation it is possible that a prosecutor may represent the state in a case against a husband for wife beating. Later the same lawyer may turn up as the wife's personal lawyer in a divorce action.

Grounds for removal from office and the procedure to accomplish it are similar to those for judges. However, these officers are not usually subject to action by the supreme court or to impeachment. The real problem is not with firing, but with trying to hold on to good people. Career opportunities for fame and fortune are greater in private practice than in public service. Thus, positions on the staffs of both public prosecutor and public defender have become training grounds for future defense lawyers.

Thus, often an inexperienced young prosecutor with a big caseload faces an experienced private defense lawyer with a smaller caseload. In recent years there has been a move toward higher salaries for lawyers in public service. However, the results have not been altogether encouraging. More than money is involved. Something in lawyers' training tends to make them see themselves as independent professionals and not as government employees.

The post of clerk of the court is generally covered by civil service regulations. Firing is difficult since the employer must show good cause. Also, the employee may have the right to appeal to the courts to test the legality of the dismissal.

Court reporters can be fired for: (1) being found to be incompetent; (2) failing to submit typed transcripts of the court proceedings within the specified time.

Research aides, bailiffs, and the clerical staff are often hired by, or with approval of, the judge they serve. They must perform to that judge's satisfaction.

PERSONAL VALUES AND PROFESSIONAL CONDUCT

Reelection weighs heavily on the minds of many judges, and political campaigns can be very expensive. Most judges do not have independent means and must rely, like any political figure, on contributions. In judicial races those funds will usually come from lawyers and private bail bonding agents. The judge whose ethics demand independence, integrity, and impartiality may find that applying those standards will drive away campaign support. This situation has led to frequent attempts to "take the judges out of politics."

Unfortunately, the alternative—a system of appointments—does not effectively remove the judge from politics. The executive officer who makes appointments may demand the judge's loyalty in a future campaign. Yet long- or life-term appointments may protect the judge from political influence. At the same time a long-term appointment prevents the people from holding him or her accountable to public concerns. Opinions differ widely on how best to select judges. We should remember they are human beings whose personal values are bound to have an effect on their professional performance.

Ours is an adversary judicial system, pitting the champion of one side against the other in the search for truth. Also, most prosecutors and defenders are the ambitious sons and daughters of the middle class. The result is seen to be a highly competitive and aggressive system. The need to win can conflict with the lawyer's role as an officer of the court. As such an officer, the lawyer is committed to the overriding goal of the proper administration of justice. To a greater or lesser degree, this conflict is one of the many tensions built into the system. Elsewhere in this book we will examine it in greater detail.

In some cases the clerk of the court is elected by the people or appointed by the local county commission rather than by the court. In such situations the clerk has an independent power base and can frustrate the judge's wishes. This rarely happens in an overt way. Clerks by training and by nature generally view the judge as the central authority in the judicial system. However, the potential for mischief is there.

THE STRUCTURE OF THE COURT SYSTEM

In this chapter we have looked at the goals of courts and at the people who staff them. Now we turn to the structure and processes of the court subsystem.

Our court system was born in rural and small-town America. The early court systems were simple, as represented in the diagram in Figure 8-2.

The supreme court was traditionally located in the state capitol. Circuit court judges literally rode the circuit, hearing the few cases that had accumulated since the judge's last visit. The major criminal and civil cases were handled by the circuit judge. The city and justice courts took care of minor matters.

As America became urbanized and litigation grew, many states added more courts. Often these were tribunals with specialized areas of subject matter authority. Today, the court system varies from state to state. We will look at several states' systems to show the general features commonly found throughout the country. Also, we will be

Figure 8-2   Simplified view of the Florida system.

able to see some of the problems that occur. Figure 8-3 shows the court structure of the State of Florida in 1973, after more than a century of development.

Infractions, or violations of city and county laws, were tried in municipal court in Florida. These were traffic violations and other minor offenses committed within the boundaries of a city. The *justice of the peace courts* had the power to: (1) judge criminal cases of a minor nature; (2) hold hearings to determine if there was adequate reason to believe the arrested person had committed the crime charged (preliminary hearings); (3) issue arrest and search warrants. Felonies other than those carrying the death penalty and misdemeanors were generally tried in the criminal court of record. Cases involving the possible application of the death penalty were tried in the *circuit court*.

The appellate process in Florida was equally confused. First, the purpose of a court of appeal is to determine if errors were made in the trial court. The appellate court decides whether the trial judge made errors during the processing and trial of the case. It also rules

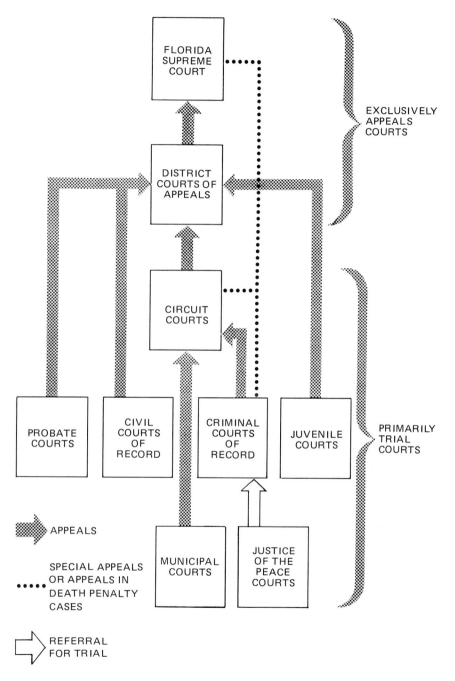

Figure 8-3   Courts in Florida.

on whether there was enough evidence to convict. In an appeal, the court basically considers the written record of witnesses' testimony, supporting physical evidence, and trial court papers. In Florida's court system, appeals from municipal court and from misdemeanor convictions in criminal court were heard by the circuit court. Convictions in felony cases were handled by the *district court of appeals* unless they involved a death sentence. If the defendant received a death sentence, the appeal went directly to the *state supreme court.* Some special kinds of appeals, called "extraordinary writs," went either directly from criminal or circuit courts to the supreme court. Others of this category went from the district court to the supreme court.

Besides notable confusion, this court system lacked flexibility and rationality. When the criminal caseload began to grow faster than the civil caseload, the criminal courts couldn't handle all the cases. They had about the only judges who could handle ordinary felony trials. So these courts floundered while the civil courts were able to keep up with the caseload. One had to have been a lawyer for seven years to be a criminal court judge. But strangely enough, one had to have been a lawyer for only five years to be a circuit court judge. Moreover, death penalty cases were tried in the circuit court while nondeath penalty cases were tried in the criminal court! Too, a judge with less time practicing law (circuit court) heard appeals in misdemeanors from cases tried by judges with more experience (criminal court). This court system was revised by constitutional amendment to look like the diagram shown in Figure 8-4.

The structure of the Federal Court of the United States is shown in Figure 8-5. It appears much the same as the revised state court system shown in Figure 8-3.

The court systems of several other states are presented in Figures 8-6, 8-7, and 8-8 for comparative purposes. New York City has civil and criminal courts at the fourth level of courts shown above. It does not have district courts, city courts, town and village courts, or county courts.

All these state court structures appear to look much like the organization of police departments described in Chapter 6. However, appearances can, as someone said, be deceiving. Police organizations attempt to be tightly organized with most of the power at the top. In courts there are two kinds of power arrangements, case review and administration. The higher courts shown on these charts have case review power. The upper court reviews the cases decided by the lower court and upholds, overturns, or modifies the lower

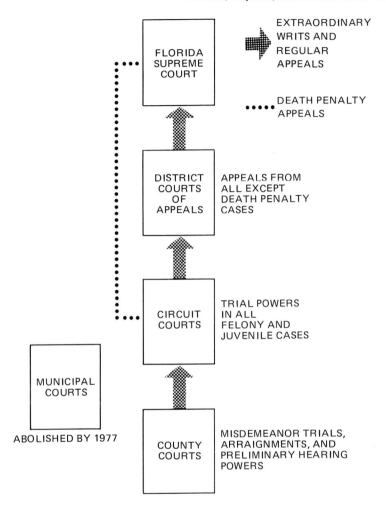

Figure 8-4   Criminal jurisdiction in Florida courts.

court's decision. In this way, the courts trace the organizational framework of the police system. But the picture of administrative power arrangement is quite different. In most courts of the United States today, the lower courts' administration is carried on by the lower courts themselves. There is a trend to centralized management, but it is fragmented and incomplete. This freedom from centralized control breeds great diversity in how cases are processed through the courts. In the next chapter the basic pattern of case processing is described.

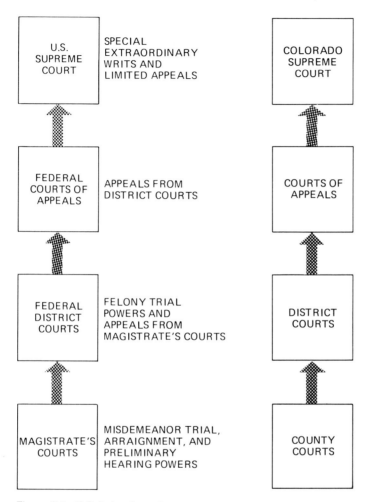

Figure 8-5 U.S. federal courts.

MUNICIPAL
COURTS

NOTE: Municipal courts
are not considered within
the state system. They are
largely state funded.

**Figure 8-6 Colorado court system.
(There are some variations from this
model in the city of Denver.)**

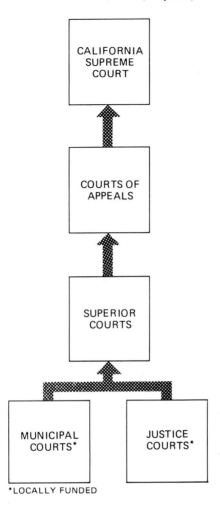

Figure 8-7   California court system.

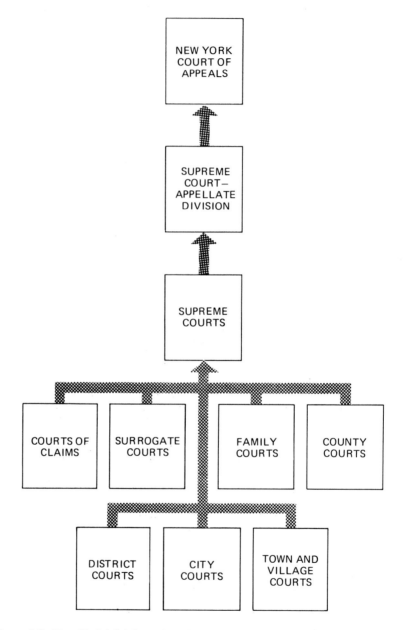

Figure 8-8   New York (state) court system.

QUESTIONS

1. What alternatives do you see to the current court system?
2. What are the attributes of an ideal judge? What selection process would be most likely to obtain ideal judges?
3. How would you propose to improve the efficiency of the public prosecutor's office?
4. How would you redesign a court structure to make the court work better?

We have considered the structure of the courts in the criminal justice system and the functions served by them. Now we turn to the question of how they actually work. Consider a clock, for example. It is possible to catalogue its functions as everything from the day's measuring stick to humanity's brief passage on earth. But that sheds little light on the intricate machinery that makes it work. The court system has two things in common with the clock. It has complicated inner works, and it needs to have something or someone to set it in motion.

To start the court working, one party to a lawsuit must present it with a document of some sort. Also, the suit must be on a matter of substance. Tradition says, in this country courts will act only on cases which present real conflicts needing resolution.

Further, a general rule is: A high appeals court will not hear a case so similar to others already decided that the outcome would be the same. There must be significant factual differences which will "distinguish" the new case from those cases which have preceded it.

We think of a court case in terms of the trial. However, the workings of the court system come into play long before the trial stage. Indeed, that is close to the end of a long and complex path strewn with stumbling blocks for the unwary. We will follow it from arrest through posttrial procedures and the appellate process.

ARREST

Arrest is imagined a simple matter of a police officer grabbing a crook and carting the criminal off to jail. It is in fact a very complicated business full of devices to protect the citizen.

If the crime is a felony, the officer with a warrant can arrest a suspect for probable cause. To arrest without a warrant, the officer must have seen the act or received information from the victim or a reliable witness.

In the case of a misdemeanor, the police officer must either (1) have personal knowledge of the offense or (2) a warrant, signed by a

chapter 9

Court Procedures

judge, for the arrest of the suspect. In minor cases the officer can issue a summons or citation requiring the accused to appear in court at a given time. If he or she fails to appear, the judge will issue a warrant for arrest.

In any case, felony or misdemeanor, an officer who feels a warrant is necessary generally must appear before a judge. The warrant may be secured (1) to protect the officer from charges of false arrest, or (2) because the victim may be unwilling to press charges unless there is a warrant. The officer can also ask the victim to join in requesting a warrant. That often sorts out the frivolous charges from the serious ones.

In order to get an arrest warrant from a judge, the police officer must make a *sworn affidavit*. That is, the officer presents the facts of the crime to the judge under oath. If the judge finds in this probable cause to believe that the accused was responsible, an arrest warrant is issued. The officer then finds and arrests the suspect.

In some states the officer can appear before the district attorney and ask that an "information" be issued. An *information* is a formal charge, on the securing of which a type of arrest warrant can be issued. An officer may also be able to appear directly before a *grand jury*. This is composed of citizens who have the power to issue formal charges, or *indictments*. As is the case with an information, after an indictment is issued an arrest warrant can be had.

It is general practice for the police to ask for arrest warrants. However, the public prosecutor or the district attorney can ask for one by seeing either an indictment or an information. This is done in such cases as public corruption and allegations of police misconduct.

After arrest, the accused is taken to jail and formally "booked": fingerprinted, photographed, and identified.

PRETRIAL PROCEDURES

Pretrial Release

Once arrested, the "accused" becomes the "defendant." The defendant is entitled to apply for release from jail before the first court appearance, provided someone posts a *bail bond*. The bond is a deposit of money or property. The purpose of the bond is to assure that the defendant will appear in court when the time comes. If the defendant fails to appear, the bond will be confiscated. The defendant will then be in a great deal of trouble.

The amount of bond required in a felony case such as burglary might be $2500. Clearly, most defendants in such a case would not have that kind of money readily available. So they will turn to a private *bail bonding agent*. Bail bonding agents turn the money over to the court. They charge the defendant a fee of 10 or 15 percent, which is called a "premium." The agent has a good reason for wanting to be sure the defendant will appear in court when due. Otherwise, the $2500 is lost, although the agent does get to keep the premium, which is small comfort.

Defendants may also post a property bond. These may be in the form of stocks, title to a house or land, an automobile, or other personal property. In any event, they will get the bail back when they appear for trial, even if they are convicted.

However, most defendants are too poor to pay the premiums required by the bonding agents. As a result they must stay in jail until their cases come up for trial. One response to this problem is being tried. Agencies are created which undertake to keep track of defendants released without bail and which see that they appear when they should. This program is called *release on recognizance*, or ROR. As when anyone guarantees a defendant's appearance in court, the judge must approve a defendant's release to such an agency. The results seem to be mixed. In some jurisdictions the rate of nonappearance is rising. This rise may be due to the release of higher risk defendants or to bigger caseloads for each staff member.

The standards for release require that a reasonable bond be set. It must be high enough to guarantee the defendant's appearance in court. But it must not be so high as to keep unconvicted people in jail unnecessarily. Since defendants are presumed innocent, they have a right to reasonable bail in all but a few categories of cases.

In *capital cases*—those punishable either by death or by life imprisonment—the defendant does not generally have an absolute right to bail. The prosecutor may demonstrate a strong likelihood that the defendant will flee the jurisdiction rather than appear at trial. The judge can then refuse to grant release on bail.

However, neither a long criminal record nor the strongest evidence of guilt is adequate reason for denying release on bond.

Case Study:
TECHNICAL LAW

The ordinary citizen rarely recognizes the skill a police officer must have before he or she can set foot on patrol. Officers have to be prepared to rescue someone from a burning building as well as know when they must take the life of a criminal. Of course, neither is a daily event in most police officers' lives.

One of the most frequent police calls involves disputes of families and neighbors. Nearly every day officers must enter into this type of dispute and make sure that the law is not being violated.

Officer John Graham, called to assist in a neighborhood dispute, pulled up at the driveway of the house of one of the parties involved. From this position he could see two women. They were shouting at each other from each of the houses while their husbands stood arguing over a hedge separating the houses. As soon as the people involved noticed Graham, each began shouting for the arrest of the other neighbor.

Graham quieted the couples and agreed to hear each side of the dispute inside each neighbor's respective house. The first neighbor, whose wife had called the police, told Graham that the dispute had its beginnings in his request of his neighbor for permission to plant a hedge between their driveways. The request had been made almost a year ago and both families had agreed.

Now the second neighbor wanted to tear out the hedge because every time he drove into the driveway, the hedge scratched the paint on his car. The first neighbor had paid several hundred dollars for the hedge. This morning when he noticed his neighbor removing the hedge, he rushed over to put a stop to it. He claimed that his neighbor then punched him in the nose and shouted for him to get back on his own property. At that point his wife had called the police.

Patrol officer Graham then went to hear the other side of the story. The other neighbor claimed that the first individual had never asked permission originally to plant a hedge, but he confirmed the rest of the first neighbor's tale of the incident, except for the assault and battery. He claimed his neighbor had approached him swinging a stick.

With an account from both sides, Graham still had to resolve the issue. The first party requested the arrest of the other for assault and battery. The second neighbor did not want anyone arrested but did charge that he was attacked by his neighbor armed with a stick.

Should Graham make the arrest? Can he arrest anyone? How can Graham be sure that the law will not be violated in the future by an identical incident?

First-Appearance Hearing

Defendants have the right to appear before a judge shortly after arrest for two purposes. They have a right to have bail set and to be informed of their rights under federal and state law. At the same time the court will consider the question of who the defense lawyer will be in each case. In criminal cases defendants have a right to a lawyer whether they can afford to pay for one or not.

In some states public defenders, hired and paid for by the state government, represent impoverished defendants. In others, private corporations, supported by a mixture of public and private funds, will provide the services of defense lawyers. Also, some bar associations have legal aide services, supported by voluntary contributions, which will furnish the defendant with legal counsel.

Preliminary Hearing

The next step after the first-appearance hearing is the *preliminary hearing*. The purpose of this hearing before a lower-court judge is to decide whether or not the case should be brought to trial. On the basis of the material presented, the judge can: (1) dismiss the case for lack of evidence; (2) "bind over" the case for trial if there is enough evidence to back up the charge against the defendant; or (3) continue the case for a later hearing if it is felt that more time is needed.

At the hearing, the judge reads the affidavits of the arresting officer and any witnesses to the crime. Depending on state law, the judge may also hear evidence from both the prosecution and the defense. If more than half the evidence points to the defendant's guilt, the judge decides there is "probable cause." The judge then binds the defendant over for trial. The term "bind over" probably comes from the old English custom of binding the hands of the defendant awaiting trial.

A case can be bound over to a higher court, where the prosecutor decides whether or not to proceed with it. It can also be bound over to a grand jury—a thing frequently done in capital cases. The grand jury then weighs the evidence and decides whether or not to indict the defendant. If the prosecutor or the grand jury decides not to proceed with the case, the defendant is freed of charges.

Arraignment

The first step in the trial process is *arraignment*, which is formal entry of a plea by the defendant. The defendant may plead guilty, not guilty, not guilty by reason of insanity, or no contest *(nolo contendere)*.

A plea of *guilty* is an admission by the defendant that all the charges against him or her are true. To plead *not guilty* is to deny all the charges. It requires the state (the prosecution) to prove that the charges are true beyond a reasonable doubt. A plea of *nolo contendere* means that the defendant neither admits nor denies having committed the crime. It has virtually the same effect as a plea of guilty. If the defendant stands mute and refuses to plead, the court will enter a plea of not guilty on his or her behalf.

At the arraignment the court may set the dates for the future stages of the case. The defendant will either demand or give up the right to a trial by jury. However, that trial is still some time away. Before it actually takes place, much work is still to be done by the lawyers on both sides of the case.

Pretrial Discovery

Essentially this is the disclosure of evidence by each side to the other; most states provide for it in some form. It is meant to: (1) eliminate surprise, (2) help lawyers to better prepare their cases, and (3) remind them that a trial is a search for the truth, not a contest. It is a fairly recent development, and many prosecutors still argue bitterly against it.

Before discovery was required, a trial was a battle between two lawyers each of whom knew little of the opponent's case. The prosecutor might not know a crucial defense witness existed until that individual appeared on the stand. The defense lawyer might not even know who the prosecution witnesses were—let alone what they had to say—until they spoke up in court. The ability to think fast on one's feet made trials more a battle of wits than a hunt for justice.

Today, the rules governing discovery vary widely from state to state. In many states the defendant is entitled to a list of the witnesses the prosecution plans to call. Defendants also have the right to know if any confessions or admissions were made by codefendants. They are entitled to have copies of such admissions in writing. The defendants may have the right to examine physical evidence the prosecution has and plans to use at the trial. They are entitled to copies of the results of scientific tests of blood, alcohol, and firearms made by the prosecution.

In some states the defense may request the identity of and sworn statements *(depositions)* from prosecution witnesses having information concerning the offense. This is ensured regardless of whether the prosecution intends to call them at the trial. The defense lawyer also agrees to give the prosecutor names of more witnesses, and more evidence, than it intends to use. This trade-off is called "reciprocal discovery."

In some states defense lawyers may be required to give the prosecution a list of witnesses for the defendant. Also, they may have to show any physical evidence that they plan to use at the trial. The district attorney then has the right to examine this evidence and make tests on it if necessary.

In a few places both sides are entitled to depositions from each other's witnesses before the trial. However, witnesses' testimony to the prosecutor or grand jury, like lawyers' trial preparation papers, are generally closed to the other side's examination.

Pretrial Motions—Legal Processes

Besides pleadings for discovery or disclosure of evidence, defense motions can challenge legality of the indictment, information, or other legal process. A basic principal of due process of law is adequate notice to the defendant of the exact nature of the charges. It is the indictment or information which gives that notice. This tells exactly what the charges are. If for some reason they are not legally sound, the defense lawyer will ask the court to dismiss them. This pleading is a *motion to dismiss the indictment* (or *information*).

A defense lawyer may feel that the grand jury was illegally formed, or that it acted illegally. The lawyer in this case may also ask for a dismissal of the charges. Grand juries must be made up of citizens who represent a cross section of the community. They cannot exclude anyone on the ground of race, sex, religion, social or economic class. The grand jury usually cannot permit spectators in the jury room during the taking of testimony or during deliberations. If the grand jury was formed illegally, or acted outside the law, the court is required to dismiss the indictment.

If the indictment or information is dismissed, it does not mean that the case against the defendant has been dropped. It just means that the whole process must start from scratch again.

Pretrial Motions—Seizure of Evidence

The rules governing police activities with regard to the defendant are strict. If the defense can prove any of these rules was broken, the prosecution's case can be seriously damaged.

For confession to be legal it must be obtained without the use of physical or psychological force. The defendant must have been advised of the rights to remain silent and to be represented by a lawyer. The defendant must have been warned that any statement given may be used in court by the prosecution. If this has not been done, the confession will be called illegal.

If the defendant appeared in an unfair line-up that led witnesses to make an identification, it can be ruled illegal. A police officer may have seized a piece of physical evidence from the defendant without a search warrant. Unless permitted by law to do so, the search will be ruled illegal. If electronic means, such as bugging or wiretapping, were used without a proper court order, they too may be illegal.

Defense lawyers who have reason to believe evidence against their clients was illegally obtained will file motions challenging the police activities. The court will then hold a hearing. At this hearing the court will take testimony from witnesses, study the law, hear arguments of both lawyers, and finally decide. If the decision is that it in fact was illegally seized, the evidence will be excluded from the trial. The judge and jury will not be allowed to consider it. If the court decides the evidence was legally taken, it can be presented at the trial. Also, it can be used to support other evidence against the defendant.

Pretrial Motions—Speedy Trial, Double Jeopardy, Discovery, Postponement

The defendant has a constitutional right to a speedy trial. Many states require a trial within a certain number of days from time of arrest or filing of formal charges. The defendant also has the right to be protected against *double jeopardy*. That is, one person can be tried only once for a crime. If the right to speedy trial or that against double jeopardy has been violated, the defense can file a motion. If at the court hearing the judge decides these rights were interfered with, the charges against the defendant will be dismissed. Such dismissals generally are final.

Both the prosecution and the defense must carry out any orders of the court having to do with discovery. Failure to do so could result in the barring of that evidence or testimony. It can even lead to outright dismissal of the charges if the failure was on the part of the prosecution.

A defense or prosecution lawyer who is not ready to go to trial may request additional time. This is done by filing a motion to continue the trial, or other matters in the case, at some future date. The court examines the reasons given and then either grants or denies the request.

PLEA BARGAINING

In large urban jurisdictions less than 10 percent of all cases go to trial. Of those, only a handful are jury trials. Trials by jury can take days or weeks or even months. However, trials without a jury—bench trials—usually take only a few hours. Most cases are closed either by (1) being dismissed or (2) having the defendant enter a plea of guilty to a charge agreed on by the defense lawyer and the prosecutor. This controversial but very widespread practice is called "plea bargaining."

The process often takes on the air of merchants haggling over price in the marketplace. The prosecutor and defense lawyer both have big caseloads and, practically speaking, cannot thoroughly prepare and try every case. Therefore, the prosecutor offers to reduce some charges, or agrees to a reduced sentence in exchange for a guilty plea. The former is called *charge bargaining*; the latter is *sentence bargaining.*

TRIAL BY JURY

If the defense decides to have the case tried before a jury, a formal and involved process begins. Trial by jury has long fascinated many Americans. Countless stories, plays, movies, and television shows have dealt with this aspect of our criminal justice system.

Jury Selection

The prospective jurors are put under oath. They may be questioned by (1) the judge, (2) the clerk of the court, and (3) lawyers for both sides, depending on the circumstances and the laws of the state. The point of the questioning is to find out if all the jurors are fair and unbiased. The judge and the clerk are assumed to have that goal in mind.

The aim of the lawyers may differ, however. Often the prosecutor really wants a juror who would convict anyone on flimsy evidence. Meanwhile the defense lawyer wants jurors who wouldn't convict anyone even in the face of overwhelmingly convincing proof of guilt.

A juror may be challenged (that is, not allowed to serve) for cause, such as already having made a decision, or on a preemptory basis. In the latter case, the lawyer does not have to give a reason for the challenge. Preemptory challenges are limited in number, while there is no limit on challenges for cause.

Opening Statements

Each lawyer is given the opportunity to make an opening statement outlining the case to the jury. Some authorities accuse lawyers of telling the jury things they cannot prove as well as things they can prove. Either side may give up the right to make an opening statement.

Case Study:
PLEA BARGAINING

City detectives had been working on a murder case involving two narcotics pushers. A five-year-old girl had been inadvertently caught in a crossfire of bullets and killed. Police knew it would be difficult for law enforcement officials to arrest the people who had ordered the gun fight, although in this state the person who ordered it could be tried as if he or she were the one who pulled the trigger.

Nearly a half-year after the shooting, detectives received their first break. A chief aide to one of the pushers fell out of grace with the boss and was cut loose from the crime ring and the group's protection. He knew members of the rival gang would be after him, so he turned to the police.

The aide told how his boss had decided to attack the other pusher's headquarters in an attempt to increase his own business. According to his former employee, the pusher himself was seated in the back seat of the car when the murder took place. Detectives wondered how the aide knew all this. Before answering, the aide asked the officers if he could make a deal. Talks between the officer, the aide, and the prosecutor resulted in the aide's pleading to a lesser charge than murder in exchange for his testimony against his boss. The aide admitted having driven the getaway car.

The witness was perfect; however, the detectives still required the gun and the person who had fired it before they could make an airtight case. Most of the officers on the force became emotionally involved since a child had been killed. Detectives were careful to be sure every fact would stand up in court.

The aide led police to a box behind the pusher's headquarters. Inside was the murder weapon. He also pointed out the gunman. Police brought in the gunman and re-covered the gun. Tests proved the gun was in fact the weapon that had killed the girl. Fingerprints on the gun matched those of the suspect named by the aide. Another round of plea bargaining, and the gunman was willing to plead to a lesser charge and turn state's evidence against his employer.

Detectives arrested the pusher. The case was airtight and the detectives were ready for trial. A month after the arrest, all the suspects appeared in court, but little testimony was taken. The defense attorney, the prosecutor, and the judge met in the judge's chamber to attempt to arrange a conclusion to the case. After a day of plea bargaining, everyone entered the courtroom to hear the pusher plead guilty to attempted murder.

Men working on the case were outraged. Here was a man who had ordered a shooting which resulted in the death of a child. He received only six months in the county jail. The prosecutor later informed the arresting officers that, although the pusher had ordered the shooting, the killing of the child had been an accident and, at the most, second- or third-degree murder. But a murder conviction would probably come only in the trial of the gunman, not in that of the pusher.

Was the prosecutor's decision right? Does plea bargaining work? Should it have been used in this case?

Case for the Prosecution

The prosecutor begins the process of calling witnesses for *direct examination*. The defense lawyer may then question the witness in *cross-examination*. After this the prosecutor may again question the witness in *re-direct examination*. As in all aspects of court proceedings, there are strict rules. The prosecutor is not allowed to call the defendant as a witness.

The defense lawyer may object to (1) a question being put to the witness, (2) the manner in which it is put, or (3) a whole line of questioning. In each case the judge will either sustain the objection (agree with the lawyer's complaint) or deny it (disagree with it).

Physical evidence is submitted, marked by the clerk. When supported by proper testimony ("yes, this is the bullet I took from the body," for example), it is put into evidence for the jury to examine.

When the prosecution has presented all its witnesses and evidence, the prosecutor will rest his or her case. Often the defense lawyer then goes before the judge and argues there is not enough evidence for a jury to convict. The defense will then bring a motion asking the judge to direct the jury to acquit without hearing the other side. The motion, in fact, is usually denied.

Case for the Defense

The defense lawyer will call witnesses, and the same process of direct, cross-, and re-direct examination will take place. A major decision facing defense counsel is whether or not to call the defendant as a witness. The defendant has a right not to take the stand. The prosecutor is not allowed to make any reference to the defendant's failure to submit to questioning. A defendant who does take the stand can be assured of a rough period of cross-examination by the prosecutor. On the other hand, the jury may view a defendant's not electing to take the stand as an admission of guilt even if the judge tells them not to. It can be a very delicate decision for the defendant's lawyer. Say the defendant was innocent of the charge but had a long string of prior convictions for similar offenses. In some states the prosecution could question the defendant about this past history and thereby cast doubt on the individual's innocence in this case.

At the close of the case for the defense, defense counsel may make motions requesting the judge to direct an acquittal. If these are denied, judge and lawyers will hold a charge conference. The lawyers will each ask the judge to give certain instructions on the law to the jury. This would be done before the jurors retire to consider their verdict.

Closing Arguments

Before the judge gives the charge to the jury, the lawyers have a final opportunity to make their closing arguments. In the federal and some state systems there are three arguments—two by the prosecutor and one by the defense. In other states, there are two arguments by the defense and one by the prosecution.

Charge, Deliberation, Verdict

The judge's charge to the jury is a short course in the criminal law as it is to be applied in that case. The jurors then retire to deliberate in total privacy. They may request that certain parts of testimony be read back for them, or that points of law be clarified. If they cannot agree on a verdict, the judge may send them back to try again. If no verdict can be reached, the judge declares a *mistrial* and the case must be tried all over again.

If the verdict is "guilty," the judge may impose sentence then or defer it to another day. If a verdict of "not guilty" is reached, the defendant walks out of the courtroom free.

POSTTRIAL PROCESSES

Sentencing

Some sentences are mandatory. That is, the law requires that on being convicted for a certain crime the prisoner must be given a certain punishment. The majority of sentences, however, are for the judge to decide.

To sentence wisely is a complicated affair. A whole list of considerations should be weighed before a judge makes a decision in each case. Among the possible sentences she or he can impose are: (1) probation; (2) fine; (3) imprisonment; (4) a suspended sentence (one which is passed, but not actually served); and (5) the experimental weekend or nighttime sentence which permits the prisoner to work while paying a penalty.

Among the things a judge should consider before passing sentence are these:

1. The effect on the prisoner
2. The effect on the community
3. The effect on the prisoner's family
4. Whether it will be a general deterrent to others who might commit that crime
5. The cost to the community

To help the judge make an intelligent decision, a probation report examining the prisoner's background and circumstances is prepared. (Forms of probation are discussed in some detail in Chapter 13; the presentence investigation, in Chapter 14.) In addition, the judge may listen to the pleas of both lawyers in the case. He or she may also hear the pleas of witnesses and the victim. Before sentence is actually passed the prisoner has the right of *allocution*. That is, the prisoner may make a statement regarding the possible sentence.

Motion for a New Trial

At the end of the trial, the lawyer for the defense may move that there be a new trial. The grounds for such a motion may be: (1) that there were legal errors committed by the judge, or (2) that the evidence was not sufficient to support the guilty verdict. In practice this motion is usually denied.

THE APPELLATE PROCESS

An *appeal* is a review, by a higher court, of the case as it has been tried in the lower court. The right of appeal is one which belongs to everyone who is convicted of a crime.

The appellate process is quite different from the jury trial we have just examined. Appellate court judges have two major functions in a criminal case: (1) They must determine whether or not there were any serious legal errors made by the trial judge; (2) they may search the record of the trial to establish whether there was enough legally valid evidence to support conviction.

The appeals process generally begins with the defense lawyer filing a *notice of appeal*. This informs both the court and the prosecutor that the client will challenge the legality of the conviction. Both sides then prepare written arguments—*briefs*—in which they analyze the facts and the law as they see it.

These things, together with (1) an *assignment of error*, in which the defense specifies the errors that are being alleged, and (2) a typed transcript of the testimony, are sent to the judges. In some appeals courts oral arguments by both lawyers are allowed. After reviewing all the facts and the law, the judges meet to discuss the case. When they reach their decision, they write the opinion of the court.

Generally a defendant is limited to one appeal. Any further review is at the discretion of the state supreme court or the United States Supreme Court. In the majority of cases that are appealed, the decision of the appellate court is the final one.

While the appeals process has been going on, the defendant may have been free on *appeal bond*. That is very like a pretrial bond, except that some public bail bonding agencies do not participate in it. The defendant does not have an absolute right to it, unlike the pretrial bond in other than capital cases. Yet it is often granted.

After the appeals court has handed down its decision, the defendant returns to the lower court. If the appeal was denied and the trial court's judgment is upheld, the defendant must start to serve the sentence. A higher court that has reversed the lower one can order a new trial. Or it can order the trial judge to reevaluate the state of the case. The trial judge then decides whether to hold a new trial or dismiss the defendant. Finally, the appeals court can reverse the conviction and order the defendant to be freed.

There are even more legal tactics that the well-informed trial lawyer can use on behalf of a client. These would aim at raising serious constitutional issues, if there appear to be any. We will not describe them in detail. The fact that they exist illustrates the lengths to which the legal system goes to protect the accused.

All these procedures of the court may seem wildly complicated and cumbersome. And so they are. But they are the best protection there is for that most fragile of treasures: justice.

INTERPRETATION OF THE LAW

The courts are often required to interpret legislation. Laws passed by the legislature are general in nature. Their precise application to particular cases may require the court to examine: (1) the way they are written, (2) the intent of the legislature, and (3) the purposes behind passage of the law.

One state's law made commission of an aggravated assault a felony. *Aggravated assault* was defined as an assault with a deadly weapon. In one case the issue presented was whether or not a stick was a deadly weapon within the meaning of the statute. The court stated what the legislature meant by the words "deadly weapon": "Any weapon that could likely produce death or great bodily injury in the manner in which it was used." Therefore, held the court, it was required to examine (1) the physical strength of the alleged violator, (2) the weakness of the intended victim, and (3) the exact manner in which the accused had wielded the stick. In another case involving the same statute, the court faced a situation where the defendant had pointed an unloaded gun at the victim. In finding the law was violated, the court reasoned thus: The law's purpose was to protect people from fear generated by threatened harm from someone using a weapon the victim thought deadly. The court held that, if the victim thought the gun was loaded and was afraid, the gun was legally a "deadly weapon." They maintained this was so even if in fact it was unloaded while the defendant aimed it at the victim.

Interpreting the Constitution

In the United States, courts must interpret constitutional provisions from time to time. An example of the development of law through constitutional interpretation exists in U.S. Supreme Court decisions on the right to counsel. Until recently, a defendant who could not afford a lawyer had no right to a free, government-paid lawyer.

The Fourteenth Amendment (1866) to the U.S. Constitution prohibited states from depriving anyone of life, liberty, or property without due process of law. Did this amendment mean: "State governments are required to provide free lawyers to poor people charged with serious crimes who could not defend themselves"? In a case in 1942, the Court held the Fourteenth Amendment requirement (that each citizen of a state was entitled to "due process of law") meant this issue had to be decided in favor of the indigent, ignorant defendant. In order to be entitled a free lawyer, the defendant had to be too poor to hire a lawyer. The defendant also had to be too ignorant to defend himself or herself.

As a result of this decision the Supreme Court was flooded with cases raising the question of defendants' capacity for self-representation. It was not until *Gideon v. Wainwright* (1963) that the Court decided: All indigents charged with serious crimes have a right to a free lawyer irrespective of the defendant's ability of self-representation. The Court reasoned: No defendant is fully capable of self-representation, given the complexity of criminal proceedings and the presence of trained prosecutors. So, failure to provide free counsel to indigents became an automatic denial of due process of law.

Now even indigent defendants who are lawyers may have the right to a free lawyer (apparently based on the legal maxim that "the lawyer who represents himself has a fool for a client"). The Court later extended the right to counsel to situations where the defendant might be sentenced to jail. Progressing from no right to free counsel to this latest ruling took less than fifty years.

THE RULES OF EVIDENCE

What facts the jury will be permitted to consider in deciding guilt or innocence has been discussed in much judicial writing. The gen-

Case Study:
EVIDENCE FOR DEFENSE

Officer Letterman was patrolling the town of Newton. She noticed three men chasing what appeared to be a teen-aged male over hedges and through front yards. With siren blasting, Letterman called for a back-up unit and proceeded to investigate the problem. By this time the three men, still in pursuit, had run to the back of a house.

Officer Letterman followed but lost her suspects. As she returned to the car, other units from her area pulled up. Letterman told the other officers what had occurred and gave a description of the three men. She then told the officers each to take a near-by block to begin a search. According to the department policy, the first officer on the scene is in charge regardless of seniority. The only time this rule changes is when a superior officer is present. In this case no superior officer was on the scene.

The other officers all followed Letterman's direction. The three patrol cars took up the search. Each vehicle drove slowly to enable the officer to view as much of the area as possible.

Ten minutes later a call from headquarters sent the patrol cars to a house. A caller had notified the department that three men were beating up someone. Officer Letterman thought these were her suspects. Again she was the first police officer at the scene.

She quickly pulled the three men from on top of a twenty-four-year-old man. "Get off of him!" she shouted. The suspects did not put up a fight. One of the men thanked her for responding so soon. She was told that the man lying on the ground had broken into a near-by house. The owner, one of the three men, had found him inside and tried to catch him.

The alleged burglar had pushed the owner away and fled. Two neighbors saw the man leave the house in a rush and gave chase. The three residents caught up with the alleged burglar and tried to hold him down until police arrived.

Officer Letterman checked the man lying near unconsciousness. His face was bloody and his nose broken. He kept holding his side, indicating a possible broken rib. Letterman called for an ambulance as her fellow officers arrived at the scene. Several neighbors had stopped one of the patrol cars and informed the driver that three men were attacking another younger person. According to these people, the three would catch up with their victim, beat him, then let him run away for a few minutes. Then they would continue the punishment.

Hours later the incident was over. Letterman determined that the burglar had entered the house and was moving goods onto the lawn. In fact, a television set was found in the driveway. The owner surprised the burglar and was pushed. From all indications the three residents did in fact attack the burglar and were not simply making a citizen's arrest. The burglar was in serious condition in the hospital, but he did identify the men.

Based upon what Officer Letterman knows, what charges can she file against the four men involved?

eral principle of law is to permit the jury to hear any fact tending to establish guilt or innocence. This general rule has many significant limitations. These limitations come from three basic sources: (1) the common law rules of evidence as established by court cases, (2) statutory limitations imposed by legislatures, and (3) those limitations springing from state and federal constitutions. The limitations in the first two categories suggest some distrust of the juries' ability to consider evidence dispassionately and intelligently. Limitations derived from the constitutions seem to stem from a desire to place restrictions on abusive police and prosecution practices.

Evidence means facts. In court, it includes: (1) the testimony of witnesses, (2) physical items, such as the murder weapon or recovered stolen property, (3) the results of tests, such as those that measure the presence of alcohol in the body, and (4) confessions made by the defendant. Legal definitions are too numerous to quote.

The common law rules of evidence exclude evidence for a number of reasons, including that: (1) it is immaterial and irrelevant to the issues in the case; (2) it is hearsay; (3) it is given by incompetent witnesses. Full treatment of these rules is far beyond the scope of this text, but a few examples are appropriate.

Assume a person is on trial for robbery allegedly committed in 1975. Evidence that the defendant cut classes five years earlier would be irrelevant. One student says the victim of the robbery said a week after it happened that the defendant was the culprit. The student could not testify because this testimony would be hearsay. The victim of the robbery might be four years old; the victim then would not be allowed to testify because he or she would be incompetent.

The constitutional limitations on the admissibility of evidence in criminal cases go beyond the issue of reliability of the evidence. The proper relationship of the government to the people is considered in the area of searches and seizures. The law now prevents the introduction in court of illegally seized evidence.

The Gault case will be discussed in Chapter 11, "The Juvenile Courts," and the court report is reproduced starting on page 280. The Court held confessions obtained from juveniles were subject to many limitations earlier placed upon the admissibility of adults' confessions. The words of the U.S. Supreme Court illustrate the Court's concern with the relationship between the citizen and the government.

The privilege against self-incrimination is, of course, related to the question of the safeguards necessary to assure that admissions or confessions are reasonably trustworthy, that they are not the mere fruits of fear or coercion, but are reliable expressions of the truth. The roots of the privilege are, however, far deeper. They tap the basic stream of religious and political principles because the privilege reflects the limits of the individuals attornment to the state and—in a philosophical sense—insist upon the equality of the individual and the state.

The U.S. Supreme Court's decision in *Schmerber v. California*[1] illustrates the problem. It attempts to balance these two issues: (1) limitations on the powers of government with (2) the need to permit critical pieces of evidence to go before the jury for consideration. After his car struck a tree, Mr. Schmerber was convicted of driving under the influence of intoxicating liquor. Part of the evidence of intoxication rested upon a blood sample taken from him after arrest and under his protest. His lawyer raised three objections to the use of the evidence in court. First, said his lawyer, Mr. Schmerber's rights under the Fifth Amendment's provision against self-incrimination had been violated. Second, he was denied his Sixth Amendment right to counsel because the blood sample was drawn against his attorney's advice. Third, the taking of blood was an unreasonable search and seizure pursuant to the provisions of the Fourth Amendment.

The Court held that, since blood was not the same as a confession—"non-testimonial," in the Court's words—the Fifth Amendment did not apply. Since he had no right to refuse to give the blood, he had no right to counsel to advise him at that time. The Court was apparently troubled by the application of the Fourth Amendment. The Court felt such an intrusion into the body was a "search" within the meaning of the Fourth Amendment. Prior cases permitted searches that followed and were related to an arrest. Since Schmerber had been legally arrested, a search could follow. But the question of whether a search warrant was required arose. Under prior case law interpreting the Fourth Amendment, the Court said, constitutional preference was for searches to be authorized by a judge prior to the search. In Schmerber, the Court noted that alcohol in the body dissipates rapidly; therefore, by the time the officer obtained a search warrant the alcohol would have disappeared. The end result was a ruling that the blood was legally valid evidence despite the absence of a search warrant.

There are statutory provisions affecting the use of evidence in court. Some of these provisions exclude evidence otherwise acceptable, while still others permit the use of evidence that might be inadmissible. An example of the former is the rule, in a few states,

1.   384 U.S. 757 (1966).

disqualifying a prospective witness who has been convicted of perjury (lying under oath before a court). On the other hand, there is the Uniform Business Records as Evidence Act. This act permits business records such as hospital or hotel records to be used in court. They are permitted even though they may not fully comply with the common law hearsay rule and some of the common law exceptions to the hearsay rule.

The law of evidence is an everchanging body of law critical to the processing of cases through the courts. Both prosecution and defense make key decisions based in part on the sufficiency and admissibility of the evidence.

The interpretation of law and the progress of individual cases through the courts is an ongoing process. In it the whole judicial system can be seen as a kind of elegant balancing act. The famous symbol of Justice is blindfolded and holds scales in her hand. This symbol becomes all the more appropriate the closer one looks at how the system works. Tension—the weight of one element pulling against another—is a basic part of the judicial process. And while it inevitably creates problems, it is that endless straining that gives the system its life and vigor.

QUESTIONS

1. Do the steps in the court process seem too numerous? What steps, if any, would you combine or eliminate? Why?
2. What do you think is the impact of pretrial discovery procedures on the processing of a criminal case?
3. Should jury trials be retained? Why or why not?
4. Should the defendant's right to refuse to testify be modified in any way? Why or why not?
5. Should the sentencing process be modified? How? Why?
6. What are the goals of the rules of evidence? Do these goals make sense today?
7. What other or more appropriate goals would you suggest?

It is difficult to measure any functioning body's effectiveness. Yet it is reasonably clear that the courts are having trouble. There are a number of reasons why this is the case, and we will examine some of them. But before we do it, we should note one thing: The traditional role of the court itself has undergone a marked change in recent years. The court used to be the setting for an adversary proceeding which resulted in a clear decision by a judge. Now the administrative handling of cases is considerably increased and jury trials are correspondingly decreased.

In addition, a host of new pretrial and posttrial activities have grown up. Most of them are only marginally under the court's supervision. For example, many pretrial practices are more and more under the virtually unregulated control of nonjudicial personnel. Alternatives to detention, discovery procedures, and plea bargaining are only a few of these. Such activities are beyond the boundaries of judicial tradition, and judges are not educated in the ways of administration.

We shall now attempt to make a fair evaluation of the effectiveness of the courts. We will look first at their procedural efficiency and then at their effectiveness in terms of achieving justice.

EFFICIENCY OF COURT PROCEDURES

The problem of measuring the degree to which courts are meeting their goals is mind-boggling in complexity. Yet many Americans, without having clearly defined standards, feel that courts are not living up to expectations.

One measure is commonly used for judging a court's efficiency. This is its backlog of cases that have not been disposed of in the required time. But even this is not a clear-cut standard. As a case in point, take courts A and B. By Law, court A must have disposed of all its cases within 60 days. Yet it has 1000 cases between 60 and 90 days old. Court B, by contrast, has a time limit of 90 days. It also has 1000 cases between 60 and 90 days old—but none older. Court A

Evaluating the Courts

would be criticized for having a backlog of 1000 cases, while court B would be blameless.

A companion question is, What factors are responsible for the backlog? The prosecutor may have an extremely heavy caseload. A defendant on pretrial release may maneuver for delays in the hope that a witness may disappear or lose interest. Or the compiling of physical evidence may take time.

Clearly, case backlog by itself is no measure of a court's effectiveness.

Problems of Inefficiency

More than the abstract question of processing as many cases as efficiently as possible without sacrificing justice concerns us here. There are also wholly innocent pawns who are at the mercy of a court's inability to handle its affairs effectively.

The juror is an indispensable element in the administration of justice. In an earlier and simpler time the judge might well have known most of the prospective jurors. Thus he would have been assured that there was a true cross section of the community represented. Today, however, a jury commissioner has the responsibility for providing a pool of possible jurors. These are ordinary men and women from all walks of life. They are disrupting their normal lives to do their duty as citizens.

Yet, modern techniques are not applied in the selection of the pool. Nor are limits on courtroom examination enforced. As a result, those called for jury duty often find much of their time has been wasted. Indeed, it frequently takes longer to pick a jury than to hear the evidence.

Witnesses, too, are often caught up in the inefficiency of a court's procedures. Frequently they make time to appear in court, are not called to testify on that date, and must return another day. It is the obligation of the prosecution and the defense to see that their witnesses testify. Yet little attention has been given to ways of sparing witnesses unnecessary trips to the courthouses. These useless trips sometimes lead to an ultimate failure of people to appear when they are needed.

Such simple things as being put on telephone notice could spare witnesses a great deal of trouble. In addition, facilities in the courthouse for the comfort of witnesses and jurors should be provided. Consideration for them as people could also contribute to overall court efficiency. The doing of a public service by a private citizen should not be made any more difficult than necessary.

Case Study:
ADMINISTRATION OF COURTS

Because of the overcrowding of prisons and the backlog of cases on the court calendar, judges had individually determined that the best method to keep the judicial system operating was to hear as few cases as possible, leaving the rest to be decided by mutual agreement between the prosecutor and defense attorneys.

In some instances, criminals who pleaded guilty to lesser crimes and received jail sentences might not have been convicted if the charges had remained the same as when the arrest took place. Judges felt this helped society.

However, police officers throughout the state were unhappy with the situation. Their leaders made public statements declaring that the current judicial practice was not protecting the public when it let criminals loose in the street. The press picked up the reports. Some reporters took up the cry and started to investigate. Sure enough, many judges were placing hardened criminals on probation or were finding them not guilty in order to keep the caseload moving.

An undercurrent was developing in the state that was slowly affecting the political arena. Before long, campaigns were run under the "law-and-order" banner. Many "law-and-order" candidates were winning. Obviously, times had changed. No longer was the public sympathetic to people in jails and prisons. An individual who committed a crime deserved to be punished, not catered to.

The influence exerted by elected officials on the courts was limited. The only method of control over the court system by elected officials was through appointments. Once a judge took a seat on the bench, it was almost impossible to remove that person until the term was up.

The real control was through the state supreme court, led by the chief justice. All judges below the rank of supreme court judge were required by law to adhere to rulings, directives, and direct orders from the chief justice. The chief justice was the one person in charge of the court system in the state.

The public was calling for the courts to be tougher with criminals. Judges, however, traditionally have been beyond the influence of the public. This was part of the objective of a fair trial for all. Judges also realized that new prisons were not being built. Some of the jails had been condemned years ago and they were still in operation.

The future did not look any better. The population increased and the rate of new cases increased proportionately. The rate at which new judges were appointed, however, lagged a year or two behind. This made the court system operate more like a factory than as a functional part of the criminal justice system. At least, this was the opinion of most of the judges in the state.

Obviously, the chief justice was saddled with a major decision which required immediate action. What suggestions would you make to remedy the situation? Is there a viable solution which the public would accept?

Management Techniques

Lack of efficiency is due to a variety of things. Perhaps at the heart of the problem lies the lack of coherent administration.

With expansion of the court system must come the employment of people trained in modern management techniques. A court consisting of 100 judges or more, with support staffs of thousands, cannot be managed solely by lawyers. The process of legal education does not emphasize such things as financial, personnel, and records systems. Judges who are well educated in the legal process of deciding cases may not be well educated in preparing budgets.

However, judges do have an obligation to take a tight rein on the judicial and semijudicial aspects of court procedures. They must not let decisions of guilt or innocence and sentencing slip from their fingers because of complicated administrative procedures. They should see that the lines of authority are clearly drawn and that they themselves are firmly in charge.

EFFECTIVENESS IN ACHIEVING JUSTICE

Different people use different yardsticks to measure success or failure. From any objective viewpoint a lawyer's won/lost record is a poor way to judge performance. Yet it is frequently used for this purpose.

Prosecutors with an outstanding records of cases won might have gained their shining reputations by shrewd screening. They prosecute only cases they are sure they can win. Clearly, this is efficient; but is it just? It is likely that some who were guilty, but whose guilt would be hard to prove, got off lightly.

By contrast, defense lawyers may have a string of losses. They may have felt committed to the fundamental principle: Everyone has a right to have his or her side of the case heard. In addition, they may well have succeeded in getting light sentences for their guilty clients.

Who is to say which is the more effective lawyer? Certainly the won/lost standard is not a reliable guide.

In the same vein, judges often like to point out that they have rarely had a decision reversed on appeal. But judges who seldom convict seldom have their decisions appealed. If one of their prime concerns is avoiding the possibility of appeal, they can probably achieve it. Once again we are faced with a goal that can be reached by strategy rather than ability. It has little to do with effectiveness. How to measure effectiveness is likely to remain open to debate.

Pretrial Release and Diversion Systems

These systems have by and large failed to meet constitutional standards, but some of the more pronounced failures have been corrected in recent years. Pretrial release programs are reducing the chances of a defendant's being detained prior to trial simply because of poverty.

Rehabilitation programs are used to divert offenders from the court process. They are one answer to the tremendous number of criminal cases that have threatened to overload the courts. However, these programs are often understaffed and must turn away qualified applicants. If these agencies take too many cases, their efforts at rehabilitation may be ineffective.

Another serious problem that can beset these programs is the possibility of discrimination in admission to them. Where the program can take only a small percentage of those qualified, favoritism could be shown to particular individuals or groups. Further, those wrongly accused might feel forced to choose entry into pretrial diversion programs rather than face the uncertainties of trial.

The answer to this dilemma is not to eliminate programs. Rather court participation in the selection or rejection of applicants for them should be required. That is part of the court's duty to see that justice is done.

Bail

Private bail bonding agents have largely been a blight on the criminal justice system. They are supposed to keep track of defendants and see to it that they are brought to trial. But too often this primary duty is neglected. In addition, it may take the court years to force the bonding agent to pay the amount of a forfeited bond—that is, should the defendant fail to appear. In any event, money is a poor substitute indeed for the presence of the defendant at trial. The criminal justice system is not supposed to make money but to see that justice is done.

Instances of bonding agents referring released defendants to particular lawyers, who pay agents for referrals, are all too common. This is not only unethical, it is illegal. In states where elected judge-ships are usual, the bail bonding agent may contribute to the judge's campaign to obligate the judge. The judge may then be reluctant to press the agent for payment of a bond should the defendant not appear.

Bail bonding agents are the ones who insure the presence of the accused. As such they may have more power over the freedom of the accused than do police officers. Bonding agents can bring the accused back to jail with barely any supervision by the court. This is another clear example of the necessity for close watching by the courts over how related functions are handled.

Other Pretrial Procedures

All the many aspects of the court system affect the administration of justice. The grand jury, for example, has been the subject of much controversy. One body of opinion praises the grand jury as the protector of the innocent from vengeful prosecution. Another group says that the grand jury itself may seek vengeance. However it is regarded, the grand jury process is costly and time-consuming. Grand juries often issue indictments in cases which cannot be proved in court. Whether the institution of the grand jury should be retained is a subject that deserves serious study.

Pretrial discovery procedures are an innovation that seems to aid the cause of justice. They require that each side reveal its evidence to the other. Many people believe pretrial discovery favors the defense over the prosecution, since the defendant is not required to give testimony. Complete pretrial discovery does reduce chances that legal tricks rather than the truth will affect the outcome of a trial.

Plea bargaining is another important practice. The practice of plea bargaining grew up because, practically speaking, all cases cannot go to trial. A judge may have 1000 cases pending. Still, under the most efficient of conditions he or she cannot try more than forty jury cases in a year. However, the judge still has an obligation to evaluate a plea secured through negotiations between the prosecution and the defense. Some courts have tended to accept such pleas indiscriminately. They have not carefully examined the quantity and quality of the evidence or the legality of the law enforcement procedures used. That both the prosecutor and defendant are satisfied does not guarantee that the public interest and justice have been served.

LEGAL FEES AND CASELOADS

By any reasonable measure, those working in the state and federal legal agencies—both prosecuting attorneys and public defenders—are underpaid and overburdened with cases. They seldom have time to prepare their cases adequately, and only adequate preparation can convict the guilty and protect the innocent.

The right of the poor to free counsel has added greatly to the strains on the court system. These strains result in situations that occasionally lead an appellate court to determine that the accused was not adequately represented in the original trial. In such a situation the trial judge has abandoned the obligation to guarantee competent representation to all accused of crime.

The problems of the privately paid lawyer are even less well understood. The attorney's fee may not allow him or her to spend adequate time on a case. Take the example of a lawyer asked to defend a client who is too well off for a public defender. The person may still be too poor to pay more than $1500 for a defense.

The lawyer has office expenses of $400 to $500 a week. This covers rent, secretarial services, office equipment, telephone, postage, utilities, etc. Despite well over forty hours of work a week, only thirty hours can be charged to clients. Like every professional, the lawyer spends many hours in administrative and other unchargeable tasks. Considering vacation time and periods of court recess, the lawyer requires $1000 to $1500 each working week to clear $25,000 after taxes. A $25,000 net income, well above the national average for all workers, is not unreasonably high for professionals.

For a fee of between $1000 and $1500 a lawyer can devote only one full working week to case preparation. This virtually eliminates the possibility of a jury trial or any other procedures that require time-consuming preparation. These pressures can only have a negative effect on the quality of justice.

POSSIBLE INNOVATIONS

The issuing of citations rather than making arrests is a device that could help in guaranteeing justice for all. It is sorely underemployed. For example, a mother may have four children in school, own a house, and have had a steady job for years. She is not likely to flee to another state to avoid prosecution for a misdemeanor or minor felony. Little good is done by keeping such a person in jail. In cases where there is no threat to the public, the citation process could well replace that of formal arrest.

Another aid in providing justice would be more careful screening of cases by the prosecution. This factor could reduce the number of weak cases that now clog the courts. The spending of more time on initial processing by experienced and well-trained prosecutors should bring better results. However, reality is a vicious circle: Poor screening makes for a clogged calendar, which puts pressure on prosecutors and leaves them insufficient time for proper screening.

Both trial and posttrial procedures could be streamlined to allow for more certainty of a fair outcome. Such techniques as the use of videotape testimony from hard-to-get, expensive expert witnesses could make such testimony more widely available.

Presentence investigation reports on the accused are designed to help the judge to pass an informed sentence. Sometimes these are less than thorough and late in being presented. In Chapter 14 we discuss the pressures on those who prepare such reports. The result of shoddy report work can be a delay in passing sentence. More important, inadequate information is supplied to the judge and, therefore, the passing of an inappropriate sentence can result.

Court control over the offender has been further eroded by new posttrial programs for some of those convicted. Courts lack much of the needed expertise to determine what is best for the individual who has been sentenced. The judge's role is unique in providing an overall view of what is best for society. The fate of the convicted offender affects the good of society as a whole to a considerable extent. To that degree, the judge must have some say in what happens to that person after his or her conviction.

The appellate process is another area that needs improvement. An appeal can drag on for years. Much of the paper work generated is the result of tradition rather than real need. In one state, for example, it is possible to file a petition for review by the state supreme court. Doing this within fifteen days of a decision by a lower appeals court automatically stops the imprisonment of the defendant. Not surprisingly, many groundless petitions are filed in order to keep a defendant out of prison a little bit longer.

The overall picture may be one of something less than dazzling efficiency and effectiveness. Still the situation might well have been worse except for some factors that appeared in the 1960s. Perhaps the most significant was the drive to enforce laws governing the use of marijuana and some other drugs. This drive greatly increased the number of new cases. More than mere numbers was involved, however.

The defendants in these cases were often solidly middle-class. Their expectations of what the justice system was all about were higher than those of the urban poor and disadvantaged. These middle-class defendants also had a lot more political skill and influence. The influx of this new breed of offender in part stimulated many reforms. Among these are pretrial diversion, treatment programs, and rules requiring prompt trials. A better and more sophisticated police force also played a role. Their expectations of the court are higher than those of past generations.

More remains to be done. The National Advisory Commission on Standards and Goals for the Criminal Justice System and the American Bar Association have made noteworthy attempts to set standards for criminal justice. But more work is needed. Reducing caseloads through decriminalization of many offenses, and increasing resources for the court system, would help. But these are not enough. A new generation of innovative thinkers must devise new ways to provide justice. Court staffs of the future must include administrators who are sensitive to due process and other court goals. They must also be efficient at managing a complex establishment. Trials should and will remain the device by which the most serious offenses and most significant legal issues are resolved. However, in order to preserve our basic values, new and imaginative court practices must also be developed. To do less is to let justice die by default.

IMPLICATIONS FOR THE FUTURE

The United States Constitution is the supreme law of the land. The federal courts are empowered to review the actions of the state courts to determine whether they meet federal constitutional standards. If there is no violation of the Constitution, the federal courts have little authority to review state criminal case activity. That is, a U.S. Supreme Court decision respecting state criminal case processes usually rests upon a violation of the U.S. Constitution. These rulings tend to take authority away from the state court systems. These decisions also tend to promote uniformity throughout the United States. The Gault case (dealing with juvenile courts), *Mapp v. Ohio* (relating to the use of illegally seized evidence), and *Miranda v. Arizona* (governing the use of confessions) all constitute pressure toward uniformity of case processing throughout the United States.

The current U.S. Supreme Court seems to be slowing the trend toward its control of state criminal courts. But no major turning back to the past seems likely. The struggle between federal and state court systems—a part of our nation's history—will likely continue into the future. Within the states the struggle by local courts against control from the state capitol goes on. The trend seems to be a slow, halting movement to centralized control. Both struggles raise the issue inherent in our system of government, "How much local diversity and local power are required and desirable?" Must the criminal courts in one portion of a state be structured and function like courts in other parts of the same state? Must criminal courts in one state be and function like courts in other states of the union? Is uniformity necessarily desirable?

There are no final answers to the questions. It has been argued that each criminally charged person should have the same basic rights anywhere in the United States. But it is felt that beyond such minimum standards, state and local government should be adjusted to peculiarly local conditions. Others argue that uniformity is good since we are a mobile society and people everywhere are entitled to the same expectations of justice. This debate will probably continue for the foreseeable future.

QUESTIONS

1. What is the first step that should be taken to reform the courts? The second step? The third? Why?
2. How could these three proposals be implemented?

The criminal justice system treats the young, or juvenile, offender differently from the adult offender. In this chapter we will look at how the courts have dealt with juvenile delinquents. Chapter 15 will take a look at corrections for juvenile delinquents.

HISTORY OF THE JUVENILE COURT

It is easier to describe what has happened than why something has happened. The history of the juvenile court in the United States can be described with some precision. Trying to establish why the juvenile court came into being, however, is to some extent a matter of speculation.

After the Civil War, America was faced with changing conditions. A number of these contributed to the eventual creation of the first juvenile court in Chicago in 1899. A wave of immigrants, particularly from Eastern Europe, during the latter nineteenth century introduced new social patterns into American life. These immigrants brought with them a close-knit family structure. Coming to the new land tested the strength of those family ties. Many of these immigrants had come from rural areas and for the first time were exposed to urban life. Besides experiencing the change from rural to city life, they found themselves adjusting to a new culture with a new language.

To a certain extent, the native American population was also coping for the first time with city life. After the Civil War, the trend toward industrialization and urbanization quickened. With urbanization, America experienced the beginning of the breakdown of the extended family. No longer were parents, grandparents, children, uncles, and aunts all living together in a close-knit group. Instead the nuclear family, which consists only of parents and children, often lived far from other kin. Close relatives were no longer available for help with child rearing. Parents worked long hours to ensure the family's survival. Now began the trend toward the employment of women outside the home. It was evident particularly in the urban

The Juvenile Courts

areas and especially at the lower end of the socioeconomic scale. In the urban areas, child labor continued to grow, although the trend was modified by state action.

All of these changing conditions placed great strains on the American community, and in response the state stepped in. Compulsory education, designed to Americanize generations of immigrants, coupled with child labor laws, impacted heavily on American family life. Children slowly drifted from the factory into the schoolhouse. Thus the state was involving itself, through the schools, in the rearing of children. Meanwhile the criminal justice system began to treat the juvenile violator separately and apart from the adult violator. As early as the 1860s, in Chicago, children were separated from adults in certain aspects of criminal court systems. By 1900 in Massachusetts, Indiana, and New York, children began to receive separate treatment by the criminal court system.

Why was a separate juvenile court system needed in the year 1899? We must look at the state of the adult criminal justice system and particularly at the adult criminal court. Many rights and procedures we now take for granted did not exist in the adult criminal court of that era. Accused persons who were indigent faced trial, conviction, and incarceration without the protection of an attorney. The only defendants who had counsel were those who could afford to hire counsel. In many states evidence that had been illegally seized by the police was fully admissible in court. It was not unusual for someone to be convicted on illegally seized physical evidence or an illegally obtained confession. Pretrial release systems were generally limited to those who had funds. Presentence investigations to assist the judge in determining what should be done with the accused after conviction were largely nonexistent.

The adult penal system was noted for its harshness. This system processed not only adults, but juveniles as well. An arrested juvenile might be placed in a cell with adults charged with rape, robbery, murder, or other violent offenses. Upon conviction, the juvenile might well be placed in the same prison with a child molester, a murderer, or a burglar. There were numerous instances of children being terrorized in these facilities.

At this time in American history, the populist movement was spreading. William Jennings Bryan was crossing the country making his famous speech, "A Cross of Gold," and America was ripe for reform. One aspect of the reform movement was increasing interest in the state of juveniles in the criminal justice system. Then, in the year 1899, the first juvenile court was born in Chicago, Illinois. The creation of the juvenile court was accompanied by enabling legislation in many state legislatures of the United States. This legislation provided a framework for the creation of juvenile courts throughout the country.

Two ancient English common law concepts provided a legal and philosophical foundation for the juvenile court and its processes. The first concept is *parens patriae* and the second is *in loco parentis*. *Parens patriae* contains the English common law notion that the monarchy stands in the relationship of parent to the country. *In loco parentis* refers to the obligation of the state to all children. It means that the state stands in the shoes of the parent in relationship to the welfare of children. These two doctrines provided a source of authority and justification for the intrusion of the state into family affairs. In particular it justified the state's interposition into the relationship between parent and child.

The juvenile court differed considerably from the adult court in philosophy, process, and terminology. The adult courts were adversarial; that is, the state accused the individual of violating the laws of the state. The burden was upon the state to prove the accused guilty beyond a reasonable doubt. In some courts, the state had the availability of prosecutors to present the state's case. Upon conviction, the court focused on the nature of the wrongdoing and the law that was being violated. It sent the accused to the penitentiary as a form of punishment. Juvenile courts, however, were formed focusing upon the child and not so much upon the nature of the child's violations. The juvenile court espoused the philosophy of helping the child become a worthwhile citizen.

Juvenile court processes were somewhat different from the processing in adult court. Rather than facing a trial, the juvenile faced a hearing. The state had to prove guilt beyond a reasonable doubt in an adversarial trial. The hearing was supposed to be conducted by a kindly judge who would inquire why the child did the alleged act. The purpose of the court was not punishment, but rather to help the child walk a correct path. By and large, there were no lawyers in the courtroom. Through the hearing the child was not considered guilty of a crime, but determined to be a delinquent or dependent child. Criminal records in adult court were public records. The philosophy of the juvenile court was that children were not fully responsible for their acts. Since there was no conviction of crimes, it was felt the records of the juvenile court proceedings should be confidential. An effect of this, so the theory went, was that there would not be a conviction on the child's record. At his or her majority, the child would stand in the position of one who had not been through juvenile court.

By the 1920s, almost every state had passed a juvenile court act providing separate treatment for juveniles in the justice system. In some states this led to the creation of separate juvenile courts. Other states provided separate processing by the same judge who might preside over civil trials or adult criminal trials as well. The tendency was for one judge to handle many different kinds of cases, including juvenile cases, in the rural areas. In some of the major cities, separate juvenile courts were created.

The typical juvenile act provided that the court's jurisdiction should fall into one of two basic classifications: delinquency and dependency. Those children abandoned by their parents or neglected by their parents came under the court's authority as dependent children. These acts gave the courts the power to remove the neglected child from the home. Or, in the case of an abandoned child, the court could order that the child receive some assistance from the state. If the child violated the law, the court had the authority by these statutes to declare the child a delinquent.

There were and still are two basic kinds of offenses within the classification of *delinquency*. The first refers to those acts which would be punishable under the adult criminal law if committed by an adult. They include such things as larceny, robbery, auto theft, and vandalism. The second kind of offense refers to those which, only if committed by a child, are violations. These are called "status offenses." Some examples of status offenses are truancy, curfew violation, and running away from home. Adults are not required to go to school. Neither, in general, do they have to be off the streets at a certain time. Nor are they punished for running away from home.

A moment's reflection on status offenses gives some picture of the reasons for the creation of the juvenile court. Because of the breakdown of the family and community control, parents were losing the ability to control their children. So, particularly through the status violation, the state stepped into the role of the parent. For the child before a juvenile court on a status violation, the state had more power over the child than did the parent.

THE JUVENILE COURT IN RECENT TIME

A typical juvenile court in the 1950s and 1960s was often staffed by a judge who had no specialized juvenile court training. The judge often was of lower status than the judges of the courts of general civil jurisdiction. Even the adult felony court judges had higher status and were very often paid more.

A typical juvenile court process began then, as now, with the police taking the child into custody. The child, in some areas, would then be brought to the police station or to an adult jail. In other areas, separate juvenile detention facilities were established and the police would transport the juvenile to those facilities. Shortly thereafter, a probation-intake officer might evaluate the case. He would decide if it was the kind of case that should go to court or might be handled informally. In some jurisdictions, the probation officer could order the child's release until a delinquency hearing would be held. This was the rule even if the probation-intake officer decided that the case should eventually go to court. (See Figure 11-1.)

In other jurisdictions, the decision to release was restricted more to the court. The probation officer might decide that the juvenile should be detained pending further proceedings. Then the court would hold a brief hearing to determine whether the juvenile should be detained until the final hearing. The final hearing would determine whether the juvenile was to be considered a delinquent. The court had the option of: (1) returning the child to the home; (2) keeping the child in the juvenile detention facility; or, (3) in some instances, releasing the child to other family members or some other responsible person. The intake officer would file a petition which might allege that the child was delinquent and in need of supervision. The case would appear on the court's calendar, the hearing would be held, and the court would render its decision. In most situations, there was neither a prosecutor nor a defense lawyer. The hearings would not be conducted in the accusatorial mode, as in an adult court. They would be based more on the inquisitorial concept of the continental court. At the conclusion of the hearing, the court might determine the child was not a delinquent. Or the court might determine that the child was a delinquent. It could order that the child be placed under the supervision of the court and sent home. Or it could select restrictions on the child's freedom of movement, including sending the child to "state reform schools."

In a few situations, the child may have been accused of committing a terrible act. Or the child may have gone through the juvenile court process many times without any apparent positive effect. In those situations, most juvenile courts could send older children to the adult felony court for trial as adult felons. While this jurisdiction existed, it was rarely utilized; only a very small percentage were referred to the adult court for trial.

During the evolutionary process of the juvenile court, things were moving in the adult court system. The Supreme Court of the United States rendered significant decisions which radically altered

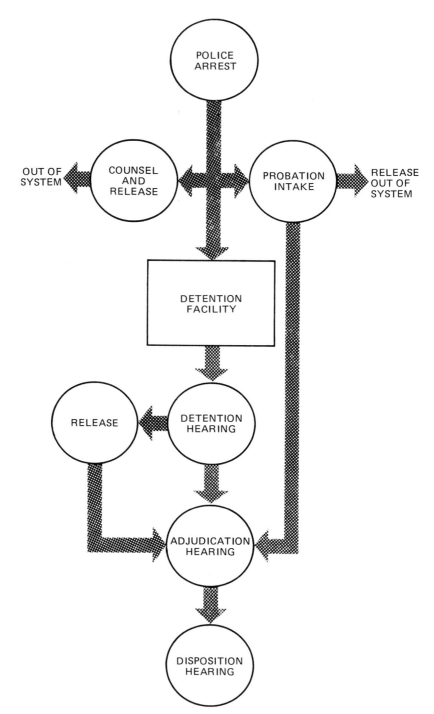

Figure 11-1 Juvenile arrest and detention.

the processes of the adult criminal court. One such case was *Gideon v. Wainwright*. Here the United States Supreme Court required that indigent adults charged with crime be furnished with an attorney free of charge. Another later case was *Mapp v. Ohio*. Here the Court required the exclusionary rule to be in full force and effect in all states of the United States. This rule stated that evidence illegally obtained could no longer be used to convict an adult charged with a crime.

In addition to U.S. Supreme Court cases, the activity of lawyers in the adult court brought about many changes. Pretrial discovery, which had been a stranger to the adult criminal court, became a reality in many of them. Defendants were entitled to have notice of the charges against them. They are guaranteed an opportunity to require the state to define the alleged offenses carefully. They also have an opportunity to challenge the legality of the seizure of the evidence. So, the adult courts were receiving a massive infusion of basic concepts of due process of law. Meantime, the juvenile courts maintained their informality.

The Gault Case

In the year 1967, the United States Supreme Court decided the Gault case. It should be noted that the Court was divided in this case. The majority opinion reflects a dissatisfaction with most aspects of the juvenile court proceedings. Minority opinions agreed in part with the majority opinion and its dissatisfaction with some juvenile court processes. But they urged that the juvenile court be largely undisturbed in its practices and procedures. The Court presented the facts as a way of demonstrating the "evils" that had befallen the juvenile court.

Some commentators have urged that the facts were unusual and did not reflect typical practices in the juvenile court. Nobody will ever really know. Prior to Gault, there were few lawyers in juvenile court and appeals were very rare. Many juvenile courts did not have any formal verbatim record of the proceedings before the court. The clerk or judge might just take a few notes as to the outcome of the hearing.

Gerald Gault was fifteen at the time of his arrest by local police. He was arrested for being a suspect in an obscene phone call violation. He was detained for several days without a hearing. His parents did not receive formal notice of Gerald's detention. Neither was there clear indication from either police officer or probation officer as to the reason for his detention. After three or four days in detention, he was released. The police officer, on a piece of plain stationery, wrote a notice for Gerald Gault to appear in court. The specific allegations of his misconduct were not clearly stated in this informal letter. The Court said that for an adult, the maximum penalty was a $50 fine or incarceration up to two months. As a juvenile, under Arizona law Gault could have been detained in the juvenile detention facility for many years. At a hearing, Mrs. Gault asked the judge to bring before the court Mrs. Cook, who allegedly received the obscene phone call. Mrs. Cook, the only witness to the event, never testified.

No record was made of the proceedings. The juvenile court judge testified at a later hearing. He had no formal record or transcript of the proceedings to refresh his memory. A subsequent hearing was held after Gault's adjudication of delinquency. The juvenile court judge could not clearly specify (1) exactly which statute Gerald was alleged to have violated and (2) which statute formed the basis of the conviction. The judge thought he remembered that Gerald Gault made an admission of guilt during the earlier hearing. This statement was hotly contested by other witnesses. During the adjudication hearing, Gault was never informed of any right to counsel and was adjudicated guilty without assistance of counsel.

The juvenile court seemed to take into consideration, in adjudicating Gerald guilty and in disposing of the case, one record. This stated that Gerald had many years before been accused of taking a baseball glove from a younger student at school. Gerald Gault was never adjudicated of that violation. The Supreme Court felt, however, that it had entered into the juvenile court judge's decision on the case. And so, Gerald Gault was adjudicated guilty of violating one or another of the laws of Arizona. He was without the benefit of notice of: (1) the charges against him, (2) the right to counsel, (3) the right to be confronted by his accuser, (4) the right to cross-examine his accuser, or (5) the right to a transcript of his proceedings. In the Supreme Court's view, Gerald Gault was denied due process of law.

The history of the American criminal justice system demonstrates a pattern of the division of functions. In its early history, a police officer handled matters now conceived to be exclusively under the control of the prosecution. The police officer would decide whether the case would go to court and would present the case to the court. The defendant, if poor, would be his or her own lawyer. The judge would decide the disposition of the defendant if convicted. Later we found: (1) The prosecutor came into the court to present the state's case. (2) The defense lawyer was in the court defending the accused. (3) The probation officer was providing the court with assistance in determining the sentence and in providing an alternative to incarceration.

While these roles and functions were being further divided and subdivided in adult court, matters were different in juvenile court. One basic proposition of law is that a person cannot perform two different and conflicting roles and do both well. In the Gault case, the Supreme Court shattered the image of the kindly, fatherly juvenile judge who dispensed justice and acted for the benefit and in the best interests of the child. That image was to some extent false. The Court said the judge could not be both judge and defense attorney. The probation officer could not be the helper of the child and the child's accuser.

The proceedings permitted sending a juvenile away to an institution for a long period of time. This was without the protection of due process of law and of a lawyer to guarantee that protection. In summary, the United States Supreme Court determined Gerald Gault was denied due process of law in "kangaroo court" proceedings. The majority in the Gault case strongly condemned the proceedings. They used some of the harshest language the Supreme Court of the United States has ever bestowed on a trial court. The minority opinion urged the majority not to interfere with the functioning of the juvenile court. It said the majority overstepped its constitutional boundaries in mandating a radical change in the nature of the local judiciary. They disagreed with the majority's assessment of the quality of processing juvenile court cases in the juvenile courts of the United States. There was some agreement to recommend more protection for the juvenile, but certainly not to the extent mandated by the majority.

The specific requirements of this decision signified a major revolution and upheaval in the juvenile court process in the United States. The court held that juveniles were entitled to certain basic rights. These rights included: (1) notification to the juvenile of the specific charges against the juvenile in writing and (2) delivery of this notification within adequate time prior to any hearing so that the juvenile might prepare his or her defense. The court further required that: (1) the juvenile be notified of his or her right to an attorney, and (2) if the juvenile is unable to hire an attorney because of lack of funds, the state must provide an attorney. Juveniles, said the court, had to be notified: (1) that they did not have to testify in juvenile court proceedings, (2) that they had the right to be confronted with those who were their accusers, and (3) that they had the right to cross-examine their accusers.

The Winship case concerned a juvenile alleged to be delinquent based upon a violation of criminal law. The Supreme Court of the United States rendered a decision respecting such cases. The juvenile cannot be found delinquent unless proven beyond a reasonable doubt guilty of committing that particular violation of the criminal law. The Court, in doing this, closed the gap between the adult trial and the juvenile hearing. The Supreme Court of the United States also made a landmark decision in *McKeiver v. Pennsylvania.* It said that, unlike an adult in Court proceedings, the juvenile had no right to a jury trial. Putting these decisions together, we have a revolution in the juvenile court.

Trends in the Future

The juvenile courts of the United States are far from having fully complied with all the requirements of the Gault decision. Yet there have been major changes in many of these courts and the beginning of other changes. These are likely to be trends in the future. A number of states have completely reorganized their court structures. They have elevated the juvenile court judges from the bottom of the judicial heap. Now they have at least equal status with the judges of other courts of general trial jurisdiction. The gap in salary between juvenile court judges, where this function is a specialized one, and other judges is closing.

Some trial courts of general jurisdiction, particularly in urban areas, as policy rotate judges from one area of specialization to another. A judge might sit on cases involving automobile accidents for a year or two, then advance to hearing adult criminal trials. Possibly from there the judge might move to hearing juvenile cases of violations. In prior years, many judges did not want transfer to the juvenile division of the court. In recent years, more and more judges are volunteering for transfer to the juvenile court. This may partially reflect the juvenile court's transformation from a separate entity with separate procedures to a miniaturized version of an adult felony trial court.

Ten years ago, juvenile prosecution was conducted largely by the police or the probation officer. Since Gault, major moves have brought the prosecutor into court to present the state's case against the juvenile. With the prosecution coming to present the state's case there is also a movement for the prosecutor: (1) To do further case screening and (2) to decide whether the case can or should be brought

Case Study:
GROWING UP VERSUS DELINQUENCY

Before joining the force, police officers were required to take up residence in town. Not only did this save them money in commuting, but the department felt the officers would have a more responsible feeling toward the community. One fact most members of the department soon understood was that any time any type of trouble started on their block, the police officer who lived there was notified immediately.

The relationship between the police officers and their neighbors became very strong over the years. An officer's family would be invited to cookouts by neighbors and the courtesy was returned. Sergeant Gamble was one of these officers. He was also the community's juvenile officer. Every time a youngster was caught in trouble, Gamble was notified to handle the procedures.

Gamble's neighbor had two young boys around thirteen and fourteen years of age. The boys were good youngsters; however, one of them, Bob, had started to get into a little trouble. He was stopped by a police officer who claimed Bob was with a group of boys who were trying to steal a car. The car was not removed; therefore, the officer released most of the group and held the youngster who was trying to pry the window down.

The officer reported the incident to Gamble and nothing else took place. Gamble made a simple note in his record books.

About six months later Bob was among a group of teen-agers picked up for possession of marijuana cigarettes. Although Bob did not have any on him, others in the group had indicated that every one of them smoked it. Even though this was a relatively minor offense, Gamble felt it was time Bob's parents were warned about the situation. The boy was released into the custody of his parents and no charges were filed. The arresting officer and Gamble decided that since no cigarettes had been found on Bob, nothing could legally be done.

Six months went by. Police were witnessing an increasing number of petty burglaries. In terms of dollars little was taken. However, with each additional break-in, public pressure mounted for the police to do something. Gamble and other officers had a good idea that youngsters were practicing what they saw on television crime shows.

A team of police officers in unmarked cars staked out various parts of the community. When they compared notes after a week of work, Gamble noticed one common factor. Bob was seen in the area of each burglary.

Gamble talked informally to Bob's parents and presented the facts as he knew them. Gamble went over Bob's past record of being indirectly involved in trouble, but the youngster's parents refused to believe anything was wrong.

What should Sergeant Gamble do now?

to the court for adjudication. Since Gault, there has been a slow infusion of the public defender into the juvenile court.

The impact of lawyers in the court cannot be overstated. One of the fears of the minority in the Gault case was: The juvenile courts would break down with the additional procedures and practices the presence of lawyers in the juvenile courtroom brought. In some areas, it is alleged, the defense bar is not capably representing the juvenile. In other areas, it is alleged, defense counsel is tying up the proceedings by insisting upon trial of too many cases.

The Gault decision has also had an impact on the police. Police officers have always engaged in diversion (routing the offender to avenues of rehabilitation outside the criminal justice system), informal though it was. The Gault decision stimulated, perhaps, more extensive and more formalized use of police diversion. With the creation of a Law Enforcement Assistance Administration, a number of police diversion programs have been funded. In addition, many jurisdictions have used much of the LEAA funds for separate diversion agencies, some operated by probation.

A significant number of cases never reach court. These diversion agencies receive the juvenile shortly after arrest. They attempt to diagnose the nature of the juvenile's problem and try to provide some informal solution. The nature of police activity in juvenile cases is changing. There is an increasing trend toward (1) the creation of separate juvenile units; (2) the training of police officers in the handling of juveniles; and (3) an attempt to improve the quality of those cases that go to court.

Gault has also had major implications for the role of the probation officer in the juvenile court. The intake decision is more and more being shifted to the prosecution. The probation officer is slowly losing many accusatorial functions that characterized his or her activity prior to the Gault decision.

The police officer, in handling the juvenile case, faces a difficult role conflict. On the one hand the officer is supposed to be the helper of the child. On the other hand he or she is the accuser of the child.

A major debate now stirs concerning the proper place of the status violation. Some authorities urge that the violations should not be violations at all. Others urge that status violations should remain on the law books. However, they want the juvenile court deprived of its jurisdiction over status violations. These authorities urge that informal neighborhood kinds of courts or social welfare agencies should deal with the juvenile status offender. Other authorities argue: Many children who become involved in purely delinquent acts

Case Study:
CONTROLLING YOUTH

Summer was upon Clarks Town once again. With the closing of school the streets were filled with teen-agers both day and night. Everyone in the department was used to the situation. It happened every year, not only in Clarks Town but all over the United States. Kids were out of school with little if anything to do but wait until the fall.

During the summer months the parks and streets were filled with not only youngsters but also a large number of senior citizens. The combination of the two groups meant the police were in for busy shifts. Either the generation gap caused irritation or the physical and mental attitudes of the two groups did not harmonize, at least for the residents of Clarks Town.

One of the first youth-against-age calls occurred in the main shopping area of the community. Four or five teen-agers were visiting a friend who lived above one of the stores. Because of the heat, the meeting took place by the front door, which opened directly to the street.

A elderly resident was pushing a shopping cart along the sidewalk and found it difficult to maneuver the cart through the group. She began to shout at a teen-ager, who in turn made a few rude comments as she walked by. The elderly citizen raised her hand containing an umbrella, exclaiming, "Why don't you bums get jobs?"

A shopkeeper became worried over the situation and thought a call to the police would solve the problem. Police arrived and asked the teen-agers to move on. The youngsters claimed they had a right to stand in front of their own house with their guests. The officer knew they were right, but he asked them to take a walk and said that they could return later.

Later in the evening, police received a call from another senior citizen complaining that youth gangs had taken over the local parks. The department arranged for the youngsters to hang around the parks in order to reduce the complaints about gangs roaming the streets.

The desk officer explained that he would have a car check out the area, but assured the caller that the community's teenagers were just congregating in the parks. He said that no harm would come to people walking through or using the parks. He also informed the caller that the teen-agers had a right to use the parks.

As one would guess, the calls continued throughout the summer months. Most of the calls were about youngsters standing around doing nothing, which is not against the law. The police department in Clarks Town could not come up with a solution and was determined to weather the storm.

What should the department do? Is there a solution to this problem?

started down the wrong path by first becoming status violators. They urge that the truant and the runaway are on the path to the commission of a criminal act. From this they conclude that juvenile courts should retain jurisdiction over status violators.

Another debate in the juvenile area has sharpened since the decision in the Gault case. It has to do with the appropriate ages for the jurisdiction of the juvenile court. There is increasing pressure to lower the age limit for prosecution as an adult. Pressure is increasing to refer more cases that are within the juvenile court's jurisdiction over to the adult court. Particularly is this desired when the juvenile is charged with having committed a serious violation. There is a perception that ever greater percentages of crime, particularly serious crime, are being committed by ever younger children.

We will recall that the original juvenile court attempted to provide confidentiality of its records. Indeed, some states passed statutes which prevented newspapers from publishing the names of juveniles alleged to be delinquent. However, the Supreme Court of the United States has recently further limited the confidentiality of juvenile records. Now, the states are beginning to modify or repeal statutes prohibiting the publication of the names of juvenile offenders.

In summary, the Gault case has stimulated a revolution. The precise direction of that revolution is, at this point, unknown. It is known that increasing attention is being paid to the juvenile justice system and, particularly, to the juvenile court. The United States Congress resounds with debate and discussion. These center upon altering the flow of federal money from the adult justice system to the juvenile justice system. Local policy boards and the Law Enforcement Assistance Administration are diverting more and more resources into the juvenile area. Programs started include: (1) education and training of juvenile officers, (2) increased use of diversion in juvenile cases, (3) changes in juvenile correctional facilities, and (4) further research in the field of juvenile justice.

In 1899, the newly established juvenile court went down one path while the adult court was going down another. By 1967, the paths were widely separated. The Gault decision turned the juvenile court in the direction that the adult courts had been taking for the preceding sixty-eight years. At the start the trend was toward the increased protection of the accused in the adult criminal justice system. The Supreme Court of the United States, since 1967, has somewhat reversed this. It may come to pass that the juvenile court and the adult court will intersect at some point in the future.

QUESTIONS

1. What will the juvenile court look like twenty years from now in terms of philosophy, procedures, and roles of the principal officials?
2. Should status violations be in the juvenile court's jurisdiction? If not, what should be done with status violations? Why?
3. What do you think is the appropriate philosophical approach for juvenile courts to take?

part 5

corrections

The area of corrections is broadly seen as the third element in the criminal justice system (after law enforcement and the judiciary). It is also viewed as the last stop on the path that starts with arrest. Also, it is seen as the last hope for the offender before turning to crime as a way of life.

GOALS

The three basic aims of corrections are punishment, rehabilitation, and deterrence. Protection of the public is a general goal that can be considered a corollary of these three. All these elements have been present throughout history, although at different times some aspect has been more emphasized than others. For example, the Lateran Council in 1214 discontinued trial by ordeal—a humanitarian step for those times of harsh punishment.

Serious efforts are being made today to analyze how best to achieve these basic goals. Much study attempts to find out how corrections fit into the overall criminal justice system. In the chapters that follow we examine how corrections works and how it could be made to work better. An aspect we will explore with special attention is alternatives to imprisonment. First, though, we will look at the relationship between corrections and the rest of the criminal justice system.

As we have seen, occasional shifting alliances as well as open hostilities appear among the branches of the criminal justice system. Police officers often complain of courts being "soft on crime." Meanwhile judges lash out against disregard for civil liberties on the part of the police. But those two bodies often join forces when they look at the third: corrections.

Frequently law enforcement officers and judges conveniently blame the failure of our whole system of criminal justice on the correctional field. The effect of such criticism, and the lack of understanding and cooperation that it reflects, is obvious. Indeed, a report of the Federal Task Force on Corrections states this attitude challenges the effectiveness of the entire system.

chapter 12

Corrections and the Criminal Justice System

A substantial obstacle to the development of effective corrections lies in its relationship to police and the courts, the other subsystems of the criminal justice system. Corrections inherit any inefficiency, inequality, and improper discrimination that may have occurred in any earlier step of the criminal justice process. Its clients come to it from the other subsystems; it is the consistent heir to their defects.

The contemporary view is to consider society's institutionalized response to crime as the criminal justice system and its activities as the criminal justice process. This model envisions interdependent and interrelated agencies and programs that will provide a coordinated and consistent response to crime. The model, however, remains a model—it does not exist in fact. Although cooperation between the various components has improved noticeably in some localities, it cannot be said that a criminal justice "system" really exists.[1]

Some friction within the criminal justice system can be traced to the different, often conflicting goals of each of its three elements.

CORRECTIONS AND THE POLICE

Essentially the tension between corrections and the police stems from differences in the populations they serve. Although the police are designated to serve society, their particular law enforcement function delegates them to work for victims and potential victims. In this role they risk their lives and concentrate their efforts to prevent crime and arrest criminals. In the process of doing this they are naturally allied with the victims. Such an alliance can often have an impact on the psychological makeup (the personality) of the officer.

The study of groups reveals one step to increase a group's cohesiveness: to designate another group or issue as alien. In sports, a team develops spirit by focusing their efforts against another team or

1. National Advisory Commission on Criminal Justice Standards and Goals, Task Force on Corrections, *Corrections* (Washington, D.C.: U.S. Government Printing Office, 1973), p. 5.

teams. During past wars, one way the generals rallied the troops was to spread word of atrocities of the opposing armies.

Another group technique to increase cohesiveness is to get group members to share the opinions of others who belong. If they share beliefs, they can then consolidate against those who don't hold them.

In the police alliance with the actual or would-be victims of crime, the police experience daily people's suffering caused by criminals. In their role as law enforcement personnel, they take chances every day to prevent crime or apprehend society's enemy—the offender.

Naturally, then, police seek to get criminals off the street in the quickest possible manner. And naturally, after this is accomplished, they want the offenders to remain incarcerated as long as possible. They are constantly exposed to social victims and encouragement of a mental set focused on apprehending the offender. The police officer naturally resists any correctional method which is based on the offender's early return to the community.

The corrections personnel, on the other hand, would like the police and society in general to take a long-range view. They want people to realize that lengthy sentences do not aid in turning the offenders from a life of crime. They emphasize that such sentences may in fact increase the person's criminal tendencies.

Whereas the police are allied with the victim, corrections personnel live much of their waking hours with the offenders. This association leads to an alliance where the corrections personnel seek ways to help successfully reintegrate offenders into the community. They see the absence of rehabilitation in institutions and the harm this can effect. They encourage—through their policies—the use of alternatives to incarceration and an increased use of community-based settings.

Police believe that letting offenders go in the hope they will correct themselves is unreasonable, especially when the police have taken chances with their own lives in getting these offenders off the street. Thus, the long-range goal of rehabilitation which prompts corrections professionals to risk early release is emotionally unacceptable to some police.

Intellectually, police officers may accept the principle. But their job has them primarily in contact with those on parole and probation who commit second crimes. So the fact that many offenders benefit from early release is not in the forefront of their minds. Consequently, in many instances the police do not work hand in hand with the corrections system. Instead, while working within their broad discretions as enforcement agents, they arrest some who could have been handled better otherwise. They sometimes too frequently "round up" ex-offenders when a crime is committed. Also they often resent the initiation of a community-based program.

Part of this conflict between the police and corrections can be alleviated. Correctional personnel can make special efforts to communicate with police. They can orient police officers to their philosophy and show them local facilities. In this way a better chance for two-way communication would be possible. For too long, corrections has isolated itself from the enforcement branch.

In addition, correctional planners must try at all cost to develop the best screening programs possible. Although a risk is present in all cases, it should be lessened as much as possible. Offenders must be carefully chosen for a program which puts them in early contact with the public again. Care must be taken to ensure decisions based on knowledge of the offender and this will increase the probability of success.

A difficulty central to the conflict between police and corrections, though, is one that will unfortunately not soon be resolved. This is in regard to the unequal advancement of police and correctional science. Criminalistics and police management technology have advanced to where law enforcement agents can see quick, observable results (i.e., quick apprehension of an offender) which are measurable. In corrections, uncertain methods and questionable results are the end products of their hard work.

So communication between these two sections of the criminal justice system can be increased. Efforts at cooperation can be enhanced somewhat in the process. Still correctional failures will continue to hamper construction of a more cohesive police-correctional team.

CORRECTIONS AND THE COURTS

The problems arising between corrections and the courts stem partly from the courts' complex role in the overall system.

The court has a dual role in the criminal justice system: it is both a participant in the criminal justice process and the supervisor of its practices. As participant, the court and its officers determine guilt or innocence and impose sanctions. In many jurisdictions, the court also serves as a correctional agency by administering the probation system.

In addition to being a participant, the court plays another important role.

When practices of the criminal justice system conflict with other values in society, the courts must determine which takes precedence over the other.[2]

It is particularly this last role that has caused a good deal of conflict between judicial and correctional professionals. The courts in some instances have had to curb the broad discretionary powers held by correctional administrators. Certain institutional policies would aid the administrator in running an institution (i.e., in the use of certain punishments for infraction of rules). Yet they also turned out to be unconstitutional; consequently, the greater good dictated prohibition of their use. Or it was decided they could be applied only after fulfilling due process of law—by having legal counsel represent the prisoner.

The courts have also proved an irritant to correctional policy through justices' manner of sentencing in various circumstances. Large inequities in sentences for different socioeconomic groups have in some instances created situations where offenders became bitter and recalcitrant. They became so not by virtue of being prisoners. They were embittered because they were sentenced to an unduly long period in comparison with the sentences of better-situated offenders. So, because of their unduly harsh sentence, such offenders are harder to handle and treat in an institution.

The above differences will not be totally resolved in the future. But steps are being taken to relieve the tension that exists in many settings between the courts and corrections. Workshops for judges are at least moving them in a more positive direction concerning equitable sentencing. On the other side, corrections professionals are becoming more and more accustomed to court involvement in the corrections field. The court has a rightful role in the administration of justice in the institutional and probation settings.

COOPERATION IN THE SYSTEM

Certainly, people in the three sections of the system—police, corrections, and the courts—are beginning to realize that a nonsystem exists. Professionals in each area are seeing what destruction a noncomplementary set of roles is doing. Seeing this (although they are not happy with the prospects of working with other subsystems) has prompted officers of each system to move further toward compromise.

2.   Ibid., p. 8.

Case Study
THREAT TO SOCIETY

Like sailors who spend their days off on a boat, Thompson Village police used their free time to play softball together, usually against the sheriff's officers who operated the jail. One Sunday afternoon the game ended in a tie and was called on account of rain. Most of the players went home, although five or six headed for a local bar.

Shop talk was on the agenda, planned or not. One of the sheriff's officers was attending college at night, working toward his B.S. degree in sociology. The officer brought up an interesting question: he wondered if the jail system was doing the right thing.

John McNally was the officer's name. He had been with the office of the sheriff for about three years. A few police officers said that after they sent an alleged criminal to McNally, he should just lock up the accused person and throw away the key. Of course, the police officers were not serious, but their comments were based on sincere feelings that criminals were too well-treated.

McNally understood the situation. He himself knew of some prisoners who had been arrested for murder and released. A day or so later they had killed again. Many times, McNally remarked, the convict does not go to jail but is released on probation to commit a similar crime. McNally was sure there were people in jail, convicted of serious crimes, who could be released without fear that they would harm society again. On the other hand, there were many petty crooks not sent to jail who were really a threat to the community.

One of the police officers asked McNally for further explanation. The sheriff's officer pointed to the fact that at present in the cells was a man convicted of killing his wife while he was drunk. This was his only offense. Before his arrest, he had not even had a traffic ticket. Furthermore, as far as the police and the courts could tell, it was the first time he had been drunk.

McNally compared this person with a burglar who had broken into twenty or thirty homes before being captured and then been released without going to jail. The burglar then broke into another thirty houses. McNally felt that, although the husband had committed murder, there was a good chance he would not commit another crime. The burglar was continuing to hurt society.

McNally based his opinion on the past record of the murderer. It was clean. He had committed a crime of passion when he did not have control of himself. The burglar had full control of the situation.

But a police officer reminded McNally that the husband did take the life of his wife. He asked about the wife's right to live. "Just the thought of leaving a killer on the streets sends chills down my spine," he concluded.

Is the police officer right? Is McNally right? What do you think of McNally's argument?

Police are being instructed in the proper use of fines and warnings in lieu of arrest. Correctional officers are becoming more acceptant of the need and reality of court supervision of treatment. And the courts are now trying to balance more carefully prisoners' constitutional rights against the realities of running an institution.

Desirably this trend toward cooperation will continue. If not, this so-called "system" will continue to do, at a greater rate, only one systematic thing. That will be to further worsen the problem of crime and the plight of society.

Possibly one of the most positive signs of greater cooperation between corrections and the courts today bears further examination. That is the growing conviction in both fields that alternatives to jail for those awaiting trial must be further developed. In order to better understand the issues involved, we will now take a look at what these alternatives are.

LOCKING PEOPLE UP

In some cases and for some offenders, prison is a necessity. But when? And for whom? Most people would probably agree on the need to lock up the extremely dangerous offender. For instance, few would argue with a decision to refuse probation to someone convicted of the sex murder of a child. But that is an extreme case in a narrow category. What about less obvious situations?

For people convicted of armed robbery, aggravated assault, and rape, should imprisonment be required or should special circumstances be considered? Where does one draw the line? In deciding whether someone should be sent to prison to punish them and to protect society, complex questions arise. When there was no alternative to prison and everyone believed offenders could be rehabilitated there, decisions were easier to make.

Today society is confronted by a body of knowledge pointing to the failure of prisons on the one hand. On the other hand are fear and frustration about crime. Studies show that in most cases imprisonment has little if any corrective impact. Yet we are still faced with the questions: What shall we do with dangerous offenders? How shall we deal with those who commit major, but not necessarily dangerous, crimes, such as grand larceny and treason? There are no easy answers. The chart in Figure 12-1 illustrates the typical route through the corrections system of a person convicted of a crime.

In the past people were primarily concerned with protecting the public and punishing the offender. The results of this position were: (1) more offenders than necessary were imprisoned; (2) less rehabili-

THE CORRECTIONS PROCESS

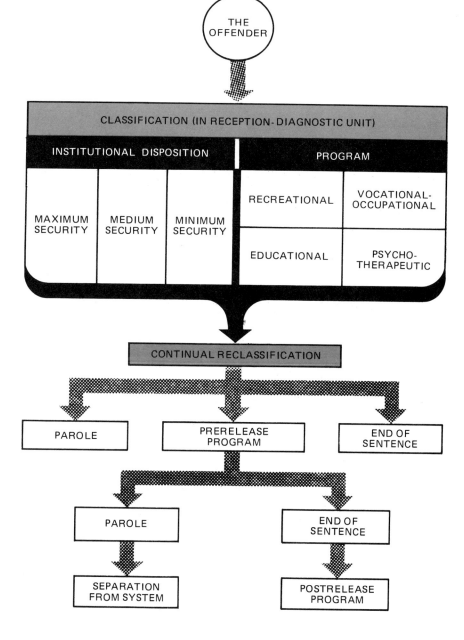

Figure 12-1

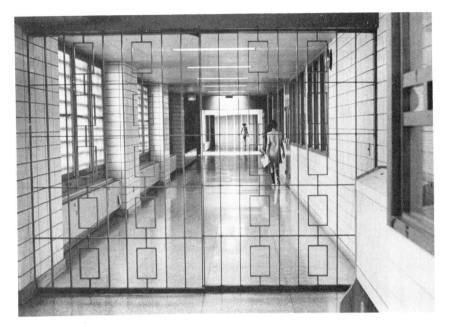

Even when locks and bars are required in an institution, efforts can be made to make conditions as pleasant as possible. This gate bears some resemblance to a room divider that might be found in a house. It is not simply the series of vertical bars that most people associate with prisons.

tation was done at a greater cost to the taxpayer; and (3) nondangerous offenders were brutalized unnecessarily by institutionalization and isolation from the community.

Now that people are realizing that prisons do not solve many problems, the pendulum is moving in the other direction. The current danger is real: In phasing out prisons and expanding community alternatives, there may be a tendency to release recidivists and dangerous offenders. The results could be: (1) the endangering of lives and property; (2) a possible increase in serious crime normally punishable by imprisonment; and (3) a vigorous outcry against the use of community alternatives. Next might come a swift and exaggerated return to the use of maximum-security prisons.

So, in encouraging rapid expansion of community-based corrections, care must be taken not to demand that prisons be abolished. Rather, we should accept their limited place in the system and encourage understanding of how they function and how they are improved. By doing this, criminal justice professionals can make the best of a necessary evil instead of avoiding the unpleasant truth: There will always be a need to lock up a certain number of offenders.

QUESTIONS

1. What steps can be taken to lessen the friction between the three subsystems of the criminal justice system?
2. Is there really a *system* of criminal justice? What are the grounds for your answer?
3. Draw up guidelines for the types of offenses, if any, which should carry mandatory imprisonment sentences. Defend your ideas.

Incarceration—shutting someone away from society—takes many different forms in the United States. A person arrested for loitering might be jailed locally overnight to await a quick hearing by a judge next day. The loiterer's incarceration will be a different experience from a felon's sentence at a state or federal facility. And even within the same system institutions vary. For example, in the federal prison system, the facility at Allenwood, Pennsylvania, with its tennis courts and open lawns—is quite different from the formidable penitentiary at Leavenworth, Kansas.

JAIL

The term *jail* here is used to refer to local institutions. When we speak of *prisons*, we mean state or federal facilities.

The United States Census Bureau's 1972 survey of jail inmates revealed the country's 3921 jails held approximately 141,600 people. Over half of these persons were either not yet arraigned, awaiting trial, awaiting sentence, or awaiting appeal.

Local jails also house convicted offenders who are serving sentences, most of them for periods of less than one year. However, some states do allow felons to serve much longer sentences in local jails, a practice which many find unsound.

Considering the deplorable physical conditions and program deficiencies in most county jails, it is at least a questionable practice to sentence any human being to such facilities for more than a few months. In fact, some authorities advocate that local jails be used for pre-adjudication detention only and that *all* sentenced defendants be transferred to state or regional facilities owned and operated by the state governments.[1]

The local jail often displays in exaggerated form the problems

1. Robert M. Carter et al., *Corrections in America* (Philadelphia: Lippincott, 1975), p. 72.

Incarceration

that plague all detention facilities to some degree: (1) overcrowding, (2) poor administration, and (3) inadequate programming. Many are archaic structures, and more than half of them have room for fewer than fifty inmates. By and large, jails are not flexible enough to handle sudden increases, nor can they accommodate offenders over ninety days. Even when not overcrowded, they are seldom sufficiently well staffed or administered to provide a healthy environment—one which would encourage a positive shift in behavior and attitude.

Staffs for small local jails are generally not made up of career people. Rather they consist of political appointees or those willing to work for low pay or on a temporary basis. As a result, although well-intentioned, the staff is often not professional and occasionally quite unsuited for this highly specialized work.

Even large municipal jails have great problems dealing with people not even tried, let alone sentenced, yet behind bars. Feelings of injustice, insecurity, and uncertainty about the future combine with idleness and overcrowded conditions to make an explosive mixture. Not surprisingly, city jail riots are common, and there is a strong movement toward finding alternatives to pretrial detention.

Local jails are still in widespread use. One authority on corrections has listed the following reasons for the continued existence of local jails:

1. Because the tax-paying public wants them and permits them to exist.
2. Because they ostensibly serve the purpose of protecting society, that same tax-paying group, from the depredations of those awaiting court action, or those serving sentences, usually as misdemeanants.
3. Because society seemingly has no alternatives for the housing of varied misdemeanants, alcoholics, drug users, vagrants, mental incompetents, and other assorted misfits—most of whom are not and should not be committed as violators of the criminal law.
4. Because in far too many areas, jails mean jobs (35,000 in 1970)—jails mean power—jails mean influence.

5. Because tradition demands, if not dictates, that many holdovers from ancient days be continued.[2]

If this is correct, a reevaluation of the practice of using jails for pretrial detention becomes urgent. In any case, there is a pressing need to (1) reexamine the philosophy behind their continued existence, and (2) improve their facilities.

ALTERNATIVES TO JAIL

There are several ways in which the population of local jails can be decreased. William L. Hickey, an analyst for the National Council on Crime and Delinquency Information Center, has suggested several measures that could work. These are decriminalization, citation and summons, diversion, release on recognizance, lessening trial delay, and alternatives to the jail sentence. We will examine some of them in turn.

Decriminalization means doing away with a law prohibiting some action. Some victimless acts, like public drunkenness, are, perhaps unnecessarily, against the law. The argument has been made that this is a factor which clogs up the flow of cases through the courts. Also, it is said, it needlessly burdens correctional facilities. A number of studies have suggested the development of other programs to deal with the problem.

A greater use of *citations and summonses* in place of arrest could also keep people out of jail. Where the accused is not dangerous and the chances of appearance at court as required are good, incarceration accomplishes little. Task forces from all branches of the criminal justice system have recommended issuing a citation and summons instead of locking up.

Diversion is routing the offender to avenues of rehabilitation outside the criminal justice system. A number of studies have explored the option of screening out by the prosecutor of those accused of minor offenses. In cases (1) where the accused is judged not dangerous, (2) where the probability of conviction is low, and (3) where alternatives to prosecution can be offered, dismissal of the charges should be considered. Using this option could well benefit both the accused and the strained court system.

Release on recognizance (R.O.R.) is a method of release without bail. Agencies are created which undertake to keep track of defen-

2. R. J. Wright, "Why Do Jails Exist?" in *Proceedings* of the American Correction Association, College Park, Md., 1972, p. 177.

dants and see that they appear when they should. Two recent reports have recommended increased use of R.O.R. One is by the Task Force on Corrections; the other is on "Standards Relating to the Administration of Criminal Justice."

Lessening Trial Delay

Some innovations in the criminal justice system mean a reduction in the time required to bring a case to trial. To significantly reduce the number held in pretrial detention will demand a sustained effort by all branches of the system.

Despite attractions of the alternatives to pretrial detention, we cannot afford to close our eyes to the problems they present. The attitude of many leaders in criminal justice is that what is needed is some constructive research in this area. Potentially humane and effective alternatives to jail exist for the accused awaiting trial. They deserve to be studied and then, if the results warrant it, to be put into effect.

TYPES OF INSTITUTIONS

Besides houses of correction and jails run by municipalities and counties, there are prison systems operated (1) by the armed forces, (2) by the U.S. Bureau of Prisons, and (3) by all the states. Each of these systems has different types of institutions with various goals. There are reception and classification centers, institutions for adult males, correctional centers for young offenders, and institutions for female offenders. They can also be grouped by their security classification: All prisons can be categorized as maximum-, medium-, or minimum-security institutions.

Maximum-Security Prisons

Maximum-security prisons were built originally with the one goal of keeping the prisoners in. Those built in the latter part of the nineteenth century relied heavily on high walls and tight internal security. They have long been condemned for being too control-conscious. They have also been disapproved for isolating prisoners from the community and providing little creative programming.

Despite this generally accepted criticism of high-security prisons, twenty-one new ones have been opened in the past fifteen years. These include one opened as recently as 1972. In fact, new versions of the maximum-security institution represent 56 percent of all state prisons in America today. Inmate control is still their primary goal.

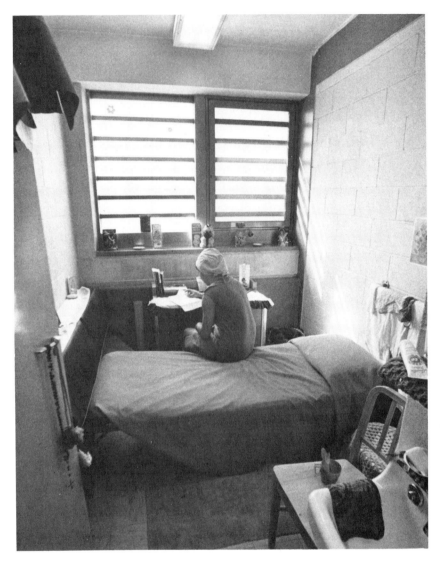

Dormitory-style housing for prisoners is often used instead of the traditional cellblocks. This inmate has decorated her room with a toy animal, several crocheted items, a rug, and a few books and pictures, just as a student living in a dormitory might do.

Even with present knowledge of the problems resulting from such confinement, rehabilitation programs are a secondary consideration. They are developed along strict security guidelines.

Medium-Security Prisons

Medium-security facilities differ from their more restrictive counterparts in one way. They invest more time and money in, and allow more scope for, rehabilitative programs. They are designed to offer inmates greater opportunity for training, treatment, and education while maintaining enough security to ensure public protection.

Minimum-Security Prisons

Prisons in the minimum-security group have few physical control features. Generally unwalled and located in remote areas, these centers offer a structured residential treatment program for nondangerous, low-risk offenders.

This kind of institutional construction seems humane. Yet there are two basic flaws in their underlying philosophy that may result in a lessening of future use. First, the expansion of community-based alternatives to prison will lead to an emptying out of minimum-security facilities. Second, most minimum-security prisons are geographically removed from the community. Therefore, easing the prisoner's way back from them into society is difficult.

Of the three types, the medium-security facility is probably the most logical one to retain for offenders requiring institutionalization. It protects the public while providing the opportunity to set up a wide variety of programs. Maximum security can be provided within a medium-security prison if it is required. There is also enough flexibility so that low-risk offenders can be put in minimum-security units. From these they may eventually be released into community programs.

CLASSIFYING PRISONERS

In order to match institutional resources with individual needs, correctional administrators must know something about the prisoner. This information may be gathered at a diagnostic center or in the prison itself. A classification is arrived at in a number of ways, depending on the practice in a given institution. In some places it may be based on nothing more than a brief personal contact. In others it may be the result of extensive testing and a series of interviews. The evaluation may be used solely to determine the offender's housing and custody classification. Or (as at the RFK Youth Center in Morgantown, West Virginia) it may be used to develop a specific treatment strategy for the individual.

At first glance the classification process seems to be a sensible procedure. Basic housing decisions can be made based on informa-

TABLE 13-1   CUSTODY CLASSIFICATIONS IN PRISON

MAXIMUM: Maximum custody requires:

1. The most secure housing, preferably inside cells with single occupancy, within the prison's main security area.
2. Assignments inside the main security area, with no early unlocks or late lockups. Day assignments only.

MEDIUM: Medium custody requires:

1. Any housing within the security area.
2. Any assignment within the security area, and outside assignment in groups of not more than twenty prisoners under frequent and direct observation by staff members.
3. Frequent and direct observation within the security area by staff members.

MINIMUM: Minimum custody requires:

1. Any established housing unit within or outside the security area or in camps.
2. Any work assignment on or off the prison reservation or on emergency fire-fighting crews.
3. "Adequate" staff supervision.

SOURCE: Louis P. Carney, *Introduction to Correctional Science,* McGraw-Hill, New York, 1974, pp. 124, 125.

tion about the person's offenses, handicaps, medical problems, and mental condition. In addition, correctional programs can be chosen based on interviews and psychological tests.

However, the reality of the classification procedure rarely fulfills its promise. One basic flaw lies in the labeling of people. Categories should guide treatment and security personnel in managing an offender's program and housing. But instead they often blind them to the individuality of the person and his or her talents and weaknesses.

Furthermore, using crude classification devices may lead to a seriously inaccurate evaluation of the offender. The result can lead to his or her assignment to an inappropriate housing area or treatment program. It can even lead the prisoner, classified as more disturbed than was the case, to react in the way apparently expected. For example, someone housed with dangerous offenders may begin to imitate their violent behavior.

Another problem is that even when the information is accurate, often it is not used effectively. Extensive educational testing is often done although no facilities for continuing education are available. Perhaps the offender is to be assigned to a prison with only one overworked psychologist. In-depth psychological testing and interviews may still be conducted routinely. It is no wonder that reception and diagnostic centers are criticized.

To counter problems such as these, a number of steps have been suggested. These recommendations include the following:[3]

1. Initial classification procedures should not be done in separate facilities (reception and diagnostic centers).
2. Reclassification should be done on a regular basis to ensure that current treatment and security fit the person's present condition.
3. Classification procedures should be in line with the reality of treatment available.
4. Current classification devices must be continually evaluated and refined so that they can become more reliable for the purpose originally intended.

INMATES WITH SPECIAL PROBLEMS

Institutional programmers must take into account the character and needs of the individual prisoner. But they must also consider the broad category into which an inmate fits.

For example, most penal systems have developed philosophies of treatment for juveniles. People found guilty of misdemeanors (minor crimes) also received a good deal of attention. (This is largely because institutions holding prisoners serving less than one year have been plagued with problems.) Other classifications of interest to correctional administrators include antisocial inmates, homosexuals, and suicidal individuals.

The Antisocial Inmate

Antisocial inmates are also called *sociopaths*. They concern prison officials because of their skill and taste for causing trouble. Dubbed by a British psychiatrist as "moral morons," antisocial offenders care only about getting what they want when they want it. They are unaffected by feelings of guilt or fear of punishment. Cellblock organizers and leaders of prison riots often are from this group. Truly practiced antisocial inmates can easily deceive wardens, correction officers, psychologists, and virtually everyone else they contact.

Case after case shows that antisocial inmates manage to avoid punishment for their acts. Still they are often the cause of conflicts between security and treatment personnel. For example, a sociopath will play up to the psychologist during therapy sessions, telling tales of the corrections officer's brutality. Back in the block, this person will appeal to the C.O. (corrections officer) by running down the

3. Stanley L. Brodsky, *Psychologists in the Criminal Justice System,* University of Illinois, Carbondale, 1972.

psychologist. The sociopath will report that the therapist constantly asks for stories of brutality by the C.O. The antisocial person does not recognize the truth and will say or do anything to gain an advantage.

The Homosexual Inmate

Classifying an inmate as a homosexual does not seem as important today as it was in the past. Administrators are not supposed to discriminate against homosexuals. Also, they should realize that the problems of prison sexuality are more complex than was previously thought.

Formerly it was believed that homosexuals were the primary instigators of sexual activity between members of the same sex. Consequently, a great effort was made to identify and isolate them. Now homosexuals are usually put in a separate dorm only at their own request.

Professionals have come to realize that prison homosexuality usually involves offenders who are heterosexual in the outside world. They see that many factors contribute to homosexual behavior in prison. Some of these are (1) overcrowding in a single-sex environment, (2) lack of opportunity to form real relationships and release sexual tensions with members of the opposite sex, and (3) little chance to redirect sex drives through creative work or recreational activities.

The Suicidal Inmate

Genuinely suicidal inmates are particularly difficult to spot. Discovering who is a real suicide risk is difficult. Cases of self-inflicted injury are common in institutions, particularly in urban detention centers.

In some parts of the inmate subculture, injury to oneself is considered a way to attract the prison officials' attention. An inmate may cut himself or herself as a cry for help. By making a suicidal gesture, medical, psychiatric, or legal aid may be secured more quickly. Injuring oneself may also be done with the intention of getting reclassified to another area. At times a wound is self-inflicted to gain sympathetic attention from peers, administrators, or the court.

Various professionals have recommended measures to stop the rising number of suicide attempts among inmates. Whether anything short of fundamental changes—from eliminating judicial inequities to overhauling correctional philosophy—will have significant effect is doubtful.

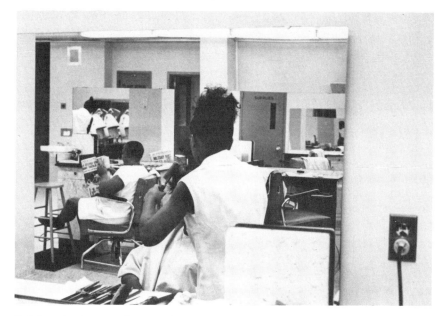

Hairdressing is a popular vocational rehabilitation program in many institutions. Many prisoners enjoy this kind of work, and after their release they can use the skills they have acquired even if they have not finished high school.

THE FEMALE OFFENDER

Recent interest in the expanding role of women in society has spurred concern about female offenders. But only a few studies have been done on women prisoners. There are several reasons for this lack of research. Some of these are (1) the relatively small number of female inmates, (2) the resistance of officials to permit investigations in women's institutions, and (3) a shortage of researchers. The result is that information which might aid in the development of more suitable correctional facilities is lacking.

Despite these problems, penologists are beginning to realize certain facts. Women's correctional institutions must offer more than the usual pep talks. The basic, outdated course in how to apply cosmetics is out. Accordingly, some institutions now offer courses in keypunch operation, nurse's aide training, and modern techniques in hair styling. There are even some opportunities for higher education. Nevertheless, the efforts to date have been half-hearted at best.

Margery Velimesis, Executive Director of the Pennsylvania Program for Women and Girl Offenders, Inc., suggests an approach for dealing with female offenders. An exerpt from her writings appears below.

Correction should forget the image of the fallen woman and, instead, view her as a woman who needs skills to change the conditions of her life. This would mean utilizing programs that already exist in the community which would provide top-quality education beyond high school and de-emphasizing the General Equivalency Diploma. A course on nurturing and early childhood development to help women become better mothers would be useful. Women's residential facilities must be located geographically close to areas that offer a variety of vocational training opportunities. Strenuous efforts should be made to place women in jobs for which they have been trained.[4]

One problem that Velimesis does not highlight is: attention must be given to motivating the female to change her lifestyle. The female offender has been exploited by society in general and men in particular. She has probably been victimized by men all through her life. Not infrequently a female offender's background reveals that she had a brutal or absent father. Other common features of many female offenders' lives are: (1) undependable husbands, (2) exploiting male employers, (3) harsh pimps and hundred of male customers for prostitutes, (4) arrest by male police officers, and (5) misunderstanding by male therapists. Is it any wonder, then, that female offenders have a negative attitude toward a society dominated by exploiting males? Unless this issue is dealt with, no number of well-intentioned programs will help.

THE INSTITUTIONAL STAFF

Prisons are staffed with professionals, paraprofessionals, and volunteers who work full- or part-time. Corrections officers, administrators, teachers, psychologists, psychiatrists, members of the clergy, and medical personnel are among those on any institutional staff.

C.O.'s

The bulk of day-to-day operations is usually delegated to the uniformed staff, mainly corrections officers (C.O.'s). In most places they are responsible for security and the general operation of the facility. The usual requirement for becoming a C.O. is a high school

4. Margery L. Velimesis, "The Female Offender," *Crime and Delinquency Literature,* vol. 7, no. 1, 1975, p. 111.

diploma. A college degree is being recommended, since the work requires the ability to deal effectively with people under stress. Promotions to sergeant, lieutenant, captain, deputy warden, and warden are made on the basis of test scores, performance, and seniority.

C.O.'s traditionally have been viewed as peace officers, guardians, and keepers of the keys. However, their role today is evolving into something much more sophisticated and complex. They are often specialists. They may be lawyers, carpenters, librarians, operators of heavy machinery, or any of many other things. The skills of today's corrections officers are virtually unlimited.

In line with this development is the need for more advanced training for C.O.'s. In answer to this need a number of municipalities, regions, and states are creating and expanding corrections academies. New York is a good example. The State Department of Correctional Services recently established a training campus for their C.O.'s. The city of New York lengthened and broadened its initial and in-service training programs. These now include applied psychology, group dynamics, techniques of interviewing, and ethnic awareness. This same trend can be seen in other states, including Virginia, California, and Connecticut.

C.O.'s can no longer get by with weapon and riot training, although this is still required for handling emergencies. It is the C.O. who is in round-the-clock contact with the prisoners. Correctional planners realize that C.O.'s need social skills to establish some type of therapeutic and generally healthy environment.

This training will not only help the uniformed staff to work with the inmates. It should also lead to improved teamwork between C.O.'s and members of the civilian staff.

Many custodial personnel are suspicious of the civilians who come to visit or work in a prison. As one senior correction officer stated, "When a civilian would come into my institution, I would always wonder what he wanted. I would smile at him and be pleasant, but at the same time I'd watch him closely to see what he was up to because civilians usually mean nothing but trouble." . . . Adding to the division between treatment and custodial staffs is the difference in how they perceive their role. The C.O. usually sees himself more as a peace officer than as an agent of correctional rehabilitation. He shies away from associating himself with the ("do-gooder") mental health staff and associates himself instead with the police officer.[5]

---

5.   Robert J. Wicks, *Correctional Psychology,* Canfield/Harper & Row, San Francisco, 1974, pp. 124–125.

It is hoped that education, staff meetings, and an integration of roles under the team concept will lessen such tensions. But progress will take time. Many C.O.'s see themselves more as guards than anything else. Their training did not emphasize the fact that their role requires participation in treatment. By the same token, many treatment staff members still resist sharing information about an offender with the C.O.'s. This in spite of the fact that such communication would make the whole program more effective.

Nonprofessionals

Nonprofessionals have been widely used in institutions, just as they have been in probation and parole work. But the reaction to them here has been less positive. Failure to prepare uniformed staff members and treatment professionals for the influx of paraprofessionals has caused trouble. C.O.'s have feared that their jobs were in jeopardy. Or it was suspected that this new group of workers would be asked to perform duties beyond their abilities. (This second concern was justified in some cases, as it turned out. Especially has this occurred where paraprofessionals were assigned as group leaders before they were adequately trained.)

Adding to these problems was the fact that there was a rapid turnover among new paraprofessionals. The causes were: (1) the negative attitude shown them by professional staff members, (2) their low salaries and boring duties, and (3) the absence of an opportunity for advancement.

In some systems the time was taken to make logical preparations for the entry of these workers into the field. This was done by creating an institutional career ladder. The procedure has led to the acceptance of paraprofessionals by the uniformed staff in those systems. Not surprisingly, this acceptance has led to increasingly effective work on their part, and the future of their role looks bright.

PROGRAMS IN CORRECTIONAL INSTITUTIONS

Institutional services vary among the facilities. Almost all fall into several basic areas: recreational, vocational and educational, and psychological.

Recreational

Recreational activities in small prisons and jails often consist of just a stretch and a walk in the yard. In a major facility recreational activities can be structured, innovative, and purposeful. Play can be

Efforts are made nowadays in many facilities to avoid the traditional appearance of cold steel and gray walls. At the Correctional Institution for Women in New York City, homey furniture, sunlight, and plants are used to minimize the dehumanizing aspects of being incarcerated.

used to control such antisocial actions as verbal and physical abuse. Thus, games are not only exercise but also a training ground for appropriate behavior. This is especially so when the games are played between inmates and members of the outside community.

Recreation may also include programs in creative writing, drama, and dance. These activities—admittedly rare in correctional institutions—help offenders become more thoughtful, expressive, and in touch with the outside community.

A carefully coordinated recreation program can lessen boredom and depression. "Basketball for everyone" and the belief that other forms of recreation are only institutional frills are now generally being discarded. In institutions still holding to those outdated ideas, violence, depression, and a range of institutionally produced problems are often encountered.

Vocational and Educational

Occupational programs for offenders are generally made up of menial tasks grandly called "on-the-job training." Furthermore, where vocational programs do exist, a number of problems hamper their effectiveness. The training they provide is frequently not related to the current job market. Inmates are often selected for training as a reward for good behavior rather than because they fit the task. There is an even more fundamental problem. The participants must have initiative in order for vocational programs to succeed. This is often lacking among the very offenders for whom the program was particularly intended.

Fortunately, some projects have recognized that learning and motivation problems exist. They are trying to provide training in a more appropriate manner. One example of this is the Draper Experiment. Here the inmates can proceed at their own pace, learning by small steps. They can be rewarded by observing their own steady advance. So far this approach has done a great deal to help previously unmotivated, difficult students.

General education of prisoners used to be confined mostly to high school equivalency programs. Now more emphasis is being put on participation in higher education programs. College courses are

Repairing motor vehicles is a useful form of vocational rehabilitation. It helps prepare inmates for jobs at which they can earn good wages after leaving prison.

Case Study:
RECIDIVISM

Early one Sunday morning Acting Governor Sand was awakened by an aide who informed him Graham Hill Prison had been taken over by inmates. The uprising had begun around midnight. Prison guards and state police units had tried to contain the situation; however, guards had been taken hostage.

Inmate leaders sent one guard out with a note for the warden. The convicts claimed they did not intend to injure anyone, and at this point no one had been hurt. But they did have major issues to resolve. Two hours after the take-over, the warden made arrangements to enter the building and discuss the matter with a group of prisoners. The meeting was less than productive.

A voice from inside one of the buildings gave the warden, now behind a state patrol car, an ultimatum: either a committee of prisoners met personally with the governor or hostages would be hurt. The warden informed the inmates that the governor was out of the state but he would reach the acting governor.

Now it was up to Sand to handle the rebellion. When confronted with similar situations, governors of other states had decided it would set a bad precedent for the state's chief executive to negotiate with convicts. However, Sand did not want a slaughter of hostages. After a half-hour of thought, he called in an aide, and suggested that he, Sand, speak to the inmate leader over the phone without making this discussion public.

Arrangements were made, and within fifteen minutes the acting governor and inmate leader were on the phone. The prisoner told Sand the uprising was their only method of getting attention to their problems. He said the men were concerned that when released no one would hire them and they would end up returning to prison.

Sand realized the inmates' problem was real. If no one would give an ex-offender a job, there was really no use teaching the prisoner a trade. The attitude of the public and employers seemed to be that, once a person had been convicted of a crime, he or she would continue in that lifestyle. A former prisoner who had no job waiting was very likely to go back to crime.

The prisoner leader knew that Sand did have a large power base in the state, which meant that whatever Sand said would stand a good chance of being accepted by the legislature. So the leader pressed for Sand to give a solution. Sand was also aware that some answer or response must be given immediately or lives might be lost. Although the inmates did have a real problem, Sand knew they were still criminals and could not be trusted under the present conditions.

If you were Sand, what would you say to the prisoners? What type of training should be started for inmates? What else could be done?

being provided in some long-term institutions. This is done through correspondence courses, live instruction, television hook-ups with colleges, and educational release programs.

However, this trend to expand advanced educational facilities is still not widespread. One reason is money. Installing television equipment linking a prison and a college can be expensive, and live instruction also requires additional funding. Consequently, one study found, not surprisingly, that only twenty-six state institutions and ten federal ones reported enrollment in live-instruction programs.

There is another thing that gets in the way of providing a college education for offenders. This is the restriction on releasing them to attend classes in the community during the day. As one speaker said in an address to the American Association for the Advancement of Science, "Education in an institutional setting like a prison is continually hampered by a number of problems, most of them human."[6]

Psychological

Most facilities offer some form of psychotherapeutic treatment using both the individual and the group approach. Individual Freudian psychotherapy may be used. Other techniques currently being tried in prisons include reality therapy, transactional analysis, and behavior modification.

Reality therapy emphasizes direct handling of the person's immediate situation. The patient is expected to form an honest, personal relationship with the therapist. The therapist is supposed to show that he or she understands, but does not accept, the patient's irresponsible behavior.

One program using reality therapy was that at Western State Hospital in Washington. The patients were sex offenders. The program encouraged honest, responsible behavior by emphasizing intensive personal involvement in patient groups and accountability to them.

Transactional analysis (TA) is designed to alert people to the principal transactions that take place in dealing with others. One method is to increase the person's awareness of the "games" people play with each other, so they can be discarded.

In correctional institutions one of the favorite games is HDIGO—How Do I Get Out? Offenders pretend to resist treat-

6. Kenneth E. Kerle, "Inmate Education: U.S. and Europe," paper delivered at the American Association for the Advancement of Science, 139th meeting, Dec. 20, 1972, p. 20.

ment at first so they can appear to have made great progress after a period of time. In this way they may gain early release. "Don't look too good too soon" and "Do some acting-out." These are two bits of advice given new inmates by other prisoners to help the new people in the game. TA aims at getting people to react honestly.

Changing of specific, observable behavior is the goal of *behavior therapists*. Behavior therapists believe that all behavior, bad as well as good, is learned. Therefore, the bad can be eliminated and replaced through a relearning process.

In penal institutions, behavior modification techniques have been applied to all sorts of goals. These aims include everything from getting offenders to keep their therapy appointments to decreasing the rate of self-injury. The techniques are also taught to C.O.'s to help them discourage disruptive behavior.

One of the most talked about applications of behavior modification techniques in corrections is the *token economy*. The way it works at the RFK Youth Center is this: Students earn points for meeting various goals in school, at work, and in the cottages where they live. All participants receive weekly paychecks in points. Their expenses, including rent, are deducted from the checks. They can use their points to buy things at the commissary and snack bar, to purchase civilian clothes, and to take part in recreational activities. They may not transfer their points to one another, and thus they are taught that they must earn what they want.

PRERELEASE PROGRAM

The minimum goal of institutional programs is to make imprisonment bearable. Ideally, they should prepare inmates for release into the free community. It was with this higher goal in mind that prerelease programs were developed. Some of these programs encourage the inmate to make contact with the community from within the institution. Others permit the offender to be released temporarily onto the street. Programs which do not permit temporary release from the institution try to train the inmate to anticipate problems. They plan in detail for ways of overcoming them.

Resource Exploration and Psychodrama

A prerelease orientation program can involve such things as resource exploration seminars or participation in psychodrama sessions. At the resource seminars the institutional staff provides information on educational and vocational opportunities. Representatives of the Veterans Administration, the state office of employment, the

Civil Service, etc., are also brought in. They discuss requirements and employment opportunities for ex-offenders.

In the psychodrama program, the session director has offenders act out expectations and fears about what they will find upon release. By playing themselves, with the director or an inmate playing the employer, they work through problems they face upon release. In role reversal they play various members of their family and other people they will come into contact with. Thus they explore the feelings others might have toward them. As one might expect, both resource seminars and psychodrama programs are rare in correctional institutions.

Furloughs

The *furlough* allows the inmate to leave the institution for study, work, or reestablishment of family ties. It is the most controversial of the prerelease plans. The Federal Bureau of Prisons has several furlough programs to help inmates get an education and vocational training. In the prison at Danbury, Connecticut, 10 percent of the population is currently enrolled in high school or vocational night school courses.

A 1967 study by the President's Commission on Law Enforcement and Administration of Justice reported work-release programs were quite successful. Cases of participants' running away were fairly rare. The major problem was that most inmates were imprisoned far from their homes. Therefore they had to give up their work-release jobs when they were paroled or discharged.

Home leave for both married and unmarried prisoners is also being tried in various penal systems. This system is believed to work better to curb prison homosexuality than permitting spouses or others to come for conjugal visits. Home leaves also allow the prisoner to maintain links with children, friends, and the community.

The difficulty with the use of furloughs is that few offenders qualify. Many systems insist upon the offender's having completed at least half of the maximum sentence. Also, correction administrators have made strict rules about the qualifications for temporary release as well. Crimes have been committed by inmates on furlough and there have been incidents where prisoners on leave have run away. This restrictive attitude is partly in answer to press and public outcry over these.

ɣPAROLE

Probation and parole are frequently confused. Each is a legal status which permits the offender "conditional liberation" from

Case Study:
REFORM OR PUNISHMENT

Years had passed since Jane Rand decided to enter politics. At the beginning Rand had wanted to make changes, and she believed the only way to bring this about was through political power. It took years of election campaigns before she was elected to the state senate. Eventually she became senate president.

Next to the governor, the president of the senate occupied the most powerful spot in the state government. Rand was able to sway votes one way or another on issues with only a few phone calls. Finally she was in a position where she could really make changes in the system. Unlike many politicians, Rand kept her original ideal. She was honest and she tried to alter the system not for the betterment of herself or her party but for the voters. She knew a large number of politicians started out with this goal but lost it somewhere along the political path.

A bill that passed the lower house was now coming to a vote on the senate floor. The bill was a financial one. This potential law would fund the corrections system in a way that would change the system's direction. The bill gave additional money to support projects experimenting in reforming prisoners and improving conditions of the almost 100-year-old jails. Three new jails would be built if the bill passed.

Opinions in the senate filled the spectrum of possibilities. Some senators thought the proposed law was a waste of money, one pointing out that if a person injured society, there was no reason for society to give the criminal good housing and food in return. The senator pointed to the fact it already cost the state $12,000 a year per prisoner, while some good, honest citizens lived on $6,000 a year.

Those who wanted prison reform, on the other hand, pushed for passage of the bill.

They stated that a convict, once in the outside world, returned to crime because no one had attempted to set that person on the right track. There is no correction in correctional institutions. The bill would provide money to begin research on finding the right method to reform convicts.

Letters from the general public were going two to one against the bill. A poll by a local radio station suggested that the taxpayers had an open ear to the reform issue but felt that additional taxpayers' money was not available for such programs. The voters preferred that the money go to build new hospitals rather than prisons.

As a professional politician, Rand knew this was a can of worms. Almost any way a senator voted, he or she was making enemies—something an elected official cannot stand too many of. Rand decided to let the senate vote without entering into the debate herself. The bill passed by one vote.

The bill was on its way to the governor's desk when, either by chance or by design, the governor was out of state. As senate president, Rand became acting governor. Her signature would make this bill law. The lack of her approval would kill the bill. The bill could not wait until the governor returned.

If you were Rand, what action would you take?

prison. They are so alike that in the federal system a probation officer also serves as a parole officer.

The main difference between parole and probation is in the timing. Probation is granted before imprisonment; parole is given after part of the sentence has been served.

Release on parole was designed to be an incentive for the inmate: (1) to stay out of trouble and (2) to make good use of the institutional programs while imprisoned. Additionally, supervision is given offenders while on parole to help them adjust to freedom and to discourage any return to criminal life.

Origin

Around 1850 Captain Alexander Maconochie, a Briton, was appointed Governor of Norfolk Island, a penal colony in Australia. The conditions he found there horrified him, and he set about making the prisoners' lives bearable. The basis of his program was a series of stages of ever-increasing freedom. The prisoners had to pass through the stages to gain their liberty.

Sir Walter Crofton adapted Captain Maconochie's idea and introduced it in Ireland. Included in his system were *tickets of license*. These were granted to prisoners who successfully progressed from heavy supervision, to doing their tasks virtually unsupervised, to full release. Since their full sentences had not been served, this release was conditional, as it is for parolees today. They were warned to work hard and not to associate with criminals. They were told to provide monthly reports to the authorities. Indeed, as we shall see, the modern parole system works in much the same way.

Procedures

Three aspects of modern parole procedures are selection and decision making, supervision, and parole revocation. Each of them is complex and gives rise to problems and injustices.

In the *selection and decision* process, problems center around people who set the standards that qualify an individual for parole. Standards differ throughout the country, and there is great variation in the way parole boards arrive at their decisions. Some are so restrictive that an offender's chances for early parole are practically nonexistent.

In most places there are three steps to the selection process:

1. The report on eligible candidates
2. The parole hearing
3. Making the decision

The report on candidates for parole may include material prepared by the institutional staff based on interviews and the prisoner's file. It may also include the presentence investigation report (if one was done) and other records. In addition, it may contain material prepared by the field parole office. Usually the institutional and parole office reports contain recommendations. Preparing a complete history takes months, and there is seldom enough time to do this. Therefore most decisions are based on incomplete information.

At the parole hearing reports are reviewed and the inmate is seen by one or more of the board members. In some jurisdictions the inmate is not seen at all. Ideally the prospective parolee should be interviewed by more than one board member to increase the chance for objective judgment.

If the decision is made not to grant parole, there may be a review by the board. This *may* by done if the inmate requests such a review. The request for the review may be denied, however.

An inmate who passes the selection and decision-making process next encounters parole *supervision*. Parole supervision seems a sensible and human program. Through counseling and social service activities the parole officer can help the offender to readjust to life in the community. Help with problems like employment and housing, as well as support through personal crises, are given. This is part of the plan the early American designers of parole had in mind. Unfortunately, it rarely works out so smoothly. All the problems that beset probation (see Chapter 14) befall parole as well.

The biggest problem in parole lies in deciding whether to revoke parole privileges and return an offender to an institution. Except in cases of serious parole violation (such as commission of a crime), the parole officer exercises a good deal of discretion. Although such flexibility allows the parole officer to consider circumstances favorable to the parolee, injustices can occur as well. The offender has little opportunity to appeal an unfavorable judgment.

The criminal justice system is full of dilemmas. Nowhere is there more conflict than while a decision is being made on whether to send someone to prison. The knowledge that imprisonment is often a destructive and useless experience only makes matters worse for everyone.

The conflicting pressures of (1) frightened citizens who want criminals punished and placed behind bars on the one hand and (2) liberal reformers urging alternatives to prison on the other have brought the correctional system to a standstill. Until the stalemate is resolved, further significant progress seems unlikely.

QUESTIONS

1. As a county executive you are given the task of upgrading the local detention facility. From what you know about the problems normally found in local detention centers, how will you go about the task?
2. What types of persons should be classified as "dangerous offenders"?
3. Is there still a need in our society for maximum-security facilities? Why or why not?

Disillusionment with the effects of prison is not new. The recidivism rate alone has been enough to arouse grave doubt about the theory that imprisonment can reform a person. (*Recidivism* is the reoccurrence of an offense for which a person has been previously imprisoned.) Indeed, the commonsense observations of the average newspaper reader have been reenforced by many studies stressing the destructive impact of imprisonment. Not only are prisons schools of crime, they also frequently strip the inmate of pride and human dignity. In only one respect have they been truly successful: they have, temporarily, physically removed the dangerous offender from the community.

But what about the nondangerous offender? Some state and federal groups have urged exploring the possibilities of using community-based resources in correctional work with these offenders. In 1972 the New Jersey Coalition for Penal Reform presented a position paper on this subject. It called for eliminating the state's large institutions. This would be done by phasing out existing facilities of that type, and halting the construction of new ones. In 1967 the President's Commission on Law Enforcement and Administration of Justice pointed out: "The goal of re-integration is likely to be furthered much more readily by work with offenders in the community than by incarceration."

More recently, the Task Force on Corrections of the National Advisory Commission on Criminal Justice Standards and Goals went even further. They stated, "Incarcerative treatment is incompatible with rehabilitative objectives." That is another way of saying that prison does not reform the prisoner.

This was strong support for the community-based movement. So it was not surprising to read, in the *Report on Corrections* published by the same task force in 1973, "The Commission considers community-based corrections as the most promising means of accomplishing the changes in offender behavior that the public expects—and in fact now demands—of corrections. Community-based corections, then, is popularly viewed by many in the field as a desirable alternative to imprisonment. It is better than confining an

chapter 14

Correctional Programs in the Community

offender in an institution that is often boring, occasionally dangerous, and almost always demoralizing."

So far, so good. But what are the realistic possibilities for
community-based corrections? Professionals in correctional work
recognize that offenders differ in their needs, offenses, backgrounds,
and personalities. This situation eliminates the possibility of using
only one kind of treatment. Therefore, a variety of choices must be
available for nondangerous offenders.

To date, the most effective forms of correction within the community have been: probation, special residential treatment, and nonresidential treatment. In examining them we will consider their
limitations and possible ways of overcoming these limitations.

PROBATION

The oldest alternative to imprisonment in this country is probation. As we noted earlier, it all began in 1841. That was when a
cobbler in Boston, John Augustus, posted bail for a man charged
with public drunkenness. When he returned the accused to court
three weeks later, the judge saw signs of reform. To the shocked
surprise of those present, the judge ordered payment of a one-cent
fine in place of the usual prison sentence.

Encouraged by this success, John Augustus went on to provide
bail, and occasionally supervision, for some 2000 offenders.

Despite this example, the first probation law was not passed until
1878, nineteen years after John Augustus' death, in Massachusetts.
The first salaried probation officer was then appointed. About
twenty years later the concept of probation was given greater recognition. Then a juvenile court in Chicago provided supervisory services for young offenders receiving suspended sentences. By 1925,
every state had probation facilities for juveniles, and by 1956, probation facilities for adults.

Modern *probation,* according to the American Correctional Association's *Manual of Correctional Standards,* "may be defined as a
sentence, as an organization, or as a process." It is a *sentence* in the
sense that the court imposes conditions—supervision by a probation
officer—offenders must observe to remain in the community. As a
structure within the criminal justice system designed to help the
offender and the court; it is an *organization.* Since certain functions
such as presentence investigations and actual supervision are performed, it is a *process.*

Probation is more than suspension of sentence so the court can
see if an offender can reform without imprisonment. It is a sophisti-

An ex-offender addressed this luncheon honoring business people who had hired former prison inmates. Participation by the public in programs aimed at reintegrating offenders into the community is necessary for those programs to succeed.

cated treatment procedure involving determination and cooperation on the part of both probation department and probationer.

Judicial decisions about the suitability of probation for an offender should be valid. To be so, they must be based on adequate, sound information about the person in question. One of the key elements in the success of probation is the *presentence investigation.*

The Division of Probation, Administrative Office of the United States Courts, describes the presentence investigation report. They specify it should be extensive enough "to focus light on the character and personality of the defendant, to offer insight into his problems and needs, to help understand the world in which he lives, to learn about his relationships with people, and to discover those salient factors that underlie his specific offense and his conduct in general."[1]

These broad guidelines presume this understanding: The decision to suspend an offender's sentence is one having important consequences for both the offender and the community. Also, even with imprisonment, a good, thorough probation report can guide institutional and parole officers in their work with the offender.

1.   Division of Probation, Administrative Office of the United States Courts, *The Pre-sentence Investigative Report* (Washington, D.C.: U.S. Government Printing Office, 1965), p. 1.

Problems with Probation

From the point of view of the offender, the advantages of probation are many: (1) It is humane; (2) it spares the nondangerous the corroding experience of prison; and (3) it allows him or her to continue to contribute to society while meeting the court's requirements of supervision. However, from the viewpoint of the probation officer, the problems are great. Among the most important of these are lack of time, limited resources, and inadequate training.

Almost invariably probation officers have a heavy caseload. This situation severely limits the time they have to devote to each probationer—usually to twenty to thirty minutes a month. It also restricts the amount of effort they can devote to preparing lengthy reports.

Usually few facilities and opportunities are open to the clients in terms of occupation, education, psychotherapy, and so on. The probation officers' own lack of time often prevents their discovering more of the community resources that may be available.

The *Manual of Correctional Standards* gives its recommendation: two years of graduate study in social work or one year of the behavioral sciences as a requirement for new probation officers. Still there is little possibility that these standards can be met. Little improvement in the training of probation officers can be expected in the near future, for these reasons: (1) The shortage of funds for probation operations, (2) a high need for personnel, and (3) little awareness on the part of the public and many professionals of the importance of increasing probation activities.

In addition to these three major deficiencies, the probation officer's caseload is often considered another problem area. Traditionally it was thought a reduced caseload leads to better supervision and probation services, which in turn lead to improved probation results. The reasoning went: If two goals of probation were to show offenders (1) that society is still interested in them and (2) that the social system is willing to provide help to those willing to help themselves, how could officers with overly heavy caseloads accomplish it? To support this position, a number of studies were done to prove that lower caseloads led to better probation results. However, the results of some of the more extensive studies were surprising. (See Table 14-1).

The message seemed to be that much of the success of probation depended on the offender: Some offenders were more likely to succeed on probation than others. A set of categories was devised: (1) low-risk, those likely to do well; (2) middle-risk, those who might

TABLE 14-1   STUDIES IN CASELOAD RESEARCH IN PROBATION AND PAROLE

Parole Research Project, Oakland, California, 1959–61
  Objective: To test whether reducing caseloads of parolees in Alameda County, California, would improve parole performance.
  Approach: Ten 36-unit caseloads were set up and compared to five 72-unit caseloads.
  Outcome: No significant differences found between performance of experimental and control groups.

California's Special Intensive Parole Unit Studies, 1953–63
  Objective: To test effects of reduced caseloads.
  Approach: Adult parolees randomly assigned to cascloads of 15, 30, 35, 72, and 90 men. In *third phase* of experiment, parolees were classified according to "risk categories."
  Outcome: No significant differences were found between low and normal caseload groups, but in third phase of experiment there seemed support for the following interpretations: regardless of caseload size, high-risk parolees violated extensively and low-risk parolees rarely violated; middle-risk cases performed significantly better when the officer's caseload was smaller.

University of California's San Francisco Project
  Objective: To test effects of reduced caseloads.
  Approach: Probationers and parolees randomly assigned to caseloads receiving one of four types of supervision: minimum, intensive, "ideal," and normal; offenders in min. supervision were required to merely submit monthly report to probation officer, but could see officer upon request; intensive caseloads consisted of 20 units each and were contacted at least weekly; ideal caseloads consisted of 50 units; normal caseloads consisted of 100 units.
  Outcome: Minimum caseloads performed as well as would be expected had they been receiving normal supervision: minimum and ideal caseloads had almost identical violation rates; intensive caseloads had 14 times the attention provided the minimum cases and had *increased* technical violation rates.

respond favorable; and (3) high-risk, those least likely to make a success of probation.

Low-risk probationers, it was shown, would succeed no matter how much or how little supervision they received. High-risk probationers would not benefit from anything less than intensive supervision.

The importance of a heavy or light caseload, therefore, has meaning only for offenders put in proper risk categories. Probation officers handling low-risk probationers can take on a comparatively large number of cases. Those with middle-risk and high-risk probationers cannot manage very many.

Solving the Problems

In the search for solutions to problems facing probation service, we look to the findings of studies done on caseloads. Categorizing each offender by risk of failure on probation would lead to a program of fitting treatment to the probationer. However, this would involve a redistribution of personnel, a procedure which might well leave gaps in various areas of probation service.

One possible support for officers would help to free more of their time: this is the use of volunteers and paraprofessionals. One authority puts it this way:

Probation must get out of the country doctor era and into the age of the clinic. We can no longer waste the training of probation officers on inappropriate tasks. We are less in need of extra probation officers than we are in need of a corps of auxiliary workers to spread the effect of the officers we already have.[2]

In 1971 a probation internship program at Anderson College examined the possible value of volunteers. They employed students on both part-time and full-time bases to work in state probation offices. The goals of this study were: (1) to see if the probationers would relate better to the students than to the regular officers, and (2) to give students an opportunity to involve themselves in a career-testing situation in criminal justice.

This program points up one fact. Nonprofessional probation programs were designed with the goal of assisting salaried probation officers. Yet they have also served to interest the community and attract students and other professionals to the probation field. One study pointed out that getting jobs as paraprofessionals in corrections could help members of underprivileged minority groups. They would gain footholds in a career that would give them professional status. They had only to perform well and get additional training and an academic degree.

Using these sources to supply additional help to the probation officers would allow officers needed time. They would be able to put into effect a program based on probationer risk categories. Some programs using this approach already exist.

Until recently a high-risk probationer—one who would probably not succeed on probation, but who was not dangerous—would have been sent to prison simply because there was no alternative. This

2.   D. L. Loughery, Jr., "Innovations in Probation Management," *Crime and Delinquency,* 15(2), 1969, p. 247.

situation has been slowly changing over the past ten years. A realization seems to be growing that putting people on probation is much less expensive than putting them in prison. It is realized this is true even in those instances where intensive intervention is required.

One good example is California's state subsidy program. Under this program the state government pays the county up to $4000 a year for each offender the county keeps out of jail and on probation. Offenders come under the program if they are referred by the court or are reinstated on probation. Since institutionalization is so expensive and imprisonment often destructive for the offender, the potential in rehabilitation and savings is impressive.

California is not the only state which has such a program; other states are experimenting with various forms of subsidized efforts. For example, Washington state has a program for participating counties. It allows for a subsidy when a county provides probation supervision for juveniles eligible for imprisonment in state institutions. As a result, such counties decreased their commitment rate by 42.8 percent in 1970, the first year of operation.

Releasing money to counties that use alternatives to prison should lead to the development of more facilities for intensive intervention. These special probation programs may involve intensive psychotherapy, counseling, behavior therapy, vocational-occupational activities, or combined treatment and rehabilitation efforts. Living accommodations may or may not be provided. This leads to our consideration of the two nonprobation forms of community programs: residential and nonresidential.

SPECIAL RESIDENTIAL TREATMENT

Foster home placement is a fairly common alternative to regular imprisonment for juveniles. According to the National Survey of Corrections, 42 percent of the 233 probation departments polled use foster homes. Judges have also traditionally used foster homes in certain circumstances: where the home environment not only hindered healthy development but might somehow have encouraged the continuation of delinquent behavior.

However, in spite of its usual superiority to institutionalization, the use of foster homes appears to be declining. Many in the criminal justice field feel it is desirable if at all possible to keep young offenders at home. Probation services can then be offered as support. However, they feel that if the delinquent is too disruptive to live at home, group homes are a better setting. There it is more possible to control them than at foster homes.

An example of a group home is PORT, Probationed Offenders' Rehabilitation Training. This was introduced in 1969 as an experiment in community-based corrections for three Minnesota counties. PORT was like other residential settings of this type. It was designed to serve those offenders who needed an intensive intervention program if they were to remain in the community. Entrance into PORT is voluntary but referral is made by the court. Participation also depends on acceptance by the staff after a three-week screening period. The original staff comprised executive and program directors, two college graduates, a former Peace Corps member, and an ex-offender.

The staff also had the services of twelve to fifteen male and female counselors, many of whom were college students. They were closely supervised and served to replace custodial and cottage treatment staff. Their three main functions were: (1) covering the building during off-duty hours, (2) helping develop a "healthy" atmosphere, and, along with the residents, (3) maintaining the building.

Initially the treatment program consisted primarily of group therapy. However, after a year of operation behavior modification techniques were also included. Basically, *behavior modification* involves rewarding people for acceptable behavior and punishing them for unacceptable behavior. These techniques were used to help teach the offenders an acceptable system of social values. These should help them function in a more positive way at work, in school, and in any daily activity. As we have said, PORT was a community-based correctional program. It was a testing ground to apply alternatives to prison. It was also a response to the need for intensive treatment resources in the community. It has gone far in demonstrating that it can help fill such needs.

Another example of an attempt to apply the group home concept is the Silverlake experiment in Los Angeles. The staff of this project use a large house set in a middle-class neighborhood. They treat up to twenty delinquent boys between the ages of sixteen and eighteen. In this semiresidential program the boys are kept at the house during the week and are released to their parents on weekends. Daily activities include school, housework, and group meetings. At these meetings staff and residents get together to discuss individual problems and responsibilities.

NONRESIDENTIAL TREATMENT

There is no such thing as a typical nonresidential program. However, two of the most widely known are Guided Group Interaction

Case Study:
RELEASE PROGRAMS

Members of the small community of Amville became concerned over rumors that their town had been selected as the location for an experimental release program for prisoners. The proposals called for selected convicts to be placed in a halfway house. Inmates approaching the end of their sentence would take up residence in the halfway house for a year. They would dress like other members of the community and even hold down regular jobs. The only special requirement was that the convicts must return to the house by 8 P.M.; they were not permitted to leave until the morning.

Corrections officials felt that this program should at least be given a chance. Funding came from the state and was readily approved by the legislators. Amville residents felt it was approved only because the site of the experiment was not in any legislator's community.

The people of Amville were up in arms. The town had a good, low crime rate and very few problems. Residents felt the state was overstepping its authority by forcing a houseful of criminals upon the Amville townspeople. The local governing body was so concerned that they managed to place the issue on the ballot as a referendum. Unfortunately for the local residents, such a move would do little about ending the situation. They could use the vote to express their anger, but they could not change the legislators' decision. The site was set and the plan was moving ahead without apparent regard for local residents.

The mayor of Amville decided that before the vote a town meeting should be held to enable residents to hear the state's views on the matter. The state director of corrections chose his assistant, Gerald Harvey, to speak to the people of Amville. Harvey was an easygoing man who could defuse almost any oncomer. He was aware that for the program to work the community must be behind it.

After Harvey explained the experiment and guaranteed that the prisoners who participated would not be those convicted of a serious crime that injured anyone, it was time for questions and answers. Harvey hoped he had all the answers. If it appeared that every aspect of the program had not been considered, any hope of community support would be lost.

One of the major fears residents had was the potential influx of crime into the community. Some of the residents had worked very hard to build their houses and raise a family in a place where they would feel safe. They did not intend their town to be the site of a prison. Others pointed out that the existence of such a house in Amville would lower everyone's property value. Apparently not only fear for safety but also the threat to homeowners' investments was a roadblock to community backing.

Do community residents have a good argument? Should the program be tried? Is there any way for the state to achieve community support?

(GGI) and the California Youth Authority's Community Treatment Project (CTP).

Guided Group Interaction

Establishing the Highfields project in New Jersey in 1949 marked the beginning of the use of GGI for treating young offenders. Offenders placed at Highfields are involved in intense group therapy sessions to examine personal and peer behavior. They are guided in examining their own feelings and problems and are encouraged to assume responsibilities equal to their abilities.

In GGI programs the peer group is used as a major treatment force once it is rebuilt around socially acceptable values. Acceptable standards of behavior are substituted for the antisocial ones causing the offenders' present situation. Then the residents should begin to support and reward that behavior in each other.

The appealing nature of the early residential experiment at Highfields led to other variations of GGI. These included a program by the Court Services Department in Hennepin County, Minnesota.

Two most publicized of the subsequent GGI-centered programs were the nonresidential ones developed at Essexfields, New Jersey, and the Provo Experiment at Pinehills in Provo, Utah. At Pinehills the boys were involved in a full day of activities that lasted until 7 P.M. They worked in the community during the day and attended group sessions at the program headquarters in the evening.

In the group sessions, agenda and decisions concerning the program's operations were established jointly by the staff and the youths. This program allowed the participants to work in the city and return home in the evening. The therapeutic sessions were especially relevant to the boys' future lives when they would no longer be in the program.

Community Treatment Project

The experimental Community Treatment Project in California is based on (1) the idea of classification of probation risk and (2) the tailoring of treatment to the offender's individual needs. Since it was started in 1961, CTP has attracted interest because of the concepts it uses. But it undertook to handle serious male and female offenders who would normally be institutionalized in state training schools.

CTP was set up to see how recently convicted youths would do in a community program offering intensive supervision. And they wanted to know if the program let them do better than they would if institutionalized. Institutionalization was the normal procedure with new wards of the California Youth Authority at that time.

Once a youth is selected for CTP, he or she is interviewed and tested. This is done to discover the individual's needs and style of dealing with peers. The youth is also evaluated in terms of level of maturity and perception of the world (perhaps he or she sees it as threatening or frustrating, for example).

The screening evaluation is completed. Then a plan is drawn to treat the individual in line with what was learned about personal strengths, problem areas, and needs. The treatment includes academic tutoring, group activities, and therapy. It is tailored to the individual and it is intensive. There is one staff member for every twelve youths.

Although CTP's overall effect has not shown it to be superior to regular confinement, it still has been a qualified success. It has done at least as well with offenders as have institutions. It has also demonstrated that more research with factors like classification, individualized treatment, caseload size, and intensive community treatment in general is warranted.

A COMMUNITY APPROACH

As we have seen, study after study has found community treatment usually at least as effective as institutionalization. This may not come as a revelation to those who have already viewed the effects of imprisonment with alarm. Still it is indeed a positive result with far-reaching implications for a society that is tired of building dungeons.

It seems that less costly and degrading alternatives to imprisonment can be employed with a majority of our current prison population. Thus, the possibilities for changing our outmoded correctional system may be endless. Large institutions can be phased out. Also, funds can be redirected to community programs which are in a better position to foster the offender's return to society.

However, for CTP to be effective, a total community approach would have to be adopted. The elements of this approach would have to include the following:

1. Diversion mechanisms and programs prior to trial and sentence.
2. Nonresidential supervision programs in addition to probation and parole.
3. Residential alternatives to prison.
4. Community resources open to confined populations, and institutional resources available to the entire community.
5. Prerelease programs.

6. Community facilities for released offenders in the critical re-entry period, with provision for short-term return as needed.[3]

The dream, however, is not without flaws. To alter the priorities of an offender treatment in a major way, wholehearted community support is going to be needed. Citizens must not merely tolerate the presence of programs for treating offenders outside of prisons—they must accept the treatment units as basic components of their communities.

QUESTIONS

1. What are the key advantages and limitations to expanding community-based correctional services?
2. You want to place a community-based facility in a middle-income area. What type of objections can you expect to receive from the neighborhood residents? How can you deal with them?
3. You are asked to set up a program with volunteers from the community enlisted as assistant probation officers. What problems can you expect once the program is established? What are the advantages of the program?

3. National Advisory Commission on Criminal Justice Standards and Goals, Task Force on Corrections, *Report on Corrections,* Washington, 1973, p. 237.

It has been said that we Americans are an impatient people. We may not always see what's wrong, but when we do, we want it fixed right away. Historically this has been a good thing. But in the area of social reform this rush for a quick cure has not always been an unmixed blessing. When we meet with disappointment, it is hard not to be discouraged. In tackling basic human problems like crime, however, there are no swift solutions. We cannot afford discouragement.

In the 1950s the question of juvenile delinquency became a matter of great national concern. Studies were beginning to show that correctional programs were, by and large, a failure. It was becoming clear that high priority should be given to efforts to prevent the young from a life of crime.

For the next ten years, in keeping with the social philosophy of the time, delinquency-prevention efforts centered on environmental change. The "disadvantaged" young should be given an opportunity to get ahead in society. Then, the reasoning went, there would be no need for them to turn to crime. Any juvenile crime, it was assumed, was largely the work of the "disadvantaged" young. They were reacting in anger and frustration against a society that didn't give them an equal chance.

Massive programs were launched to provide opportunities for the young of all ages within certain social and economic groups. A stinging disappointment was in store later for those who had designed such programs. Not only was juvenile delinquency in fact not declining, but it was on the rise.

Studies which were conducted in the 1960s revealed that:

1. Delinquency is a problem besetting society as a whole. Although many sociologists and the general public believe lower socioeconomic backgrounds produce juvenile delinquents, this is not so.
2. Along with all other criminal activity, juvenile crime continued to increase. This was true despite prevention programs that had been undertaken and despite increased correctional efforts with delinquents.

chapter 15

Juvenile Corrections

RADICAL NONINTERVENTION

Reformers took stock of the situation and came to the unexpected conclusion that doing less might achieve more. They reasoned that, since heavy interference had failed, perhaps the time for radical nonintervention had come. In other words, "Leave the kids alone."[1]

The feeling grew that the criminal justice system should be used as sparingly as possible for juveniles. The aim was to use every means at hand to divert the young from the correctional system. Efforts were now made to keep young offenders out of the system. This would prevent their being labeled criminals, and their being subjected to a correctional system which didn't really correct. In effect, the principle of radical nonintervention held to this theory: "If a young person has a problem, ignore it and maybe it won't get worse; pay attention to it and it will surely become more serious."

The years have passed. Once again the prevention and treatment of juvenile crime has been reevaluated. A significant study of total nonintervention was made by T. Hirschi in 1969 and another by W. Gold in 1970.[2] These have led professionals in the field to conclude that the concept, although of value, needs some changes.

Hirschi and Gold confirmed that juvenile crime occurs in all socioeconomic groups. But they went on to demonstrate that only a small number of young people commit major crimes or are recidivists. This finding suggested that efforts at delinquency prevention and control should be concentrated selectively. The belief grew that delinquency prevention efforts should be directed toward the few juveniles who are frequent and serious offenders. The young person who commits one minor offense should be kept out of the criminal justice system if possible.

The National Advisory Commission on Criminal Justice Standards and Goals described the idea of limited intervention in the paragraphs that appear below.[3]

Court and detention practices for juveniles throughout the country are characterized by great disparity and frequently a total lack of services. The

1. E. Schur, *Radical Non-Intervention: Rethinking the Delinquency Problem* (Englewood Cliffs, N.J.: Prentice-Hall, 1973), pp. 154, 155.
2. T. Hirschi, *Causes of Delinquency* (Berkeley: University of California Press, 1969); M. Gold, *Delinquent Behavior in an American City* (San Francisco: Brooks-Cole, 1970).
3. President's Commission of Law Enforcement and Administration of Justice, *Task Force Report: Juvenile Delinquency and Youth Crimes* (Washington, D.C.: U.S. Government Printing Office, 1967), p. 6.

common concept of the detention center, with its overemphasis on secure custody and relative neglect of other purported objectives—such as programs, guidance, and observation—is counterproductive. Court intake services and detention activities should be integrated and organized if the goal of delinquency [prevention] is to be achieved.

Many children who commit offenses, and many whose actions would not constitute crimes if committed by adults, are brought before the courts even though they could be helped better through other means. Often the court is used as a substitute when needed services either do not exist in the community or have not been made available to these children. This practice not only has destructive effects on children but also adds unnecessarily to the workload of the court.

Intake screening services should be made available to every child who is referred to the court. These services should assess the child's situation and in every possible instance arrange for diversions to alternate programs and agencies outside the juvenile justice system. The services also should avoid the detention of children whenever possible. . . .

Children should be referred for court action only when there are compelling reasons for doing so—at the request of the child or his parents, when there is a denial or significant discrepancy in the allegations of a serious offense, or when the protection of the community dictates.

The idea, then, is to screen out those who are not serious offenders or persistent recidivists. But what about the ones caught in the net? These harder cases must be dealt with by the juvenile correction system, and there are only a certain number of options available within it.

PROBATION OFFICERS

Probation has been discussed in Chapter 14. It is one of the most widely used methods of handling juvenile offenders. Probation officers for juveniles perform a wide variety of functions. They have a wider range of responsibilities than do adult probation officers. Their two major duties are studying cases referred to the court and supervising juveniles placed on probation. They may also screen cases referred to the court and decide whether detention is necessary. In some places they are responsible for running the juvenile detention center as well as clinics, camps, halfway houses, and community residential facilities.

One of the heaviest responsibilities the juvenile probation officer has is conducting what is called an "intake." An *intake* is a thorough study of a juvenile offender's case history and a recommendation for a course of action to be taken. Unless the intake reveals a good reason for holding the offender, the only alternatives are immediate dismissal of the case or referral to a social assistance agency. The referral cannot be made without the offender's cooperation.

In the case of a juvenile, the "intake" process differs somewhat from that of an adult.

Intake is set apart from the screening process used in adult criminal courts by the pervasive attempt to individualize each case and the nature of the personnel administering the discretionary process. In adult criminal proceedings at the post-arrest stage, decisions to screen out are entrusted to the grand jury, the judge, or usually to the prosecutor. The objective is screening as an end in itself: attempts to deliver service to those screened out are rare. . . . At intake in the juvenile courts, screening is an important objective, but referral to, if not insistence upon, service and imposition of controls are additional goals. Thus, the expressed function of intake is likely to be more ambitious than that of its criminal law counterpart and the function is performed chiefly by persons who are neither legally trained nor significantly restricted in the exercise of their discretionary authority by procedure requirements comparable to those of the criminal law.[4]

The result of the intake procedure may lead to probation for the juvenile. Or it may lead to commitment to a juvenile institution. Many of these institutions are similar to their adult counterparts. But there is one kind of facility which is peculiar to the juvenile system—the training school or reformatory.

TRAINING SCHOOLS

Young offenders used to be sent to reform schools. Now they go to training schools, and there are those who say it is a distinction without a difference. In the past the emphasis throughout the correctional system was on security, and juvenile institutions, whatever they were called, were no exception. Today the emphasis has shifted to treatment, at least in theory. However, many training schools today still put security first, with treatment running a poor second.

Yet, there are some juvenile institutions with an enlightened, therapeutic approach to treatment which offer educational and vocational programs as well. In some cases these training schools have made great efforts to establish a working relationship with the community. Through encouraging members of the community to partici-

---

4. Ibid., p. 15.

Some juvenile facilities have sophisticated equipment available for a variety of purposes. A videotape camera might be used by inmates for vocational-recreational programs as a medium for self-expression. It might also be used to record role-playing exercises in a therapy program, so that the subjects could later look at themselves to get an idea of how other people see them.

pate in institutional programs, the administrators hope to break down the traditional isolation of such places. By the same token, having training school residents participate in educational and athletic events in the community tends to break down the barrier of mistrust and makes their eventual reentry into normal society easier. Another way in which the juvenile offender's return to the community can be eased is through juvenile parole.

These correctional officers at a juvenile detention center use many of the same types of devices in their work as business people. Using communications equipment, maps, and monitoring devices efficiently requires intelligence and training.

JUVENILE PAROLE

From the point of view of the offender, parole is a middle ground between the close supervision of institutional life and the freedom of the open community. It is meant to provide support during what can be a difficult transition period. From the point of view of those concerned with prevention of juvenile delinquency, however, it is the last chance the criminal justice system has to keep the trouble-prone young person from a life of crime. If juvenile crime cannot be prevented, informal probation is possible. If informal probation fails, juvenile-court–ordered probation is possible. If this does not work, the young offender can be sent to a correctional institution and eventually put on parole. If in the end parole fails, society must then cope with an adult criminal.

Case Study:
JUVENILE SENTENCING

Educators have found that usually a student who does poorly in school is the one in trouble with the police. There have been theories suggesting that the youngster in trouble is also a child in a broken home environment. It is known that a juvenile in trouble does not have to be a poor student from a broken home. Good students also get into trouble, according to the juvenile courts.

Just this type of situation existed in Ridge Park. A youngster—an average student—was arrested for stealing a woman's pocketbook. While he attempted to escape down the main street, the youth walked right into a police officer who was patrolling on foot. Screams from the victim alerted the police officer to the incident. The boy was taken into custody and the pocketbook was returned to the victim.

The officer, with the woman as a witness, signed the juvenile complaint against the boy, who was later released in the custody of his parents. The investigation by the police and a court representative before the case arrived at the courtroom revealed the youth was carrying through on a dare by friends. His family was not poor and the youth did receive an above-average allowance.

As most juvenile judges contend, reaching a determination involving a juvenile is not easy. Should the youth be sent to a juvenile home? Should psychiatric care be imposed? Should the youth be returned to the community? Many choices are available, and each has a different effect on the child.

However, in this case the juvenile judge decided to return the boy to the community. In this state, a community group, usually composed of ministers, a police representative, an educator, and a physician is formed to oversee minor juvenile offenders. The conference committee, as it is called, has power only to suggest to the court. The suggestions, if within the law, are usually accepted by the judge.

The youngster had his day before the judge. A meeting with the committee determined that the boy must report to a local counselor once a week for help—a form of probation. In general, the juvenile could have been: (1) simply released by the police with a warning; (2) released by the judge with merely a warning; (3) sent to the conference committee; (4) placed on probation by the judge; (5) placed in a home for psychiatric diagnosis; (6) sent to a hospital for treatment; or (7) sent to a juvenile care facility—a better title for juvenile jail.

About four months later, the police officer who originally arrested the boy noticed the youth carefully examining a parked car. The officer knew the boy was up to mischief. When the youth made an attempt to break into the vehicle, the officer made the arrest. The system started all over again. A complaint was signed and the boy released in the custody of his parents while awaiting an appearance in court. Again the boy claimed his friends dared him to steal the car.

If you were the judge, what would you select as the proper course of action in this case? Why?

PRERELEASE

The idea of *prerelease*—allowing an offender to spend short periods of time in the community before release from an institution—is attractive. It allows the juvenile some time, from a few hours to a few days, without supervision, during which he or she can begin to adjust to the freedom of the outside world. It can give the young person an opportunity to start to take charge of his or her own life by enrolling in school, hunting for a job, and readjusting to family life. At the very least, it can lessen the shock of total freedom after imprisonment and scale down unrealistic expectations.

The biggest problem with prerelease programs is their scarcity. There is a great resistance on the part of institutional personnel to prerelease. The reason for this negative view is probably a combination of concerns. For one thing, an inmate with a poor home environment, or no home at all, is not eligible. This is unfair to young people who, through no fault of their own, must serve their sentence while others around them are enjoying periods of freedom.

Harsh punitive attitudes may play a part in resistance to establishing prerelease programs. But correctional authorities also worry about the danger of their charges' running away or committing crimes while on release. Such things do happen from time to time, and they have the effect of discouraging other juvenile corrections authorities from experimenting with the programs.

Why would a juvenile on prerelease commit a crime, thereby risking his or her freedom? There are a good many psychological explanations, but there are also administrative reasons, such as:

- Inadequate screening of candidates
- A disruptive family environment
- Insufficient preparation for prerelease
- Prerelease permitted during a time of crisis or depression caused by some problem in the juvenile's personality or environment
- Prerelease conducted as a matter of routine, or as an administrative method of temporarily lowering the inmate population

AFTERCARE

Aftercare programs, unlike prerelease, can be and are being undertaken by a wide range of community organizations. Among these are volunteer groups, state agencies, adult parole authorities, public and private casework agencies, the juvenile court, and the training school itself. The programs are designed to help newly released prisoners and offenders on parole. However, these programs cannot prevent a certain number of young offenders from renewing their criminal activity as soon as they are free. Researchers in criminal justice are constantly looking for new ways to approach this old problem. One of the most promising is the method used in the *Street-corner Research Project.*

In the late 1950s researchers at Harvard University ran an experimental program designed to reduce juvenile delinquency by using a behavior modification approach. This was called the "Streetcorner Project." In the study male offenders between the ages of sixteen and twenty-one with records of serious delinquency were hired. All had served at least six months in a prison or reformatory. The young men were told that they were being hired to help the researchers learn about crime, and they were paid not only with money, but with food and reenforcement in the form of praise.

Using behavior modification techniques, the researchers tried to establish good relationships for the subjects in an open, honest, secure environment. The aim of the program was to get the young men to talk about their lives and then explore new ways of thinking, feeling, and acting. One-hour sessions were held two to five times a week. As the program progressed, the sessions became more and more painful for the participants because the discussions grew more personal. Most of the subjects, however, kept at it. In other words, youths with bad records, who were given physical and psychological rewards for working, stuck to difficult and worthwhile jobs.

The findings suggest that community efforts to treat youths with serious, sometimes violent delinquency records can succeed. The results also support using direct methods to encourage the individual to change behavior, rather than relying on the traditional and time-consuming approach of trying to change a personality.

Given a willingness to experiment with new ideas and new techniques, students of criminology will learn more about the prevention and treatment of juvenile crime. Attention should be focused on those who commit serious crimes and have a record of recidivism. Young people who commit minor offenses should be diverted from the juvenile court and its consequences whenever possible.

This is just one approach which shows promise and which therefore should be pursued. The important thing is not to expect miracles, but to keep working for steady improvement.

QUESTIONS

1. Should juveniles who commit serious or repeated offenses be treated differently from the way adult offenders are treated? Why or why not?
2. Which is more important—and therefore, should receive more *financial* support—treatment or research and evaluation?

part 6

progress

Under our system of government all behavior is legal unless there is a specific law declaring it illegal. This century has witnessed an enormous growth in the number of laws making various kinds of behavior criminal, including behavior that harms only the one who does it: so-called victimless crimes.

This growth in law has come from legislative bodies which react to both public pressure and the individual views of their members. Rarely is it the result of profound research into the causes of the behavior in question and the far-reaching consequences of making it a crime. Ideally, a set of standards would be established, and before proposed legislation was passed into law, it would have to meet those standards. One obvious advantage to such a procedure would be that intelligent discussion would replace emotionalism as a basis for enactment of the laws governing the behavior of our citizens.

The classic example of a law which reflected the prejudices and emotions of pressure groups rather than serious study and evaluation is that which outlawed the sale and consumption of alcohol. Had the right questions been asked, and then given well-researched answers, the disasterous era of Prohibition would never have come to pass.

Following is a list of questions which could lead to less and better law, were legislatures to ask them about every piece of proposed criminal legislation. Where law is concerned, more is not better.

1. Would the proposed law provide an effective deterrent to the behavior in question?
2. Can the law be enforced effectively?
3. What will be the financial cost of enforcing the law effectively?
4. To what extent would enforcement of the law result in increased invasion of privacy?
5. Would the law encourage corruption among public officials?
6. Would there be significant harm to the public if the activity in question was lawful?
7. Is there a victim apart from the offender? If not, how significant is the harm to the victim-offender himself or herself?
8. Would the proposed law be popular?

chapter 16

Overcriminalization

9. Are there ways, other than criminalization, which would deter the undesirable behavior?
10. After answering these questions, is criminalization the most effective way to deter the behavior in question?

AN EXAMPLE: PROSTITUTION

For the purposes of demonstrating the impact of asking these questions, we will suppose that a state legislature is to consider whether or not a law should be enacted making it a criminal offense, punishable by fine and/or imprisonment, for two adults to engage in sexual acts where one of the partners is paid for his or her participation—in other words, Prostitution. The answers will necessarily be incomplete and speculative, since more thorough answers must wait for further research. However, unless such questions are asked and answered, there will be no incentive to research and make the badly needed changes in the law.

1. Would the proposed law provide an effective deterrent to the behavior in question?

Prostitution has been called the oldest profession. There is good reason for believing that that may be a perfectly accurate description. Indeed, it is not unreasonable to assume that our earliest ancestors offered clamshells or animal skins in return for favors received.

The threat of various methods of punishment, both spiritual and physical, has been used over the centuries in an effort to curb promiscuity. None has had any noticeable effect on the always flourishing trade in sex.

A study of history can only lead the observer to conclude that there is little reason to believe that where threats of hell fire and broken marriages have failed, the threat of committing a criminal offense against the state will succeed.

2. Can the law be enforced effectively?

Prostitution is basically a private transaction. Only one aspect of it, the soliciting of clients by some prostitutes, takes place in public.

It is reasonable to assume that, with adequate manpower assigned to the task, public soliciting of this sort could be controlled. However, brothels, networks of call girls, and the widespread massage parlors all provide clients with services. The problems of enforcing what goes on inside a building, or on a telephone line, as opposed to what happens on a public street, are infinitely greater and more complex. Realistically, the answer must be that it is unreasonable to suppose the law can be enforced effectively. Prostitution is, essentially, a private transaction.

3. What will be the financial cost of enforcing the law effectively?

The mind reels at the thought of the major undertaking to try to stamp out prostitution. Armies of men and women would have to be recruited to do surveillance, physical and electronic, as well as to arrest the offenders in such a way that their civil rights were not violated, leading the courts to reject the evidence against them.

In another chapter we examined the cost to a sheriff's office of reassigning personnel from one department to another. It was staggering. A serious attempt to wipe out prostitution would require the allocation of vast sums of money. A further consideration, of course, would be one of priorities: Given the resources available, is this the best way to spend them?

4. To what extent would enforcement of the law result in increased invasion of privacy?

As has already been indicated, since the behavior in question takes place in private, invasion of privacy is virtually inevitable in enforcing the law.

Houses of prostitution can be made illegal, but how is one to know what goes on inside a house without hearing, seeing, or being informed of it? The arresting officer must then get evidence by securing a warrant and entering the building himself or herself. Indeed, that is what takes place when a brothel is "raided." But the question of whether public enforcement of personal morality must be asked: Is it worth the damage to every citizen's right to privacy?

5. Would the law encourage corruption among public officials?

Since enforcement of a law against prostitution presents such a range of problems, the temptation for police officers to close their eyes to this offense is great. However, since it is an offense against the law, and since police officers have the power to enforce that law, a more dangerous temptation presents itself: demanding payment for turning a blind eye.

Law enforcement officers are notoriously underpaid considering their responsibilities and importance to the community. It is not surprising that some of them give in to the opportunity to "make a little on the side" by accepting, if not demanding, payment for their silence. Like any other form of corruption, this is an insidious thing. The first step into wrongdoing can lead, very quickly, to more and bigger steps. There are few things as frightening, or as dangerous to the health of a society, as a corrupt official of the law.

6. Would there be significant harm to the public if the activity in question was lawful?

The argument has often been made that it would be the wisest course to recognize that prostitution has always been with us and always will be. It would be better, the argument runs, to control it and see that it is a properly run business than to try to stamp it out—so far, a fruitless undertaking.

As it is now, the prostitutes themselves are often the victims of those who exploit them by taking part of their earnings in exchange for procuring clients for them and protecting them from the law. In addition, the health factor is of critical importance to the community as a whole. There is an epidemic of venereal disease in this country. If prostitutes were required to register and have regular checkups to prevent the spread of the disease, a start could be made on controlling it.

In giving an answer to the question of the public good, it is necessary to weigh moral against practical considerations: Is the official disapproval of behavior the police cannot control more important than the opportunity to attack a source of at least two social diseases, police corruption and venereal infection?

7. Is there a victim apart from the offender? If not, how significant is the harm to the victim-offender himself or herself?

Prostitution is an excellent example of the victimless crime. Both parties to the transaction are willing participants, so neither is the victim of the other. We are not here discussing white slavery or other forms of forced participation in illegal activities. The prostitute, for whatever reasons, chooses to earn money trading in sex.

It has been argued that millions of people every day do themselves serious harm by indulging in smoking and drinking alcohol. Indeed, Prohibition was the disastrous attempt to prevent people from harming themselves with alcohol. Not only did it fail to achieve its aim, but many authorities say it spawned a generation of alcoholics, along with a criminal underworld which is still with us today.

Doubtless it would be better for male and female prostitutes if they would go into some other line of work. But at what point is it up to the state to make that decision for its citizens?

8.   Would the proposed law be popular?

The conventional wisdom is that prostitution undermines the fabric of our society, which is built on the strength and sanctity of the family. But not making specific behavior a crime is not the same as approving of that behavior.

Further, the argument has been made by some psychologists that prostitution is less destructive to marriages than other alternatives. If one partner to a marriage is driven to someone other than his or her spouse for sexual satisfaction, the impersonal relationship of prostitute and client can be a safer alternative than the danger to the marriage presented by a relationship based on something more fundamental than money.

Beyond that, the rising consciousness of women has made the whole concept of branding the prostitute, most frequently in our society a woman, as a criminal. As the law is enforced virtually everywhere, it is the woman who is arrested, fined, or imprisoned. Her client goes free. Since without the demand for it the service would not be for sale, the injustice of the situation is leading many women to reconsider what was traditionally viewed as a law designed to protect them in their role as wives.

9.   Are there ways, other than criminalization, which would deter the undesirable behavior?

The answer to this question is to try to understand the wellsprings of human nature. However, more open and direct view of relationships between men and women and free discussion of sex and its implications are leading toward a reevaluation of accepted standards.

The buying and selling of bodies is a concept that is inherently offensive. The greater the sense of dignity among those who have traditionally sold their bodies—primarily women with little opportunity or education—the less attractive the business is likely to become. Raising standards and providing greater opportunities for everyone is a very real way to deter prostitution, along with a host of other undesirable activities.

10.   After answering these questions, is criminalization the most effective way to deter the behavior in question?

Our answer, in short, would have to be, no. Indeed, to us it would appear that criminalization is counterproductive. The harm it does to individuals and society outweighs any advantages it could have.

That is one example of how the asking of a short list of questions could lead to an objective, closely reasoned evaluation of a proposed law. But in the wake of the sexual revolution of the 1960s and 1970s, prostitution is not really the burning social issue that it was in earlier decades. How, then, would this technique of question and answer work when applied to something which engages the emotions or touches one's pride? Take, for example, something as common as drunk driving or as controversial as the use of marijuana.

AN EXAMPLE: DRUNK DRIVING

Consider the following proposal:

1. First offenses of driving under the influence of between 80 and 160 milligrams of alcohol per milliliter of blood would lead to a one-year suspension of one's driving license and up to six months in a county jail. Driving under the influence of over 160 milligrams per milliliter of blood would result in up to five years in a state penitentiary.

   Second and third offenses would incur proportionately more severe penalties.
2. Special facilities would be constructed for those convicted of this offense.
3. Funds would be appropriated to launch a publicity campaign informing all drivers of the new legislation and penalties.

The same list of questions will be applied to this proposed legislation as were applied to that regarding prostitution. While considering the answers, imagine yourself to be an elected representative of your state. Then bear in mind that a very high percentage of licensed drivers have at one time or another driven cars while intoxicated to some degree. These same drivers are the voters who can keep you in or throw you out of your job.

Ideally, one's selfish concerns should not influence the answers in such serious matters. However, legislators are human, and appreciating those concerns will help lead to an understanding of why some of them would rather not take this kind of objective view.

1. Would the proposed law provide an effective deterrent to the behavior in question?

More rigid enforcement of drunk driving laws in England and Denmark has resulted in a decrease in alcohol-related injuries and deaths. Until such a law had been in force for a period of time, it would not be possible to say whether or not its enforcement would have a deterrent effect in our society.

2. Can the law be enforced effectively?

The past ten years have seen a significant increase in the numbers of police patrolling the roads. In some metropolitan areas an average of one and one-half traffic citations per driver are issued each year. Furthermore, the methods used to determine the level of alcohol in the blood are easy and reasonably accurate. The manpower and the means are there, so there is good reason to think that effective law enforcement is possible.

3.   What will be the financial cost of enforcing the law effectively?

Even a superficial look at the proposed law shows that effective enforcement would be an expensive business. New facilities would have to be built and staffed, and a wide publicity campaign would have to be mounted.

Studies would have to be made to arrive at reliable figures, and then methods would have to be found to raise money in a least burdensome way to the taxpayer. In Sweden, those convicted of drunk driving work during the day to pay for their keep, and any amount above that goes to the maintenance of their families while they are in prison.

Once the basic hurdle has been cleared, whether or not the community will support the law, one way to get reliable answers would be to run a pilot project in a single state's county. However, the mechanics and economics would be complicated and would have to be considered very carefully.

4.   To what extent would law enforcement result in increased invasion of privacy?

Since laws are already on the books permitting blood tests for alcohol, there would be little if any additional invasion of privacy.

5.   Would the law encourage corruption among public officials?

There might be an added incentive on the driver's part to try to bribe the arresting officer, but the risk of encouraging additional corruption is small.

6.   Would there be significant harm to the public if the activity in question was lawful?

The single greatest cause of death among people under twenty-five is automobile accidents. The majority of these result from drunk driving. More Americans have been killed because of drunk driving than in all the wars our country has fought. The property damage is staggering, and the cost of work-hours lost runs into the billions of dollars annually.

7.   Is there a victim apart from the offender?

There are far too many victims, apart from and including the violator.

Case Study:
SOCIAL IMPACT

Patrol officers meet with every type of individual. Some of these individuals are innocent residents in need of help. Others are people who have been trouble for years. Unfortunately, police officers deal with more of the latter than of the former. After a year on the force, most officers know who their steady customers are and about when they will be needing attention.

Late one evening Officer Pappas was working the south end of town. She would stop the car and check vacant houses from time to time to make sure that no one had an invitation out to a criminal. Headquarters reported a call from a home owner in her area. The caller claimed that four children were gathered outside his house making all sorts of noise and that they had broken a first-floor window with a stone.

Pappas arrived at the scene to find the children, ranging from eight years old to twelve. They were dirty and playing on the caller's lawn. Pappas thought the children should have been in bed by this time, or at least in the house. She proceeded to bring the children to their home, which was down the block.

A knock on the door produced a thirty-year-old woman with a young baby in her hands. The officer learned that the four children were hers and that they had just walked out of the house. The woman was busy with her other two young children at the time and did not notice that her older ones were missing.

The woman informed Officer Pappas that her husband, a truck driver, was not home, and that she was left with their six children in the four-room house. The officer realized that there were major problems facing the family. So, following assurances from the woman that the window would be paid for, the officer returned to patrol.

Officer Pappas, while traveling on Main Street, noticed a car swerving. She quickly stopped the vehicle and asked the driver for the required papers. The driver had problems understanding the officer and finding his license. Officer Pappas was sure the man was drunk. After obtaining his license, Pappas realized that the driver was the wayward husband and the father of the six children she had seen earlier. Pappas also remembered having stopped this man for drunk driving a few months before. That time the officer had let the driver off with just a warning.

If this man were found guilty of drunk driving, he would lose his driving privilege. He would not be allowed to operate his truck. This was state law, and nothing could alter the penalty. Pappas knew that not only would the driver be punished, but his family would lose their only income.

On the other hand, Officer Pappas remembered an accident in which a drunk driver had lost control of the vehicle and had killed an elderly woman.

If you were Pappas, what action would you take?

8. Would the proposed law be popular?

Human beings suffer from a wide range of illusions about themselves. One of the most common among those who drink is that they hold their liquor well. That could result in poor support for a law with an arbitrary level of alcohol as a signpost for drunkenness. However, any rational person wants to see a reduction of automobile accidents. Proof that this law would achieve it would be the best propaganda for supporting it.

Public opinion polls and surveys could be conducted to measure the popularity of such a measure. If it was found to be unpopular, more thought would have to be given to how to show citizens the importance of wiping out this form of irresponsible behavior.

9. Are there ways, other than criminalization, which would deter the undesirable behavior?

In theory there are more desirable ways of arriving at the same ends, but not in practice. An effective alternative would be the long-term suspension, or total revocation, of a driver's license. However, the automobile has become a practical and economic necessity in American life. Such an action could result in the offender's loss of the means of making a living and the basic disruption of family life. If there were extensive public transportation systems in all parts of the country, such action would be far preferable to those other steps suggested here.

Putting people in jail, as we have tried to demonstrate in a variety of ways in this book, is at worst a disaster and at best the lesser of two evils. However, until public transport becomes a reality everywhere, criminal penalties for drunk driving would seem to be the best alternative.

10. After answering these questions is criminalization the most effective way to deter the behavior in question?

The only way to answer this question is by posing another. What is it worth to the citizens of the state to reduce the level of slaughter on their highways? Every person who is asked that question is a potential victim or killer. The answer may literally be a matter of life and death.

AN EXAMPLE: MARIJUANA

The question of marijuana is a highly charged emotional issue still. Part of the problem is lack of information about every aspect of drugs: their physical effect, in the short term and over the long range; their social impact; and, not least, the hazards of legalizing them as opposed to outlawing them altogether.

In addition, somewhere along the line during the last fifteen years marijuana became a symbol of youth in rebellion. To be against the war in Vietnam and for the legalization of marijuana was all tied up with long hair and protests against an off-the-track society.

In the face of that it was difficult to sit down and have a reasoned discussion about decriminalization of the drug. The lines were too sharply drawn. One was for it or against it—and "it" really meant far more than the legalization of marijuana.

The climate has cooled somewhat. Although it was still held to be a criminal offense, by 1974 every state in the nation had reduced the crime of smoking marijuana from a felony to a misdemeanor. Let's expose marijuana to the same ten questions we have posed before, in an effort to see whether or not the basic concept of criminalization of that drug is wise.

This time, however, we will provide a list of things to be considered, but here we will leave the business of answering to the reader. Once again, it is well to take as broad a view as possible, looking at the issue from the point of view of the legislator, the young citizen, the older person, those who enforce the laws, and those who pay the bill. Society is everybody, and in this country, everybody has equal rights in it.

The proposed law states that the possession and use of marijuana will be considered to be crimes carrying with them penalties ranging from heavy fines to periods of imprisonment, depending on whether it is a first or subsequent offense.

1. Would the proposed law provide an effective deterrent to the behavior in question?
    a. On October 28, 1919, the Volstead Act was passed by Congress, prohibiting the sale and use of alcoholic beverages.
    b. The birth and growth of the Mafia have been traced directly to the illegal supplying of alcohol to those who would not obey the law.
    c. The great increase in concern over the use of marijuana has come as a direct result of the great growth in its use.
    d. Marijuana has come to symbolize youth and protest, while opposition to its use represents "The Establishment."
2. Can the law be enforced effectively?
    a. Prohibition was repealed within a few years of its passage.
    b. The use of marijuana has increased each year.
3. What will be the financial cost of enforcing the law effectively?
    a. Wide disregard of a law requires increased numbers of personnel to enforce it.
    b. A law widely disregarded will result in high rates of arrest and subsequent imprisonment.
4. To what extent would enforcement of the law result in increased invasion of privacy?
    a. Marijuana use, like prostitution, is essentially a private affair.

    b. Since Marijuana is available only illegally, surveillance and search procedures have to be employed.

5. Would the law encourage corruption among public officials?
   a. If the enforcer of the law is not in sympathy with the aims of that law, he may not do his duty.
   b. Marijuana is a highly portable substance and could be planted on the premises, or person, of someone wanted by an officer of the law for some other offense for which he has no evidence.
   c. There is money in illegal drugs—lots of it. Police officers are underpaid and, by the nature of their profession, in contact with the underworld.

6. Would there be significant harm to the public if the activity in question was lawful?
   a. The immediate effects of marijuana are a sense of well-being and laziness. Marijuana is recognized as a depressant, rather than a stimulant. It reduces aggressive behavior. In this respect it has the opposite effect of alcohol, which stirs up aggression.
   b. The effects of long-term use of marijuana are not fully known. The danger areas are: impotence in men; a possible effect on DNA, a basic building block of the body; the effect on the fetus in a pregnant woman; its relation to diabetes; and its impact on academic motivation and performance.
   c. It is not addictive.
   d. One potent, mind-altering, addictive drug, alcohol, is already legal and widely used and abused.

7. Is there a victim apart from the offender? If not, how significant is the harm to the victim-offender himself or herself?
   a. Studies done of those driving an automobile under the influence of marijuana have found these effects: marijuana increases braking time; it increases starting time; it interferes with attention and concentration; and it lowers the ability to perform divided-attention tasks.
   b. See the things to be considered under point 6, above.

8. Would the proposed law be popular?
   a. Increased efforts by law enforcement bodies across the country have led only to more arrests.
   b. At rock festivals and other places where the young gather there is conspicuous indulgence in marijuana.
   c. Arrest for possession or use of marijuana leaves the same stigma as arrest for any other criminal offense, making one ineligible for a wide variety of jobs and social benefits.

9. Are there ways, other than criminalization, which would deter the undesirable behavior?
   a. Legalization of alcohol has taken many forms, including the state control of the sale of the drug.
   b. Penalties are imposed for driving under the excessive influence of alcohol.

Case Study:
CHANGES IN LAW

When John Adams first joined the force fifteen years ago, everything seemed to be different from the present. Hair was shorter; the kids listened to and respected parents and law officers; the young people supported the government. But apparently that isn't the case now.

Adams recalled an incident occurring two nights ago. While on patrol, he stopped a car with a young driver and passenger. The vehicle jumped the light. It wasn't anything serious, and Adams just gave the kids a warning. When the patrolman was waiting for the driver's operator's license, he made a normal check of the car. One of the youngsters angrily asked the police officer what he was doing. "You can't search the car without a warrant or a crime happening," the youth exclaimed. The boy was right.

When Adams was their age, he would never even have thought of talking back to a police officer. In fact, he recalled that he did not know the law the way young people do today. Times have changed, Adams thought. He was wondering if he himself had changed.

The chief had contemporary ideas and held monthly departmental meetings. During one session, the chief asked the officers to remember that time has not stood still. He indicated that police officers are in a business that cannot stand still. The department and its members must alter their action on the job to conform with the new concepts of society. The chief made sure it was clear that his comments were not policy or orders but just remarks in passing.

Adams did not have to agree. However, he felt that changes must come from the legislators and not the police. The police must enforce the laws equally. Alterations of police behavior before the laws have been either removed or redesigned would be illegal, at least in his eyes.

A few weeks following the meeting, Adams was placed in a situation which called for a decision involving these issues. Adams had stopped a car with young people. When he asked for the driver's license, it was almost impossible for him not to smell the marijuana smoke that filled the passenger compartment. Adams noticed two of the youths actually smoking the cigarettes.

After calling for a back-up unit, he asked the youngsters to step out of the car while he made a search. The examination uncovered four additional cigarettes under the front seat. Under the law, marijuana cigarettes are illegal, although efforts have been launched to repeal this rule. In his day as a teenager, Adams was brought up to believe that smoking marijuana was highly wrong and that those using it must be punished.

Since Adams was the first officer at the scene, department policy demanded that he decide whether or not to make an arrest and what charges to file.

If you were Adams, what action would you take? Would Adams be justified in making the arrest for the cigarettes? Would he be justified in letting the young people go?

    c. Prohibition created alcoholics. One reason was that it was illegal to drink alcohol, and so it became attractive to some people. Eve, they say, ate the apple because she was told she shouldn't, not because she was hungry.

10. After answering these questions, is criminalization the most effective way to deter the behavior in question?

The reader must answer the question for himself or herself. We have tried to provide objective information, because there are pros and cons in every difficult area. Personal experience and observation will add more.

ALTERNATIVES TO CRIMINALIZATION

There are alternatives to deterring undesirable behavior by turning it into criminal behavior. One of the most effective and most accessible is the use of the civil law. In such cases as a breach of contract (where one party to a legal agreement fails to carry out his or her role), landlord-and-tenant disputes, illegal trespass and many other "torts" or civil wrongs, the law steps in to correct the situation but does not turn the guilty party into a criminal.

Probably the most common form of deterrent to undesirable behavior is social pressure. Erving Goffman in *Behavior in Public Places* and *The Presentation of Self in Everyday Life* explores the elaborate structure of rules of behavior that has grown up with nothing but the usually unspoken disapproval of others as the instrument of enforcement. The force of it should not be overlooked.

Codes of ethics which have some muscle behind them are also effective ways to encourage people to stay within the bounds of acceptable behavior. Lawyers and doctors can be deprived of their right to practice their professions if they are found to have engaged in unethical conduct. It is a form of deterrent that could be applied to a wide range of occupations and activities.

In short, there are numerous ways to shape behavior to fit the needs of society, and all that is required is the imagination to investigate them. Before rushing to agree with the outraged cry, "There ought to be a law!" legislators should ask some hard and searching questions and look for imaginative answers.

QUESTIONS

1. Do you think legislatures are quick to pass laws and slow to repeal them? If so, why? If not, why not?
2. What other alternatives to criminalization exist?
3. Should gambling be decriminalized? Why or why not?

SUGGESTED READINGS

PART 1

Bopp, William J., and Donald C. Schultz, *A Short History of American Law Enforcement.* Springfield, Ill.: Charles C. Thomas, 1972.
——, *Principles of American Law Enforcement and Criminal Justice.* Springfield, Ill.: Charles C. Thomas, 1972.
Churchman, C. West, *The Systems Approach.* New York: Delta Books, Dell Publishing Co., 1969.
Emery, F. E., editor, *Systems Thinking.* Baltimore: Penguin Books, 1969.
Fosdick, Raymond B., *American Police Systems.* New York: The Century Company, 1921.
President's Commission on Law Enforcement and Administration of Justice, *Task Force Report: Science and Technology.* Washington: U.S. Government Printing Office, 1967.
Richardson, James F., *The New York Police.* New York: Oxford University Press, 1970.
Van Gigch, John P., *Applied General Systems Theory.* New York: Harper & Row, 1974.

PART 2

Barnes, Harry Elmer, and Negley K. Teeters, *New Horizons in Criminology,* 3rd ed. Englewood Cliffs, N.J.: Prentice-Hall, 1959.
Blumberg, Abraham S., *Criminal Justice.* Chicago: Quadrangle Books, 1967.
Clark, Ramsey, *Crime in America: Observations on Its Nature, Causes, Prevention and Control.* New York: Simon and Schuster, 1970.
Cressey, Donald R., editor, *Crime and Criminal Justice.* Chicago: Quadrangle Books, 1971.
Crimes and Victims—A Report on the Dayton-San Jose Pilot Survey of Victimization. Washington: U.S. Department of Justice, 1974.
Criminal Victimization, Surveys in 13 American Cities. Washington: U.S. Department of Justice, 1975.
Doleschal, Eugene, and Nora Klapmuts, "Toward a New Criminology." *Crime and Delinquency Literature,* 5(4), 1973.
Firestone, Ross, editor, *Getting Busted.* A Douglas Book, World Publishing Co., 1970.
Johnson, Elmer Hubert, *Crime, Correction, and Society.* Homewood, Ill: Dorsey Press, 1968.
McLennon, Barbara, editor, *Crime in Urban Society.* New York: Dunellen Publishing Co., Inc., 1970.
Menninger, Karl, *The Crime of Punishment.* New York: Viking Press, 1966.
Netter, Gwen, *Explaining Crime.* New York: McGraw-Hill, 1974.
Parker, Herbert L., *The Limits of the Criminal Sanction.* Stanford, Calif.: Stanford University Press, 1967.

President's Commission on Law Enforcement and Administration of Justice, *Task Force Report: Crime and Its Impact—an Assessment.* Washington: U.S. Government Printing Office, 1967.

———, *Task Force Report: The Challenge of Crime in a Free Society.* Washington: U.S. Government Printing Office, 1967.

Roger, A. J., III, *The Economics of Crime.* Hinsdale, Ill.: Dryden Press, a division of Holt, Rinehart & Winston, 1973.

Uniform Crime Reporting, 2d ed. New York: International Association of Chiefs of Police, 1929.

Sutherland, Edward, and Donald R. Cressey, *Principles of Criminology.* Philadelphia: J. P. Lippincott, 1973.

Vetter, Harold J., and Jack W. Wright, Jr., *Introduction to Criminology.* Springfield, Ill.: Charles C. Thomas, 1974.

PART 3

Bard, Norton, *Training Police as Specialists in Family Crisis Intervention.* Washington: U.S. Government Printing Office, 1970.

Bittner, Egon, *The Functions of the Police in Modern Society.* Rockville, Md.: National Institute of Mental Health, 1970.

Bopp, William J., *Police Community Relationships: An Introductory Undergraduate Reader.* Springfield, Ill.: Charles C. Thomas, 1972.

Dix, George E., and M. Michael Sharlot, *Basic Criminal Law: Cases and Materials.* St. Paul, Minn.: West Publishing Co., 1974.

Eldefonso, Edward, editor. *Readings in Criminal Justice.* Beverly Hills, Calif.: Glencoe Press, 1973.

Felkenes, George T., and Paul M. Whisenand, *Police Patrol Operations* Berkeley, Calif.: McCutchan Publishing Co., 1972.

Horgan, John J., *Criminal Investigation.* New York: McGraw-Hill, 1974.

Munro, Jim L., *Administrative Behavior and Police Organization.* Cincinnati: W. H. Anderson, 1974.

National Advisory Commission on Criminal Justice Standards and Goals, *The Police.* Washington: U.S. Government Printing Office, 1973.

Radelet, Louis, *The Police and the Community.* Beverly Hills, Calif.: Glencoe Press, 1973.

Skolnick, Jerome H., *Justice without Trial.* New York: John Wiley, 1966.

Skolnick, Jerome H., and Thomas C. Grey, *Police in America.* Boston: Little Brown, 1975.

Stuckey, Gilbert B., *Evidence for the Law Enforcement Officer,* 2d ed. New York: McGraw-Hill, 1974.

Sullivan, John L., *Introduction to Police Science,* 3rd ed. New York: McGraw-Hill, 1977.

The Urban Police Function. New York: American Bar Association, 1972.

Wilson, O. W., and Roy McLaren, *Police Administration,* 3rd ed. New York: McGraw-Hill, 1972.

PART 4

Finkelstein, M. Marvin, et al., *Prosecution in the Juvenile Courts.* Washington: U.S. Department of Justice, 1973.

Fox, Sanford J., *Juvenile Courts.* St. Paul, Minn.: West Publishing Co., 1973.

Frank, Jerome, *Courts on Trial: Myth and Realty in American Justice.* New York: Atheneum, 1971.

Franks, John, *American Law—The Case for Radical Reform.* New York: Macmillan, 1961.

Fremlin, Ronald H., editor, *Modern Judicial Administration—A Selected and Annotated Bibliography.* Reno, Nev.: Court Studies Division, National College of the State Judiciary, 1973.

Friesen, Ernest C., Jr., et al. *Managing the Courts.* New York: Bobbs-Merrill, 1971.

Galles, Edward C., "The Courts as a Social Force." *Public Administration Review,* March/April 1971, pp. 125–133.

Greenwood, Peter, et al., *Prosecution of Adult Felony Defendants in Los Angeles County: A Policy Perspective.* Santa Monica, Calif.: Rand Corporation, 1973.

Israel, Gerald H., *Criminal Procedure—Constitutional Limitations.* St. Paul, Minn.: West Publishing Co., 1975.

James, Howard, *Crisis in the Courts,* New York: David McKay, 1971.

Karlen, Delmar, *Judicial Administration: The American Experience.* Dobbs Ferry, N.Y.: Oceana Publications, 1970.

Mullen, Joan, *The Dilemma of Diversion.* Washington: U.S. Department of Justice, 1975.

National Advisory Commission on Criminal Justice Standards and Goals, *The Courts.* Washington: U.S. Government Printing Office, 1973.

Nelson, Dorothy W., *Judicial Administration in the Administration of Justice.* St. Paul, Minn.: West Publishing Co., 1974.

Uviller, H. Richard, *Adjudication.* St. Paul, Minn.: West Publishing Co., 1975.

Wildhorn, Sorrel, et al., *Indicators of Justice: Measuring the Performance of Prosecution, Defense, and Court Agencies Involved in Felony Proceedings.* Santa Monica, Calif.: Rand Corporation, 1976.

Wright, J. Skelley, "The Courts Have Failed the Poor." *The New York Times Magazine,* March 9, 1969.

PART 5

Allen, Harry E., and Clifford E. Simonsen, *Corrections in America: An Introduction.* Beverly Hills, Calif.: Glencoe Press, 1975.

Arnold, William R., and Bill Stiles, "A Summary of Increasing Use of 'Group Methods' in Correctional Institutions." *International Journal of Group Psychotherapy,* 22(1), 1972.

Bradley, H. B., "Community Based Treatment for Young Adult Offenders." *Crime and Delinquency,* 15(3), 1969.

Brodsky, Stanley L., *Psychologists in the Criminal Justice System.* Carbondale, Ill.: University of Illinois, 1972.

Carney, Louis J., *Introduction to Correctional Science.* New York: McGraw-Hill, 1974.

Carter, Robert M., et al. *Corrections in America.* Philadelphia: J. B. Lippincott, 1975.

Clarke, Steven H., "Juvenile Offender Treatment Programs and Delinquency Prevention." *Crime and Delinquency Literature,* 6(3), 1974.

Cormier, Bruno M., "Therapeutic Community in a Prison Setting." *International Annals of Criminology,* 9(2), 1970.

Criminal Justice and Behavior, 1(4), 1974. The entire issue is devoted to the female offender.

Danto, Bruce L., editor, *Jail House Blues.* Orchard Lake, Mich.: Epic, 1973.

Downie, Leonard, Jr., *Justice Denied.* Baltimore: Penguin Books, 1971.

Hickey, William L., "Depopulating the Jails." *Crime and Delinquency Literature,* 7(2), 1975.

Kerle, Kenneth E., "Inmate Education: U.S. and Europe." Paper presented at the American Association for the Advancement of Science, 139th meeting, December 30, 1972.

Klapmuts, Nora, "Diversion from the Justice Systems." *Crime and Delinquency,* 6(1), 1974.

National Advisory Commission on Criminal Justice Standards and Goals, *Corrections.* Washington: U.S. Government Printing Office, 1973.

Nicholson, Richard C., "Transactional Analysis: A New Method for Helping the Offender." *Federal Probation,* 34(3), 1970.

Riots and Disturbances. Washington: American Correctional Association, 1970.

Schmideberg, Melitta, "Reality Therapy with Offenders." *International Journal of Offender Therapy and Comparative Criminology,* 14(1), 1970.

Trojanowicz, Robert C., *Juvenile Delinquency: Concepts and Control.* Englewood Cliffs, N.J.: Prentice-Hall, 1973.

Velimesis, Margery, "The Female Offender." *Crime and Delinquency Literature,* 7(1), 1975.

Warren, Marguerite Q., "The Case of Differential Treatment of Delinquents." *Canadian Journal of Corrections,* 12(4), 1970.

Wenk, Ernst, "Schools and Delinquency Prevention." *Crime and Delinquency Literature,* 6(2), 1974.

Wicks, Robert J., *Correctional Psychology: Themes and Problems in Correcting the Offender.* San Francisco: Canfield Press, Harper & Row 1974.

PART 6

Bruckner, Edward, *Licit and Illicit Drugs.* Boston: Little, Brown; Consumer's Union, 1970.

Morris, Norval, and Gordon Hawkins, *The Honest Politician's Guide to Crime Control.* Chicago: The University of Chicago Press, 1970.

President's Commission on Law Enforcement and Administration of Justice, *Task Force Report: Drunkeness.* Washington: U.S. Government Printing Office, 1967.

——, *Task Force Report: Narcotics and Drugs.* Washington: U.S. Government Printing Office, 1967.

Ross, Lawrence, "The Scandinavian Myth: The Effectiveness of Drinking and Driving Legislation in Sweden and Norway." *Journal of Legal Studies,* 4(2), June 1975, p. 285.

admissibility of evidence: Whether evidence will be permitted to be presented to the trier of fact. In jury trials, the jury is the trier of fact while in non-jury trials the judge performs this function. (*See also* "evidence.")

affidavit: A voluntary written statement made under oath on affirmation, taken before a person having legal authority to take the oath on affirmation.

aftercare: The supervision and treatment provided to juveniles as an alternative to incarceration. Aftercare programs are usually run by or in conjunction with a probation department.

aggravated assault: One person's unlawful attack upon another for the purpose of inflicting severe bodily injury. Usually involves use of a weapon.

allocution: A formal court procedure in which an accused is asked to state if she or he has any legal reason why the judgment of guilt should not be entered.

appeal: An action brought in a higher court to test the legality of the procedures and rulings made by the judge in a lower court. In general, appeals are decided upon a written record of the proceeding in the lower court, the higher court not usually hearing any testimony by witnesses.

appeal bond: A bail bond pending the conclusion of an appeal. (*See also* "bail bond.")

arraignment: The stage in a criminal case in which the accused states whether she or he is guilty, is innocent of the charges, or does not contest their truth.

assignment of error: An assertion, made by a party to an appeal, of error committed by the judge in the lower court action.

Auburn system: Model of prison behavior, started in New York, which imposed strict rules of silence, prohibited communication among inmates, and allowed them to remain out of their cells with one another only during working hours. Also known as the "separate system."

bail bond: A contract entered into by the accused and another person in which the other person agrees to pay a sum of money to the court if the accused fails to appear in court.

bail bonding agent: A person who represents the insurance company that will actually pay the bond money to the court upon the failure of the accused to appear in court.

bailiff: A person who helps keep order in the court, has custody of the jury while it is kept separate from other people, and in general assists the judge in the performance of his or her duties.

behavior modification: Using a system of rewards and/or punishments to encourage desired actions and to discourage undesired ones.

bench trial: A trial in which the judge, rather than a jury, is the trier of fact.

bind over: Transfer a criminal case from a court of inferior jurisdiction to a court of superior jurisdiction after the lower court judge finds that there is probable cause to believe that the defendant committed a crime.

brief: A written document prepared by the attorney, which is presented to a higher court and contains the facts, law, and argument upon which the attorney relies to persuade the court to rule in favor of the attorney's client.

capital case: Any crime which, upon conviction, may be punishable by death.

case review: The examination of the outcome of a case by another court.

charge to the jury: Judge's instructions to the jury concerning the law to be applied to the case by the jury.

citation: Written allegation of the violation of a law in which the party is ordered to appear in court instead of being immediately taken into custody by the issuing officer.

civil law: A system of law which rests upon statutes or codes generally created by legislative bodies. (*Compare* "common law.")

clerk of court: A person who keeps the official records of the court.

common law: A body of law created by judicial decisions, originally resting upon old and acceptable customs, often of English origin. (*Compare* "civil law.")

confession: A voluntary statement by an accused person acknowledging that he or she committed a crime.

congregate system: (See "Pennsylvania system.")

court of inferior jurisdiction: Usually a lower court where trials for petty offenses are held in volume.

court reporter: A person who writes, types, or records all the words spoken during the proceedings in court.

crime: Any act or failure to act which is forbidden by law and which is punishable by fine, imprisonment, or loss of the right to hold public office.

crisis intervention: A brief action, due to the presence of undesirable symptoms, to alleviate a person's distress.

cross-examination: Questioning of a witness by the attorney opposing the one who called the witness to testify. It occurs after the direct examination and is limited to material covered in the direct examination.

decriminalization: Making once illegal conduct lawful through elimination of a law.

delinquency: An offense committed by a juvenile.

defendant: A person or corporation charged with a violation of law.

defense counsel: An attorney who represents a defendant.

deposition: An oral or written statement made under oath, usually outside of court by a person in response to questions asked by an attorney representing one of the parties to a criminal action.

deterrence: An action or measure taken to prevent another's (often hostile or undesirable) action.

direct examination: The first interrogation of a witness in court by the party who has called the witness to testify.

disclosure: The duty of an attorney and/or the client to disclose facts to the opposing attorney or the opposing attorney's client.

dismissal of charges: Removing the case from the court. Dismissal with leave is for a refiling of the charges. Dismissal with prejudice precludes refiling the charges.

diversion: An action which turns aside something or someone, such as diversion of juveniles from the courts by employing helping organizations so the youngsters don't become enmeshed in the criminal justice system.

double jeopardy: The constitutional rule that forbids the government from trying an accused more than once for the same violations of law or upon the same facts.

due process: Fundamental fairness of legal procedures and of law in general.

evidence: Any means which tends to prove a fact. More narrowly, the testimony of witnesses, physical objects, or inferences drawn from either which tend to prove or disprove the guilt of the accused.

exclusionary rule: A legal rule which precludes the use in court of evidence that has been illegally obtained by an agent of the government, either directly or indirectly.

felony: A crime more serious than a misdemeanor. A felony is punishable by at least one year in jail.

first appearance hearing: The first stage in a criminal case, in which the accused is advised of his or her rights, is arraigned, is informed of the criminal charges lodged against him or her, and generally is given an opportunity either to obtain a lawyer or to have a defense lawyer appointed by the court. In addition, the court may set conditions for the release of the accused pending trial.

furlough: Temporary release from prison, usually for work, education, or a short home visit.

grand jury: A body of private citizens that has power to investigate the activities of government officials and to file formal charges against almost anyone for violating the criminal law.

grand larceny: The theft of property of a value— designated by law—exceeding the limits of petty larceny. (*Compare* "petty larceny.")

incarceration: Confinement of a criminal or of a person accused of a crime to an institution in such a manner as to prevent him or her from freely interacting with society.

indictment: A formal charge of a crime by a grand jury.

infraction: An offense against institutional law, such as when a prisoner refuses to be locked in his or her cell at the time designated by the prison's regulations. More generally, a minor crime.

information: A formal charge of a crime by a prosecutor.

in loco parentis: In the place of a parent. Refers to the idea that the state stands in the place of a parent in certain relationships to a child. (See "parens patriae.")

intake: Initial evaluation of a person admitted to a correctional facility to determine his or her status and to plan a short- or long-term program for that individual.

judicial review: In general, the legal doctrine that courts may review the legality of actions of other branches of government.

legal aid: A system of providing free lawyers to indigent persons charged with crimes.

malum in se: Something evil or wrong by itself, such as robbery or homicide. (Plural: mala in se.)

malum prohibitum: Something that is not inherently evil or wrong but that is determined to be wrong as a result of the passage of a law, such as income tax evasion. (Plural: mala prohibita.)

manslaughter: Unlawful killing of a person without malice, such as through negligence.

maximum security prison: A facility which has as its primary goal stringent security. To maintain security, single cells located in the inner compound are usually employed. Assignments are usually not permitted after evening lock-up, and surveillance is extremely strictly enforced throughout the day.

medium security prison: Prison which permits some congregation of prisoners for work and recreation, but with frequent supervision. Though supervision is not constant, as in the maximum security prison, it is still a primary activity of the correctional staff.

minimum security prison: A correctional facility which emphasizes its treatment program rather than its security. Supervision is provided primarily to offer the prisoners support and guidance. Surveillance is not continual, even when the prisoner is on an outside detail.

misdemeanor: A minor offense, less serious than a felony, usually punishable by no more than a year in jail and/or a small fine.

Missouri plan: A system of selecting persons to become judges in which a panel of lawyers and sometimes others selects a small number of candidates from those who apply for a judgeship. A governmental body then selects one person from those selected by the panel.

mistrial: The termination of a trial by the judge due to some grave error committed during the trial. If the mistrial is properly declared, the accused may be tried again without violating the double jeopardy rule.

nolo contendere: A plea given by the accused in which the accused does not contest the validity of the charges. It almost amounts to an admission by the accused of the validity of the charges.

no contest: A popular term for the plea of nolo contendere.

parens patriae: Father of the nation. In Old English law the king was deemed the father and his subjects were considered his children. This doctrine in America was one of the primary legal justifications for the extensive power of the courts over neglected and delinquent children. (See "in loco parentis.")

parole: Conditional release from prison of a convicted offender who has served some part of his or her sentence.

P-CR: Police-community relations.

Pennsylvania system: A philosophy of corrections involving solitary confinement, visits from model citizens, working in one's cell instead of a day-room, solitary exercise, and exposure to the Bible. From their blindfolded entry into the prison until ultimate release, painstaking efforts were taken to shield prisoners from all but "beneficial" outside influences. This was done while providing for hard work, religious study, and self examination. Also known as the "congregate system."

peremptory challenge: The right of an attorney or his/her client to exclude a prospective juror from becoming a juror in a particular case without stating the reason for the exclusion. Usually limited in number in each case.

petty larceny: The theft of property of a value determined by law to be less than that of grand larceny.

plea bargaining: An informal procedure in which the defendant pleads guilty to a lesser offense than the one with which he or she was originally charged, in exchange for an informal guarantee by the prosecutor to the defense lawyer that the charge or sentence will be reduced.

preliminary hearing: A hearing before a judge during which the judge determines if there is sufficient evidence to believe the accused guilty of the crime charged to hold the accused for a later trial.

prerelease: A program in which the prisoner is allowed out of the institution—usually just during the day or on weekends—prior to the completion of the sentence, such as for a prerelease work program or for weekend furloughs.

presentence investigation: An investigation made to assist the judge in determining the appropriate sentence.

pretrial discovery: A process, prior to trial, during which the attorneys or their clients disclose facts they know about the case.

probate: The process of proving the validity of a will. More broadly, the jurisdiction of courts involved in wills and the administration of the property of deceased persons.

probation: Suspension of an offender's sentence with no provision for incarceration unless the offender's behavior in the community is in conflict with rules set down by the court. The court, for example, may order the offender to stay out of fights. (*Compare* "suspended sentence.")

probation report: Presentence report prepared by the court or its representative with recommendations regarding probation after analysis of the convicted individual's resources (family environment, willingness to participate in a treatment program, past drug history, job opportunities, and so on).

public prosecution: An agent of the government who represents the government in the prosecution of criminal cases.

recidivism: Criminal behavior that is repetitive.

reciprocal discovery: Rules of pretrial discovery that require the attorney or client seeking facts from the opposing attorney or client to give certain facts to the opposition in exchange for getting the requested facts.

redirect examination: The second period of questioning of a witness by the party who has called the witness to testify. It is usually limited to bolstering the witness's testimony on a point that has been challenged by the opposing lawyer or client during cross-examination.

reformatory concept: The belief that youthful offenders should be incarcerated with other young people and not be put in an institution with adult offenders, who, it is felt, would corrupt them.

rehabilitation: The use of recreation, work, therapy, and/or educational programs in an effort to enhance and restore an offender's chance of becoming a constructive member of society.

release on one's own recognizance (ROR): Release from jail without the necessity of posting bail, with the expectation that the released person will perform some act in the future, such as appear in court at a designated time.

rules of evidence: That body of law or rules governing the admissibility of evidence. Common law rules of evidence are those made by judicial decision based upon the common-law. Legislatures have passed laws affecting and adding to the common-law rules of evidence.

sample survey: A research technique in which a representative part of a total is selected for examination.

search: Looking into a closed place for the purpose of discovering evidence of criminal activity.

separate system: (*See* "Auburn system.")

social control: Formal or informal mechanisms to discourage deviant behavior.

stare decisis: The policy of courts to follow a principle of law as applied to a certain set of facts in similar cases in the future.

suspended sentence: A sentence which does not involve incarceration unless the offender fails to follow the judge's prescription. The offender may, for example, be given a three-year prison sentence, suspended under the condition that he or she seek psychiatric help. (*Compare:* "Probation.")

team policing: A method of decentralizing police services in which a police unit is responsible for providing crime reduction activities and other services to a discrete geographical area.

third-degree methods: The use of such tactics as physical force by police to extract confessions or admissions.

time in grade: The amount of time a person is in a particular pay range. Most government employment has several levels, each of which has its own salary range.

token economy: A behavior modification technique in which a person is rewarded for specified actions by being given tokens which can then be turned in for available rewards. In prison the rewards may take the form of a carton of cigarettes, advancement to a less stringent housing area, or an increase in recreation time.

victimless crime: A crime in which the perpetrator and victim are the same person, or in which the victim is a willing participant, such as possession of drugs or gambling.

THE CONSTITUTION OF THE UNITED STATES, INCLUDING THE BILL OF RIGHTS AND THE FOURTEENTH AMENDMENT

We the People of the United States, in Order to form a more perfect Union, establish Justice, insure domestic Tranquility, provide for the common defence, promote the general Welfare, and secure the Blessings of Liberty to ourselves and our Posterity, do ordain and establish this Constitution for the United States of America.

ARTICLE I

Sec. 1. All legislative Powers herein granted shall be vested in a Congress of the United States, which shall consist of a Senate and House of Representatives.

Sec. 2. The House of Representatives shall be composed of Members chosen every second Year by the People of the several States, and the Electors in each State shall have the Qualifications requisite for Electors of the most numerous Branch of the State Legislature.

No Person shall be a Representative who shall not have attained the Age of twenty five Years, and been seven Years a Citizen of the United States, and who shall not, when elected, be an Inhabitant of that State in which he shall be chosen.

Representatives and direct Taxes shall be apportioned among the several States which may be included within this Union, according to their respective Numbers, which shall be determined by adding to the whole Number of free Persons, including those bound to Service for a Term of Years, and excluding Indians not taxed, three fifths of all other Persons. The actual Enumeration shall be made within three Years after the first Meeting of the Congress of the United States, and within every subsequent Term of ten Years, in such Manner as they shall by Law direct. The Number of Representatives shall not exceed one for every thirty Thousand, but each State shall have at Least one Representative; and until such enumeration shall be made, the State of New Hampshire shall be entitled to chuse three, Massachusetts eight, Rhode-Island and Providence Plantations one, Connecticut five, New York six, New Jersey four, Pennsylvania eight, Delaware one, Maryland six, Virginia ten, North Carolina five, South Carolina five, and Georgia three.

When vacancies happen in the Representation from any State, the Executive Authority thereof shall issue Writs of Election to fill such Vacancies.

The House of Representatives shall chuse their Speaker and other Officers; and shall have the sole Power of Impeachment.

Sec. 3. The Senate of the United States shall be composed of two Senators from each State, chosen by the Legislature thereof, for six Years; and each Senator shall have one Vote.

Immediately after they shall be assembled in Consequence of the first Election, they shall be divided as equally as may be into three Classes. The Seats of the Senators of the first Class shall be vacated at the Expiration of the second Year, of the second Class at the Expiration of the fourth Year, and of the third Class at the Expiration of the sixth year, so that one third may be chosen every second Year; and if Vacancies happen by Resignation, or otherwise, during the Recess of Legislature of any State, the Executive thereof may make temporary Appointments until the next Meeting of the Legislature, which shall then fill such Vacancies.

No Person shall be a Senator who shall not have attained to the Age of thirty Years, and been nine Years a Citizens of the United States, and who shall not, when elected, be an Inhabitant of that State for which he shall be chosen.

The Vice President of the United States shall be President of the Senate, but shall have no Vote, unless they be equally divided.

The Senate shall chuse their other Officers, and also a President pro tempore, in the Absence of the Vice President, or when he shall exercise the Office of President of the United States.

The Senate shall have the sole Power to all Impeachments. When sitting for that Purpose, they shall be on Oath or Affirmation. When the President of the United States is tried, the Chief Justice shall preside: And no Person shall be convicted without the Concurrence of two thirds of the Members present.

Judgment in Cases of Impeachment shall not extend further than to removal from Office, and disqualification to hold and enjoy any Office of honor, Trust or Profit under the United States: but the Party convicted shall nevertheless be liable and subject to Indictment, Trial, Judgment and Punishment, according to Law.

Sec. 4. The Times, Places and Manner of holding Elections for Senators and Representatives, shall be prescribed in each State by the Legislature thereof; but the Congress may at any time by Law make or alter such Regulations, except as to the Places of chusing Senators.

The Congress shall assemble at least once in every Year, and such Meeting shall be on the first Monday in December, unless they shall by Law appoint a different Day.

Sec. 5. Each House shall be the Judge of the Elections, Returns and Qualifications of its own Members and a Majority of each shall constitute a Quorum to do Business; but a smaller Number may adjourn from day to day, and may be authorized to compel the Attendance of absent Members, in such Manner, and under such Penalties as each House may provide.

Each House may determine the Rules of its Proceedings, punish its Members for disorderly Behaviour, and, with the Concurrence of two thirds, expel a Member.

Each House shall keep a Journal of its Proceedings, and from time to time publish the same, excepting such Parts as may in their Judgment require Secrecy; and the Yeas and Nays of the Members of either House on any question shall, at the Desire of one fifth of those Present, be entered on the Journal.

Neither House, during the Session of Congress, shall, without the Consent of the other, adjourn for more than three days, nor to any other Place than that in which the two Houses shall be sitting.

Sec. 6. The Senators and Representatives shall receive a Compensation for their Services, to be ascertained by Law, and paid out of the Treasury of the United States. They shall in all Cases, except Treason, Felony and Breach of the Peace, be privileged from Arrest during their Attendance at the Session of their respective Houses, and in going to and returning from the same; and for any Speech or Debate in either House, they shall not be questioned in any other Place.

No Senator or Representative shall during the Time for which he was elected, by appointed to any civil Office under the Authority of the United States which shall have been created, or the Emoluments whereof shall have been encreased during such time; and no Person holding any Office under the United States, shall be a Member of either House during his Continuance in Office.

Sec. 7. All Bills for raising Revenue shall originate in the House of Representatives; but the Senate may propose or concur with Amendments as on other Bills.

Every Bill which shall have passed the House of Representatives and the Senate, shall, before it became a Law, be presented to the President of the United States; If he approve he shall sign it, but if not he shall return it, with his Objections to that House in which it shall have originated, who shall enter the Objections at large on their Journal, and proceed to reconsider it. If after such Reconsideration two thirds of that House shall agree to pass the Bill, it shall be sent, together with the Objections, to the other House, by which it shall likewise be reconsidered, and if approved by two thirds of that House, it shall become a Law. But in all such Cases the Votes of both Houses shall be determined by yeas and Nays, and the Names of the Persons voting for and against the Bill shall be entered on the Journal of each House respectively. If any Bill shall not be returned by the President within ten Days (Sundays excepted) after it shall have been presented to him, the Same shall be a Law, in like Manner as if he had signed it, unless the Congress by their Adjournment prevent its Return, in which Case it shall not be a Law.

Every Order, Resolution, or Vote to which the Concurrence of the Senate and House of Representatives may be necessary (except on a question of Adjournment) shall be presented to the President of the United States; and before the Same shall take Effect, shall be approved by him, or being disapproved by him, shall be repassed by two thirds of the Senate and House of Representatives, according to the Rules and Limitations prescribed in the Case of a Bill.

Sec. 8. The Congress shall have Power To lay and collect Taxes, Duties, Imposts and Excises, to pay the Debts and provide for the common Defence and general Welfare of the United States; but all Duties, Imposts and Excises shall be uniform throughout the United States;

To borrow Money on the credit of the United States;

To regulate Commerce with foreign Nations, and among the several States, and with the Indian Tribes;

To establish an uniform Rule of Naturalization, and uniform Laws on the subject of Bankruptcies throughout the United States;

To coin Money, regulate the Value thereof, and of foreign Coin, and fix the Standard of Weights and Measures;

To provide for the Punishment of counterfeiting the Securities and current Coin of the United States;

To establish Post Offices and post Roads;

To promote the Progress of Science and useful Arts, by securing for limited Times to Authors and Inventors the exclusive Right to their respective Writings and Discoveries;

To constitute Tribunals inferior to the supreme Court;

To define and punish Piracies and Felonies committed on the high Seas, and Offences against the Law of Nations;

To declare War, grant Letters of Marque and Reprisal, and make Rules concerning Captures on Land and Water;

To raise and support Armies, but no Appropriation of Money to that Use shall be for a longer Term than two Years;

To provide and maintain a Navy;

To make Rules for the Government and Regulation of the land and naval Forces;

To provide for calling forth the Militia to execute the Laws of the Union, suppress Insurrections and repel Invasions;

To provide for organizing, arming, and disciplining, the Militia, and for governing such Part of them as may be employed in the Service of the United States, reserving to the States respectively, the Appointment of the Officers, and the Authority of training the Militia according to the discipline prescribed by Congress;

To exercise exclusive Legislation in all Cases whatsoever, over such District (not exceeding ten Miles square) as may, by Cession of particular States, and the Acceptance of Congress, become the Seat of the Government of the United States, and to exercise like Authority over all Places purchased by the Consent of the Legislature of the State in which the Same shall be, for the Erection of Forts, Magazines, Arsenals, dock-Yards, and other needful Buildings;—And

To make all Laws which shall be necessary and proper for carrying into Execution the foregoing Powers, and all other Powers vested by this Constitution in the Government of the United States, or in any Department or Officer thereof.

Sec. 9. The Migration or Importation of such Persons as any of the States now existing shall think proper to admit, shall not be prohibited by the Congress prior to the Year one thousand eight hundred and eight, but a Tax or duty may be imposed on such Importation, not exceeding ten dollars for each Person.

The Privilege of the Writ of Habeas Corpus shall not be suspended, unless when in Case of Rebellion or Invasion the public Safety may require it.

No Bill of Attainder or ex post facto Law shall be passed.

No Capitation, or other direct, Tax shall be laid, unless in Proportion to the Census or Enumeration herein before directed to be taken.

No Tax or Duty shall be laid on Articles exported from any State.

No Preference shall be given by any Regulation of Commerce or Revenue to the Ports of one State over those of another: nor shall Vessels bound to, or from, one State, be obliged to enter, clear, or pay Duties in another.

No Money shall be drawn from the Treasury, but in Consequence of Appropriations made by Law; and a regular Statement and Account of the Receipts and Expenditures of all public Money shall be published from time to time.

No Title of Nobility shall be granted by the United States: And no Person holding any Office of Profit or Trust under them, shall, without the Consent of the Congress, accept of any present, Emolument, Office, or Title, of any kind whatever, from any King, Prince or foreign State.

Sec. 10 No State shall enter into any Treaty, Alliance, or Confederation; grant Letters of Marque and Reprisal; coin Money; emit Bills of Credit; make any Thing but gold and silver Coin a Tender in Payment of Debts; pass any Bill of Attainder, ex post facto Law, or Law impairing the Obligation of Contracts, or grant any Title of Nobility.

No State shall, without the Consent of the Congress, lay any Imposts or Duties on Imports or Exports, except what may be absolutely necessary for executing it's inspection Laws: and the net Produce of all Duties and Imposts, laid by any State on Imports or Exports, shall be for the Use of the Treasury of the United States; and all such Laws shall be subject to the Revision and Controul of the Congress.

No State shall, without the Consent of Congress, lay any Duty of Tonnage, keep Troops, or Ships of War in time of Peace, enter into any Agreement or Compact with another State, or with a foreign Power, or engage in War, unless actually invaded, or in such imminent Danger as will not admit of delay.

ARTICLE II

Sec. 1. The executive Power shall be vested in a President of the United States of America. He shall hold his Office during the Term of four Years, and, together with the Vice President, chosen for the same Term, be elected, as follows.

Each State shall appoint, in such Manner as the Legislature thereof may direct, a Number of Electors, equal to the whole Number of Senators and

Representatives to which the State may be entitled in the Congress: but no Senator or Representative, or Person holding an Office of Trust or Profit under the United States, shall be appointed an Elector.

The Electors shall meet in their respective States, and vote by Ballot for two Persons, of whom one at least shall not be an Inhabitant of the same State with themselves. And they shall make a List of all the Persons voted for, and of the Number of Votes for each; which List they shall sign and certify, and transmit sealed to the Seat of the Government of the United States, directed to the President of the Senate. The President of the Senate shall, in the Presence of the Senate and House of Representatives, open all the Certificates, and the Votes shall then be counted. The Person having the greatest Number of Votes shall be the President, if such Number be a Majority of the whole Number of Electors appointed; and if there be more than one who have such Majority, and have an equal Number of Votes, then the House of Representatives shall immediately chuse by Ballot one of them for President; and if no person have a Majority, then from the five highest on the List the said House shall in like Manner chuse the President. But in chusing the President, the Votes shall be taken by States, the Representation from each State having one Vote; A quorum for this Purpose shall consist of a Member or Members from two thirds of the States, and a Majority of all the States shall be necessary to a Choice. In every Case, after the Choice of the President, the Person having the greatest Number of Votes of the Electors shall be the Vice President. But if there should remain two or more who have equal Votes, the Senate shall chuse from them by Ballot the Vice President.

The Congress may determine the Time of chusing the Electors, and the Day on which they shall give their Votes; which Day shall be the same throughout the United States.

No Person except a natural born Citizen, or a Citizen of the United States, at the time of the Adoption of this Constitution, shall be eligible to the Office of President; neither shall any Person be eligible to that Office who shall not have attained to the Age of thirty-five Years, and been fourteen Years a Resident within the United States.

In Case of the Removal of the President from Office, or of his Death, Resignation, or Inability to discharge the Powers and Duties of the said Office, the Same shall devolve on the Vice President, and the Congress may by Law provide for the Case of Removal, Death, Resignation or Inability, both of the President and Vice President, declaring what Officer shall then act as President, and such Officer shall act accordingly, until the Disability be removed, or a President shall be elected.

The President shall, at stated Times, receive for his Services, a Compensation, which shall neither be increased nor diminished during the Period for which he shall have been elected, and he shall not receive within that Period any other Emolument from the United States, or any of them.

Before he enter on the Execution of his Office, he shall take the following Oath or Affirmation:—"I do solemnly swear (or affirm) that I will faithfully execute the Office of President of the United States, and will to the best of my Ability, preserve, protect and defend the Constitution of the United States."

Sec. 2. The President shall be Commander in Chief of the Army and Navy of the United States, and of the Militia of the several States, when called into the actual Service of the United States; he may require the Opinion, in writing, of the principal Officer in each of the executive Departments, upon any Subject relating to the Duties of their respective Offices, and he shall have Power to grant Reprieves and Pardons for Offences against the United States, except in Cases of Impeachment.

He shall have Power, by and with the Advice and Consent of the Senate, to make Treaties, provided two thirds of the Senators present concur; and he shall nominate, and by and with the Advice and Consent of the Senate, shall appoint Ambassadors, other public Ministers and Consuls, Judges of the supreme Court, and all other Officers of the United States, whose Appointments are not herein otherwise provided for, and which shall be established by Law: but the Congress may by Law vest the Appointment of such inferior Officers, as they think proper, in the President alone, in the Courts of Law, or in the Heads of Departments.

The President shall have Power to fill up all Vacancies that may happen during the Recess of the Senate, by granting Commissions which shall expire at the End of their next Session.

Sec. 3. He shall from time to time give to the Congress Information of the State of the Union, and recommend to their Consideration such Measures as he shall judge necessary and expedient; he may, on extraordinary Occasions, convene both Houses, or either of them, and in Case of Disagreement between them, with Respect to the Time of Adjournment, he may adjourn them to such Time as he shall think proper; he shall receive Ambassadors and other public Ministers; he shall take Care that the Laws be faithfully executed, and shall Commission all the Officers of the United States.

Sec. 4. The President, Vice President and all civil Officers of the United States, shall be removed from Office on Impeachment for, and Conviction of, Treason, Bribery, or other high Crimes and Misdemeanors.

ARTICLE III

Sec. 1. The judicial Power of the United States, shall be vested in one supreme Court, and in such inferior Courts as the Congress may from time to time ordain and establish. The Judges, both of the supreme and inferior Courts, shall hold their Offices during good Behaviour, and shall, at stated Times, receive for their Services, a Compensation, which shall not be diminished during their Continuance in Office.

Sec. 2. The judicial Power shall extend to all Cases, in Law and Equity, arising under this Constitution, the Laws of the United States, and Treaties made, or which shall be made, under their Authority;—to all Cases affecting Ambassadors, other public Ministers and Consuls;—to all Cases of admiralty and maritime Jurisdiction;—to Controversies to which the United States shall be a Party;—to Controversies between two or more States;—between a State and Citizens of another State;—between Citizens of different States—between Citizens of the same State claiming Lands under Grants of different States, and between a State, or the Citizens thereof, and foreign States, Citizens or Subjects.

In all Cases affecting Ambassadors, other public Ministers and Consuls, and those in which a State shall be Party, the supreme Court shall have original Jurisdiction. In all the other Cases before mentioned, the supreme Court shall have appellate Jurisdiction, both as to Law and Fact, with such Exceptions, and under such Regulations as the Congress shall make.

The Trial of all Crimes, except in Cases of Impeachment, shall be by Jury; and such Trial shall be held in the State where the said Crimes shall have been committed; but when not committed within any State, the Trial shall be at such Place or Places as the Congress may by Law have directed.

Sec. 3. Treason against the United States, shall consist only in levying War against them, or in adhering to their Enemies, giving them Aid and Comfort. No Person shall be convicted of Treason unless on the Testimony of two Witnesses to the same overt Act, or on Confession in open Court.

The Congress shall have Power to declare the Punishment of Treason, but no Attainder of Treason shall work Corruption of Blood, or Forfeiture except during the Life of the Person attained.

ARTICLE IV

Sec. 1. Full Faith and Credit shall be given in each State to the Public Acts, Records, and judicial Proceedings of every other State. And the Congress may by general Laws prescribe the Manner in which such Acts, Records and Proceedings shall be proved, and the Effect thereof.

Sec. 2. The Citizens of each State shall be entitled to all Privileges and Immunities of Citizens in the several states.

A Person charged in any State with Treason, Felony, or other Crime, who shall flee from Justice, and be found in another State, shall on Demand of the executive Authority of the State from which he fled, be delivered up, to be removed to the State having Jurisdiction of the Crime.

No Person held to Service or Labour in one State, under the Laws thereof, escaping into another, shall, in Consequence of any Law or Regulation therein, be discharged from such Service or Labour, but shall be delivered up on Claim of the Party to whom such Service or Labour may be due.

Sec. 3. New States may be admitted by the Congress into this Union; but no new States shall be formed or erected within the Jurisdiction of any other State; nor any State be formed by the Junction of two or more States, or Parts of States, without the Consent of the Legislatures of the States concerned as well as of the Congress.

The Congress shall have Power to dispose of and make all needful Rules and Regulations respecting the Territory or other Property belonging to the

United States; and nothing in the Constitution shall be so construed as to Prejudice any Claims of the United States, or of any particular State.
Sec. 4. The United States shall guarantee to every State in this Union a Republican Form of Government, and shall protect each of them against Invasion; and on Application of the Legislature, or of the Executive (when the Legislature cannot be convened) against domestic Violence.

ARTICLE V

The Congress, whenever two thirds of both Houses shall deem it necessary, shall propose Amendments to this Constitution, or, on the Application of the Legislatures of two thirds of the several States, shall call a Convention for proposing Amendments, which, in either Case, shall be valid to all Intents and Purposes as Part of this Constitution, when ratified by the Legislatures of three fourths of the several States, or by Conventions in three fourths thereof, as the one or the other Mode of Ratification may be proposed by the Congress; Provided that no Amendment which may be made prior to the Year One thousand eight hundred and eight shall in any Manner affect the first and fourth Clauses in the Ninth Section of the first Article; and that no State, without its Consent, shall be deprived of it's equal Suffrage in the Senate.

ARTICLE VI

All Debts contracted and Engagements entered into, before the Adoption of this Constitution, shall be as valid against the United States under this Constitution, as under the Confederation.

This Constitution, and the Laws of the United States which shall be made in Pursuance thereof; and all Treaties made, or which shall be made, under the Authority of the United States, shall be the supreme Law of the Land; and the Judges in every State shall be bound thereby, any Thing in the Constitution or Laws of any State to the Contrary notwithstanding.

The Senators and Representatives before mentioned, and the Members of the several State Legislatures, and all executive and judicial Officers, both of the United States and of the several States, shall be bound by Oath or Affirmation, to support this Constitution; but no religious Test shall ever be required as a Qualification to any Office or public Trust under the United States.

ARTICLE VII

The Ratification of the Conventions of nine States, shall be sufficient for the Establishment of this Constitution between the States so ratifying the Same.

Done in Convention by the Unanimous Consent of the States present the Seventeenth Day of September in the Year of our Lord one thousand seven hundred and Eighty seven and of the Independence of the United States of America the Twelfth. In witness whereof We have hereunto subscribed our Names,

G⁰ WASHINGTON—Presidᵗ
and deputy from Virginia

Articles in addition to, and Amendment of the Constitution of the United States of America, proposed by Congress, and ratified by the Legislatures of the several States, pursuant to the fifth Article of the original Constitution.

[The first ten amendments went into effect November 3, 1791.]

ARTICLE I

Congress shall make no law respecting an establishment of religion, or prohibiting the free exercise thereof; or abridging the freedom of speech, or of the press; or the right of the people peaceably to assemble, and to petition the government for a redress of grievances.

ARTICLE II

A well regulated Militia, being necessary to the security of a free State, the right of the people to keep and bear Arms, shall not be infringed.

ARTICLE III

No Soldier shall, in time of peace be quartered in any house, without the consent of the Owner, nor in time of war, but in a manner to be prescribed by law.

ARTICLE IV

The right of the people to be secure in their persons, houses, papers, and effects, against unreasonable searches and seizures, shall not be violated, and no Warrants shall issue, but upon probable cause, supported by Oath or affirmation, and particularly describing the place to be searched, and the persons or things to be seized.

ARTICLE V

No Person shall be held to answer for a capital, or otherwise infamous crime, unless on a presentment or indictment of a Grand Jury, except in cases arising in the land or naval forces, or in the Militia, when in actual service in time of War or public danger; nor shall any person be subject for the same offence to be twice put in jeopardy of life or limb; nor shall be compelled in any criminal case to be a witness against himself, nor be deprived of life, liberty, or property, without due process of law; nor shall private property be taken for public use, without just compensation.

ARTICLE VI

In all criminal prosecutions, the accused shall enjoy the right to a speedy and public trial, by an impartial jury of the State and district wherein the crime shall have been committed, which district shall have been previously ascertained by law, and to be informed of the nature and cause of the accusation; to be confronted with the witnesses against him; to have compulsory process for obtaining witnesses in his favor, and to have the Assistance of Counsel for his defence.

ARTICLE VII

In Suits at common law, where the value in controversy shall exceed twenty dollars, the right of trial by jury shall be preserved, and no fact tried by a jury, shall be otherwise re-examined in any Court of the United States, than according to the rules of the common law.

ARTICLE VIII

Excessive bail shall not be required, nor excessive fines imposed, nor cruel and unusual punishments inflicted.

ARTICLE IX

The enumeration in the Constitution, of certain rights, shall not be construed to deny or disparage others retained by the people.

ARTICLE X

The powers not delegated to the United States by the Constitution, nor prohibited by it to the States, are reserved to the States respectively, or to the people.

[*The fourteenth amendment went into effect July 28, 1868.*]

ARTICLE XIV

Sec. 1. All persons born or naturalized in the United States, and subject to the jurisdiction thereof, are citizens of the United States and of the State wherein they reside. No State shall make or enforce any law which shall abridge the privileges or immunities of citizens of the United States; nor shall any State deprive any person of life, liberty, or property, without due process of law; nor deny to any person within its jurisdiction the equal protection of the laws.

Sec. 2. Representatives shall be apportioned among the several States according to their respective numbers, counting the whole number of persons in each State, excluding Indians not taxed. But when the right to vote at any election for the choice of electors for President and Vice President of the United States, Representatives in Congress, the Executive and Judicial officers of a State, or the members of the Legislature thereof, is denied to any of the male inhabitants of such State, being twenty-one years of age, and citizens of the United States, or in any way abridged, except for participation in rebellion, or other crime, the basis of representation therein shall be reduced in the proportion which the number of such male citizens shall bear to the whole number of male citizens twenty-one years of age in such State.

Sec. 3. No person shall be a Senator or Representative in Congress, or elector of President and Vice President, or hold any office, civil or military, under the United States, or under any State, who, having previously taken an oath, as a member of or as an officer of the United States, or as a member of any State legislature, or as an executive or judicial officer of any State, to support the Constitution of the United States, shall have engaged in insurrection or rebellion against the same, or given aid or comfort to the enemies thereof. But Congress may by a vote of two-thirds of each House, remove such disability.

Sec. 4. The validity of the public debt of the United States, authorized by law, including debts incurred for payment of pensions and bounties for services in suppressing insurrection or rebellion, shall not be questioned. But neither the United States nor any State shall assume or pay any debt or obligation incurred in aid of insurrection or rebellion against the United States, or any claim for the loss or emancipation of any slave; but all such debts, obligations and claims shall be held illegal and void.

Sec. 5. The Congress shall have power to enforce, by appropriate legislation, the provisions of this article.

CORRECTIONS AND THE CRIMINAL JUSTICE SYSTEM

In 1971, the National Advisory Commission was instituted to study how the criminal justice system operates and how it could be improved. The commission published a number of reports, including one on the police, one on the courts, and one on corrections. In these reports, current trends are discussed and recommendations are made. Because these reports are influential and are frequently referred to in writing about criminal justice, we have included an excerpt from the Report on Corrections. *The student may want to read more of this report or others published by the Commission.*

The pressures for change in the American correctional system today are building so fast that even the most complacent are finding them impossible to ignore. The pressures come not only from prisoners but also from the press, the courts, the rest of the criminal justice system, and even practicing correctional personnel.

During the past decade, conditions in several prison systems have been found by the courts to constitute cruel and unusual punishment in violation of the Constitution. In its 1971–72 term, the U.S. Supreme Court decided eight cases directly affecting offenders, and in each of them the offender's contention prevailed.

The riots and other disturbances that continue to occur in the Nation's prisons and jails confirm the feeling of thoughtful citizens that such institutions contribute little to the national effort to reduce crime. Some maintain that time spent in prisons is in fact counterproductive.

It is clear that a dramatic realignment of correctional methods is called for. It is essential to abate use of institutions. Meanwhile much can be done to eliminate the worst effects of the institution—its crippling idleness, anonymous brutality, and destructive impact. Insofar as the institution has to be relied on, it must be small enough, so located, and so operated that it can relate to the problem offenders pose for themselves and the community.

These changes must not be made out of sympathy for the criminal or disregard of the threat of crime to society. They must be made precisely because that threat is too serious to be countered by ineffective methods.

Many arguments for correctional programs that deal with offenders in the community—probation, parole, and others—meet the test of common sense on their own merits. Such arguments are greatly strengthened by the failing record of prisons, reformatories, and the like. The mega-institution, holding more than a thousand adult inmates, has been built in larger number and variety in this country than anywhere else in the world. Large institutions for young offenders have also proliferated here. In such sur-

SOURCE: The National Advisory Commission on Criminal Justice Standards and Goals, *Corrections* (Washington: Government Printing Office, 1973).

roundings, inmates become faceless people living out routine and meaningless lives. And where institutions are racially skewed and filled with a disproportionate number of ill-educated and vocationally inept persons, they magnify tensions already existing in our society.

The failure of major institutions to reduce crime is incontestable. Recidivism rates are notoriously high. Institutions do succeed in punishing, but they do not deter. They protect the community, but that protection is only temporary. They relieve the community of responsibility by removing the offender, but they make successful reintegration into the community unlikely. They change the committed offender, but the change is more likely to be negative than positive.

It is no surprise that institutions have not been successful in reducing crime. The mystery is that they have not contributed even more to increasing crime. Correctional history has demonstrated clearly that tinkering with the system by changing specific program areas without attention to the larger problems can achieve only incidental and haphazard improvement.

Today's practitioners are forced to use the means of an older time. And dissatisfaction with correctional programs is related to the permanence of yesterday's institutions. We are saddled with the physical remains of last century's prisons and with an ideological legacy that has implicitly accepted the objectives of isolation, control, and punishment, as evidenced by correctional operations, policies, and programs.

Corrections must seek ways to become more attuned to its role of reducing criminal behavior. Changing corrections' role from one of merely housing society's rejects to one of sharing responsibility for their reintegration requires a major commitment on the part of correctional personnel and the rest of the criminal justice system.

Behind these clear imperatives lies the achievable principle of a much greater selectivity and sophistication in the use of crime control and correctional methods. These great powers should be reserved for controlling persons who seriously threaten others. They should not be applied to the nuisances, the troublesome, and the rejected who now clutter our prisons and reformatories and fill our jails and youth detention facilities.

The criminal justice system should become the agency of last resort for social problems. The institution should be the last resort for correctional problems.

Of primary importance as the pressures for change gain force are definition of corrections' goals and objectives, articulation of standards to measure achievement, and establishment of benchmarks to judge progress. That is the purpose of this report on corrections.

DEFINITION AND PURPOSES OF CORRECTIONS

Technical terms can be defined as they arise later in this report, but to begin with a definition of corrections is needed. Corrections is defined here as the community's official reactions to the convicted offender, whether adult or juvenile.

This is a broad definition and it suffers, as most definitions do, from several shortcomings. The implications of the definition for the management of juveniles and for pretrial detention require further discussion. So does the fact that it states no purpose for corrections.

Juvenile Corrections

Use of the term "convicted offender" in a definition of corrections would seem to exclude all juveniles who pass through the juvenile court process, since that process is noncriminal and no conviction may result from it. Juvenile court operations are based on the parens patriae concept in which the state assumes responsibility for a juvenile only to protect "the child's best interests." There is no charge or conviction; rather there is a hearing and a finding as to what action is in the child's interests. Only when the juvenile is tried as an adult on a criminal charge can he be termed a "convicted offender."

But the definition is worded with full understanding of the problem it creates. Juveniles who have not committed acts considered criminal for adults should not be subject to the coercive treatment that vague labels such as "juvenile delinquency" now allow. This is most obvious in the case of such categories as "minors in need of supervision," "dependent and neglected" children, or youths "lapsing into moral danger." The distinction is less clear for the groupings of "delinquent," "beyond parental control," or "habitually unruly." The point here, however, is that if we are concerned with helping the child rather than with the child's noncriminal act, then such help is not a proper function of the criminal justice system.

To define away corrections' role in the treatment of juveniles, however, is not automatically to change the current situation in which correctional systems are deeply enmeshed in juvenile programs, both in the community and in institutions. Regardless of propriety, corrections has accepted the role of "treating" and "helping" juveniles. By so doing, corrections has assumed a responsibility it cannot now evade, responsibility for reforming the manner and processes of treating juveniles. Such an assumption implies that reform must be approached realistically, recognizing current practice and the systems supporting it.

This report, therefore, will discuss the diversion of juveniles from the criminal justice system, juvenile intake and detention, juvenile institutions, and community programs for youth. As a long-range objective, juveniles not tried as adults for criminal acts should be removed from the purview of corrections. However, the current investment in juvenile corrections and the attitudes acquired by correctional staff over the years indicate that the ultimate goal is not immediately feasible.

Jails and Pretrial Detention

The second major difficulty raised by the definition used here is that it would seem to include the jailing of convicted misdemeanants but would not cover pretrial detention. Again, the wording is intentional. This report does discuss the elimination of jails in their present form and the development of community correctional centers. These centers would serve some functions traditionally performed by jails and some new ones, with most functions being "correctional." Jails have not traditionally been part of the correctional system but rather have been run by law enforcement agencies. Still, as long as convicted offenders require services, provision of those services should be the responsibility of the correctional system, regardless of the type of conviction or sentencing disposition.

In addition, what happens to the offender through every step of the criminal justice process has an effect on corrections. If he has been detained before conviction, the nature and quality of that detention may affect his attitude toward the system and his participation in correctional programs. Corrections, therefore, has a very real interest in how pretrial detention is conducted and should make its concerns known.

Detention before trial should be used only in extreme circumstances and then only under careful judicial control. The function of detention prior to trial is not correctional. However, as long as pretrial detention is used at all, it should be carried out in the recommended community correctional centers because of the resources that will be available there. Thus, by implication, corrections is assuming responsibility for the pretrial detainee, even though this is not properly its function as defined here.

Varying Purposes of Corrections

The definition of corrections as the community's official reactions to convicted adult and juvenile offenders neither states nor implies what corrections should try to achieve. This is essential if realism is to replace rhetoric in the field. In particular, corrections is not defined here as being directed exclusively toward the rehabilitation (or habilitation, which is more often the case) of the convicted offender.

If correctional processes were, or could be, truly rehabilitative, it is hard to see why they should be restricted to the convicted. Corrections is limited to the convicted because there are other justifications for coercively intervening in their lives in addition to helping them. Clearly, the penal sanctions imposed on convicted offenders serve a multiplicity of purposes, of which rehabilitation is only one.

Even when correctional purposes are both benevolent and rehabilitative, there is no reason to assume they are so viewed and experienced by the convicted offender. He may believe our intent is to punish, to deter others from crime, or merely to shut him up while he grows older and the fires of violence or criminality die down. Furthermore, insofar as the word "rehabilitation" suggests compulsory cure or coercive retraining, there is an impressive and growing body of opinion that such a purpose is a mistaken sidetrack that corrections has too long pretended to follow.

In the new view, crime and delinquency are symptoms of failure and disorganization in the community as well as in the offender himself. He has had too little contact with the positive forces that develop law-abiding conduct—among them good schools, gainful employment, adequate housing, and rewarding leisure-time activities. So a fundamental objective of corrections must be to secure for the offender contacts, experiences, and opportunities that provide a means and a stimulus for pursuing a lawful style of living in the community. Thus, both the offender and the community become the focus of correctional activity. With this thrust, reintegration of the offender into the community comes to the fore as a major purpose of corrections.

Corrections clearly has many purposes. It is important to recognize that correctional purposes can differ for various types of offenders. In sentencing the convicted murderer we usually are serving punitive and deterrent rather than rehabilitative purposes. Precisely the contrary is true with respect to the deprived, ill-educated, vocationally incompetent youth who is adjudged delinquent; with him, rehabilitative and reintegrative purposes predominate.

There is no doubt that corrections can contribute more than it does to the reduction and control of crime, and this is clearly one of its purposes. What is done in corrections may reduce recidivism. To the extent that recidivist crime is a substantial proportion of all crime, corrections should be able to reduce crime. A swift and effective criminal justice system, respectful of due process and containing a firm and humane corrections component, may provide useful deterrents to crime. Through these mechanisms corrections can contribute to the overall objective of crime reduction. This is an entirely worthy objective if it can be achieved without sacrificing other important human values to which this society is dedicated.

There are other limits to the overreaching purpose of reducing crime and the extent to which it can be accomplished. The report of the President's Task Force on Prisoner Rehabilitation (April 1970) was surely correct when it stressed that:

some of the toughest roots of crime lie buried in the social conditions, especially poverty and racial discrimination, that prevail in the nation's inner cities. These conditions not only make it difficult for millions of Americans to share in America's well-being, but make them doubt society's good faith toward them, leaving them disposed to flout society. America's benefits must be made accessible to all Americans. How successfully America reduces and controls crime depends, in the end, upon what it does about employment and education, housing and health, areas far outside our present mandate or, for that matter, our particular competence. This is not to say that improvements in the correctional system are beside the point . . . . Our point is that improvements in the correctional system are necessarily tactical maneuvers that can lead to no more than small and short-term victories unless they are executed as part of a grand strategy of improving all the nation's systems and institutions.[1]

It is a mistake to expect massive social advance to flow either from corrections or from the criminal justice system as a whole. That system can

1. President's Task Force on Prisoner Rehabilitation, *The Criminal Offender—What Should Be Done?* (Washington: Government Printing Office, 1970), p. 7.

be fair; it can be humane; it can be efficient and expeditious. To an appreciable extent it can reduce crime. Alone, it cannot substantially improve the quality and opportunity of life. It cannot save men from themselves. It can be a hallmark of a harmonious and decent community life, not a means of achieving it.

There is another limitation on corrections' potential to reduce and control crime. Corrections is only a small part of a social control system applied to define, inhibit, reduce, and treat crime and criminals. It is but a subsystem of the criminal justice system. And it is the inheritor of problems created by the many defects in the other subsystems.

Corrections alone cannot solve the diverse problems of crime and delinquency confronting America, but it can make a much more significant contribution to that task. Correctional planning and programs must be closely related to the planning and programs of police and courts. Corrections' goals must be defined realistically and pursued with determination by application of achievable and measurable standards.

STANDARDS AND GOALS IN CORRECTIONS

It may be objected: Here is still another list of uplifting aspirations for corrections. Will they never learn that rhetoric is not self-fulfilling? It will be argued: More emphatic reaffirmations of the obvious are not needed; the need is for implementation of what we already know. The argument has force, but it misses the distinction between general principles that abound in corrections and specific standards that have been dismally scarce. Precise definition of goals, and of standards marking steps toward their achievement, is no waste of energy. Operating without them invites, if it does not guarantee, failure.

Standards vs. Principles

A comprehensive and soundly based body of guiding principles to direct correctional reform has existed ever since the American Prison Association's "Declaration of Principles" in 1870. The principles, revised in 1930 and reformulated in more modern language in 1960 and 1970, still remain a contemporary document. We have yet to achieve the aspirations of 1870. And there have been many subsequent attempts in this country to guide those who would improve corrections.

Both the Wickersham Commission's report in 1931 and the report in 1967 of the President's Commission on Law Enforcement and Administration of Justice (often referred to as the Crime Commission) contain a wealth of recommendations. Many of them continue to attract substantial support but have yet to be implemented. With such a treasury of past recommendations, why should there be further effort to articulate standards and goals for corrections? Quite apart from the need to be clearer in purpose and direction in a time of rapid change, there is a compelling practical reason for the present definition of standards and goals.

The reason is this: Principles and recommendations are neither self-fulfilling nor self-interpreting. Standards and goals may be much more precise, while retaining sufficient flexibility to allow agencies some freedom. When clearly formulated and precisely stated in measurable terms, they can serve as the basis for objective evaluation of programs as well as development of statutes and regulations relating to correctional services.

Standards and goals set forth in this report may lack automatic enforcing machinery, but it has been the Commission's intention to minimize vagueness in definition. Correctional administrators can readily discern whether or not standards have been achieved. All concerned with running or observing an institution, agency, or program will know whether the standard has been applied or the goal achieved. That was not true of the 1870 Declaration of Principles or of the several series of Commission recommendations that followed. The range for individual interpretation has been too great in view of endemic political and social problems confronting correctional administrators.

The standard has another important practical advantage over the principle and the recommendation. It supports more strongly and authoritatively the passage of legislation, promulgation of regulations, and development of other quality control mechanisms that provide an element of enforcement. It encourages public opinion to focus on and press for correctional reform. It prevents all of us from concluding that what we have is right simply because we have it. It reduces room for rationalization.

Achieving Standards

As a State moves from accepting these standards and goals to achieving them, new legislation may be required. More often, merely administrative and regulatory expression will be needed. The recent promulgation by the State of Illinois of an extensive system of administrative regulations for adult correctional institutions is a step of great significance toward the introduction of an enforceable rule of law into a penal system. The regulations were discussed with the staff before adoption and made readily available to the prisoners when instituted. They contain what are in effect self-enforcement mechanisms. For example, they include well-defined provisions concerning disciplinary offenses and hearings and a grievance procedure available to all prisoners. Indeed, one of the most effective methods of attaining standards and achieving goals is to add to them mechanisms for their enforcement.

Standards and goals must be realistic and achievable, but that certainly does not mean that they need to be modest. The American culture has not only a bursting energy but also a remarkable capacity for adapting to change. What was unthinkable yesterday may be accepted as common practice today. In the criminal justice system, such changes have been observable in recent years with respect to the treatment of narcotics addiction and in the law's attitude toward a range of victimless crimes. They have been seen in the remarkable sweep of the movement toward procedural due process in all judicial and quasi-judicial hearings within the criminal justice system. When the courts abandoned the "hands-off" doctrine that led them to avoid inquiry into prison conditions, this was another aspect of change.

In recent years the Federal Government and many of the States have begun to demonstrate in budgets their seriousness of purpose in correctional reform. For whatever reason, more money is now being allocated to this task. The low priority traditionally assigned to budgetary support for the penal system and to prisoners generally is being changed. It is being supplanted by realization that the quality of life depends in part on creation of a humane, just, and efficient criminal justice system. Coupled with this realization is the knowledge that achievement of such a system must entail substantial correctional reform.

On the other hand, it must be recognized that the road to correctional reform is littered with discarded panaceas. Politically, there has been no great incentive to invest in correctional reform. Until quite recently, there was scant public recognition of the importance of the criminal justice system to community life, and so fiscal support for corrections was little more than a pittance grudgingly doled out. These attitudes have not disappeared completely. Simple solutions are still offered with the promise of dramatic consequences. Correctional reform has lacked both a constituency and a sound political base. Such support as it is now attracting flows in part from the increasing recognition that, if there is to be an effective criminal justice system, an integral part of it must be an effective, humane correctional system.

Formulation and specification of standards and goals can be a step of permanent significance in moving from admirable rhetoric toward a working blueprint for correctional reform with built-in quantitative and qualitative yardsticks of progress.

OBSTACLES TO CORRECTIONAL REFORM

Fragmentation of Corrections

One of the leading obstacles to reforming the criminal justice system is the range and variety of governmental authorities—Federal, State, and local—that are responsible for it. This balkanization complicates police planning, impedes development of expeditious court processes, and divides responsibility for convicted offenders among a multiplicity of overlapping but barely intercommunicating agencies. The organizational structure of the criminal justice system was well-suited to the frontier society in which it was implanted. It has survived in a complex, mobile, urban society for which it is grossly unsuited. Accordingly, this report seriously addresses large-scale organizational and administrative restructuring of corrections.

One set of solutions is to accept the present balkanization of corrections, recognizing its strong political support in systems of local patronage, and to prescribe defined standards, buttressed by statewide inspection systems to attain those standards. Local jails provide a good example. At the very least, if they are to be retained for the unconvicted, they must be subject to State-controlled inspection processes, to insure the attainment of minimum standards of decency and efficiency. A further control and support that might be added is State subsidy to facilitate attainment of defined standards and goals by the local jails, the carrot of subsidy being added to the stick of threatened condemnation and closure. However, these measures are but compromises.

The contrasting mode of organizational restructuring of corrections is an integrated State correctional system. There is much support for movement in that direction. For example, it is recommended in this report that supervision of offenders under probation should be separated from the courts' administrative control and integrated with the State correctional system.

If prisons, probation, parole, and other community programs for adult and juvenile offenders are brought under one departmental structure, there is no doubt of that department's improved bargaining position in competition for resources in cabinet and legislature. Other flexibilities are opened up; career lines for promising staff are expanded, to say nothing of interdepartmental inservice training possibilities. Above all, such a structure matches the developing realities of correctional processes.

An increasing interdependence between institutional and community-based programs arises as their processes increasingly overlap; as furlough and work-release programs are expanded; as institutional release procedures grow more sophisticated and graduated; and as more intensive supervisory arrangements are added to probation and parole supervision. Institutional placement, probation, and parole or aftercare grow closer together and structually intertwine. This is true for both adult and juvenile offenders.

Development of further alternatives to the traditional institution, and diversion of offenders from it, will increase this pressure toward an integrated statewide correctional system, regionalized to match the demography and distribution of offenders in the State. Administrative regionalization of such structurally integrated statewide correctional systems may be necessary in the more populous or larger States to link each regional system with the needs, opportunities, and social milieu of the particular offender group. Regionalization greatly facilitates maintaining closer ties between the offender and his family (as by visits, furloughs, and work release) than is possible otherwise.

In sum, the task of achieving an effective functional balance between State and local correctional authorities is complex and uncertain, yet it offers opportunity. It will require political statesmanship that transcends partisan, parochial, and patronage interests. But whatever the interagency relationships may be, the enunciation of precisely defined standards and goals for those agencies will aid in attainment of effective and humane correctional processes.

Overuse of Corrections

The correctional administrator (and for the present purposes, the sentencing judge too) is the servant of a criminal justice system quite remarkable in its lack of restraint. Historically, the criminal law has been used not only in an effort to protect citizens but also to coerce men to private virtue. Criminal law overreaches itself in a host of "victimless" crimes; that is, crimes without an effective complainant other than the authorities. This application of the law is a major obstacle to development of a rational and effective correctional system.

When criminal law invades the sphere of private morality and social welfare, it often proves ineffective and criminogenic. What is worse, the law then diverts corrections from its clear, socially protective function. The result is unwise legislation that extends the law's reach beyond its competence. Manifestations are seen in relation to gambling, the use of drugs, public drunkenness, vagrancy, disorderly conduct, and the noncriminal aspects of troublesome juvenile behavior. This overreach of criminal law has made hypocrites of us all and has confused the mission of corrections. It has overloaded the entire criminal justice system with inappropriate cases and saddled corrections with tasks it is unsuited to perform.

The unmaking of law is more difficult than the making; to express moral outrage at objectionable conduct and to urge legislative proscription is politically popular. On the other hand, to urge the repeal of sanctions against any objectionable conduct is politically risky since it can be equated in the popular mind with approval of that conduct. But corrections, like the rest of the criminal justice system, must reduce its load to what it has some chance of carrying. Too often we are fighting the wrong war, on the wrong front, at the wrong time, so that our ability to protect the community and serve the needs of the convicted offender is attenuated. It is for this reason that a major emphasis in this report is placed on developing diversions from and alternatives to the correctional system.

It is particularly urgent to evict from corrections many of the alcoholics and drug addicts who now clutter that system. They should be brought under the aegis of more appropriate and less punitive mechanisms of social control. The same is true of truants and other juveniles who are in need of care and protection and have not committed criminal offenses. They should be removed from the delinquency jurisdiction of the courts as well as corrections.

At the same time, the rapid expansion of those diverse community-based supervisory programs called probation and parole is needed. Most States still lack probation and parole programs that are more than gestures toward effective supervision and assistance for convicted offenders. Standards and goals for correctional reform depend largely on the swift, substantial improvement of probation and parole practices.

Overemphasis on Custody

The pervasive overemphasis on custody that remains in corrections creates more problems than it solves. Our institutions are so large that their operational needs take precedence over the needs of the people they hold. The very scale of these institutions dehumanizes, denies privacy, encourages violence, and defies decent control. A moratorium should be placed on the construction of any large correctional institution. We already have too many prisons. If there is any need at all for more institutions, it is for small, community-related facilities in or near the communities they serve.

There is also urgent need for reducing the population of jails and juvenile detention facilities. By using group homes, foster care arrangements, day residence facilities, and similar community-based resources, it should be possible to eliminate entirely the need for institutions to hold young persons prior to court disposition of their cases. Likewise, by other methods discussed in this report, it will be practicable to greatly reduce the use of jails for the adult accused. By placing limitations on detention time and by freely allowing community resources, agencies, and individuals to percolate the walls of the jail, it will be possible to minimize the social isolation of those who must be jailed.

Nevertheless, it must be recognized that at our present level of knowledge (certainly of adult offenders) we lack the ability to empty prisons and jails entirely. There are confirmed and dangerous offenders who require protracted confinement because we lack alternative and more effective methods of controlling or modifying their behavior. At least for the period of incarceration, they are capable of no injury to the community.

Even so, far too many offenders are classified as dangerous. We have not developed a means of dealing with them except in the closed institution. Too often we have perceived them as the stereotype of "prisoner" and applied to all offenders the institutional conditions essential only for relatively few. Hence, this report stresses the need for development of a broader range of alternatives to the institution, and for the input of greater resources of manpower, money, and materials to that end.

Community-based programs are not merely a substitute for the institution. Often they will divert offenders from entering the institution. But they also have important functions as part of the correctional process. They facilitate a continuum of services from the institution through graduated release procedures—such as furloughs and work release—to community-based programs.

Large institutions for adult and juvenile offenders have become places of endemic violence. Overcrowding and the admixture of diverse ethnic groups, thrown together in idleness and boredom, is the basic condition. Race relations tend to be hostile and ferocious in the racially skewed prisons and jails.

Increasing political activism complicates inmate-staff relations. Knives and other weapons proliferate and are used. Diversion of the less violent and more stable from institutions will leave in the prisons and jails a larger proportion of hardened, dangerous, and explosive prisoners. The correctional administrator thus confronts a stark reality. While making needed changes to benefit the great majority of inmates, he must cope with a volatile concentration of the most difficult offenders, whose hostility is directed against the staff.

For these reasons and others, continuing attention must be paid to conditions within the remaining institutions. Although the institution must be used only as a last resort, its programs must not be neglected. Such attention is essential if the institution is to serve as the beginning place for reintegration and not as the end of the line for the offender.

The principle of community-based corrections also extends to prisons and jails. We must make those institutions smaller, for only then can they cease to hold the anonymous. We must make them more open and responsive to community influences, for only thus can we make it possible for prisoners and staff alike to see what the community expects of them.

Lack of Financial Support

The reforms envisioned in this report will not be achieved without substantially increased government funds being allocated to the criminal justice system and without a larger portion of the total being allocated to corrections. There is little sense in the police arresting more offenders if the courts lack the resources to bring them to trial and corrections lacks the resources to deal with them efficiently and fairly. Happily, the Federal Government, followed by many States, already is providing important leadership here.

Budgetary recognition is being given to the significance of crime and the fear it produces in the social fabric. For example, statutory provisions now require that at least 20 percent of the Federal funds disbursed by the Law Enforcement Assistance Administration to the States to aid crime control be allocated to corrections. It is clearly a proper role for the Federal Government to assist States by funds and direct services to increase the momentum of the movement toward community-based corrections and to remedy existing organizational inefficiencies.

Two other obstacles to reform merit mention in this litany of adversity and the means of overcoming it. Like the other impediments to change, these obstacles are not intractable, but, like the rest, they must be recognized as genuine problems to be reckoned with if they are not to frustrate progress. They are, first, the community's ambivalence, and second, the lack of knowledge on which planning for the criminal justice system can be firmly based.

Ambivalence of the Community

If asked, a clear majority of the community would probably support halfway houses for those offenders who are not a serious criminal threat but still require some residential control. But repeated experience has shown that a proposal to establish such a facility in the neighborhood is likely to rouse profound opposition. The criminal offender, adult or juvenile, is accorded a low level of community tolerance when he no longer is an abstract idea but a real person. Planning must be done, and goals and standards drafted, in recognition of this fact.

Responsible community relations must be built into all correctional plans. The antidote to intolerance of convicted offenders is the active involvement of wide segments of the community in support of correctional processes. With imagination and a willingness to take some risks, members of minority groups, ex-offenders, and other highly motivated citizens can play an effective supporting role in correctional programs.

Part of this process of opening up the institution to outside influences is the creation of a wider base for staff selection. Obviously, recruitment of members of minority groups is vitally important and must be energetically pursued. Of parallel importance, women must be employed in community-based programs and at every level of the institution (for men and women, for adults and youths) from top administration to line guard. Corrections must become a full equal opportunity employer.

Correctional administrators have tended to isolate corrections from the general public—by high walls and locked doors. In light of the community's ambivalence toward corrections, lack of effort at collaboration with community groups and individual citizens is particularly unfortunate. In almost every community there are individuals and social groups with exceptional concern for problems of social welfare whose energies must be called upon. A lobby for corrections lies at hand, to be mobilized not merely by public information and persuasion, but also by encouraging the active participation of the public in correctional work.

There are yet other advantages in such a determined community involvement in corrections. Obstacles to the employment of ex-offenders will be lowered. Probation and parole caseloads could be reduced if paraprofessionals and volunteers, including ex-offenders, assist. And the "nine-to-five on weekdays" syndrome of some probation and parole services can be cured, so that supervision and support can be available when most needed.

Lack of Knowledge Base for Planning

. . . Lack of adequate data about crime and delinquency, the consequences of sentencing practices, and the outcome of correctional programs is a major obstacle to planning for better community protection. It is a sad commentary on our social priorities that every conceivable statistic concerning sports is collected and available to all who are interested. One can readily find out how many lefthanders hit triples in the 1927 World Series. Yet if we wish to know how many one-to-life sentences were handed out to the 1927 crop of burglars—or the 1972 crop for that matter—the facts are nowhere to be found.

Baseline data and outcome data are not self-generating; no computer is self-activating. Research is of central significance to every correctional agency. It is not, as it so often is regarded, merely a public relations gimmick to be manipulated for political and budgetary purposes. It is an indispensable tool for intelligent decisionmaking and deployment of resources.

It is time we stopped giving mere lip service to research and to the critical evaluation of correctional practices. To fail to propound and to achieve ambitious research and data-gathering goals is to condemn corrections to the perpetual continuance of its present ineptitude. . . .

THE GAULT CASE

The Gault case, which is printed below, is significant in the development of juvenile justice. In this case the Supreme Court reversed a decision reached in the juvenile courts regarding a fifteen-year-old Arizona boy. The Supreme Court's action is a reflection of increasing criticism of the way juvenile offenders have been handled by the criminal justice system.

In re. GAULT

387 U.S. 1 (1967)

MR. JUSTICE FORTAS delivered the opinion of the Court.

This is an appeal under 28 U.S.C. § 1257(2) from a judgment of the Supreme Court of Arizona affirming the dismissal of a petition for a writ of habeas corpus. 99 Ariz. 181, 407 P.2d 760 (1965). The petition sought the release of Gerald Francis Gault, appellants' 15-year-old son, who had been committed as a juvenile delinquent to the State Industrial School by the Juvenile Court of Gila County, Arizona.

We begin with a statement of the facts.

I.

On Monday, June 8, 1964, at about 10 a. m., Gerald Francis Gault and a friend, Ronald Lewis, were taken into custody by the Sheriff of Gila County. Gerald was then still subject to a six months' probation order which had been entered on February 25, 1964, as a result of his having been in the company of another boy who had stolen a wallet from a lady's purse. The police action on June 8 was taken as the result of a verbal complaint by a neighbor of the boys, Mrs. Cook, about a telephone call made to her in which the caller or callers made lewd or indecent remarks. It will suffice for purposes of this opinion to say that the remarks or questions put to her were of the irritatingly offensive, adolescent, sex variety.

At the time Gerald was picked up, his mother and father were both at work. No notice that Gerald was being taken into custody was left at the home. No other steps were taken to advise them that their son had, in effect, been arrested. Gerald was taken to the Children's Detention Home. When his mother arrived home at about 6 o'clock, Gerald was not there. Gerald's older brother was sent to look for him at the trailer home of the Lewis family. He apparently learned then that Gerald was in custody. He so informed his mother. The two of them went to the Detention Home. The deputy probation officer, Flagg, who was also superintendent of the Detention Home, told Mrs. Gault "why Jerry was there" and said that a hearing would be held in Juvenile Court at 3 o'clock the following day, June 9.

Officer Flagg filed a petition with the court on the hearing day, June 9, 1964. It was not served on the Gaults. Indeed, none of them saw this petition until the habeas corpus hearing on August 17, 1964. The petition was entirely formal. It made no reference to any factual basis for the judicial action which it initiated. It recited only that "said minor is under the age of eighteen years, and is in need of the protection of this Honorable Court; [and that] said minor is a delinquent minor." It prayed for a hearing and an order regarding "the care and custody of said minor." Officer Flagg executed a formal affidavit in support of the petition.

On June 9, Gerald, his mother, his older brother, and Probation Officers Flagg and Henderson appeared before the Juvenile Judge in chambers. Gerald's father was not there. He was at work out of the city. Mrs. Cook, the complainant, was not there. No one was sworn at this hearing. No transcript or recording was made. No memorandum or record of the substance of the proceedings was prepared. Our information about the proceedings and the subsequent hearing on June 15, derives entirely from the testimony of the Juvenile Court Judge, Mr. and Mrs. Gault and Officer Flagg at the habeas corpus proceeding conducted two months later. From this, it appears that at the June 9 hearing Gerald was questioned by the judge about the telephone call. There was conflict as to what he said. His mother recalled that Gerald said he only dialed Mrs. Cook's number and handed the telephone to his friend, Ronald. Officer Flagg recalled that Gerald had admitted making the lewd remarks. Judge McGhee testified that Gerald "admitted making one of these [lewd] statements." At the conclusion of the hearing, the judge said he would "think about it." Gerald was taken back to the Detention Home. He was not sent to his own home with his parents. On June 11 or 12, after having been detained since June 8, Gerald was released and driven home.[1] There is no explanation in the record as to why he was kept in the Detention Home or why he was released. At 5 p. m. on the day of Gerald's release, Mrs. Gault received a note signed by Officer Flagg. It was on plain paper, not letterhead. Its entire text was as follows:

"Mrs. Gault:
"Judge McGhee has set Monday June 15, 1964 at 11:00 A.M. as the date and time for further Hearings on Gerald's delinquency

"/s/Flagg"

At the appointed time on Monday, June 15, Gerald, his father and mother, Ronald Lewis and his father, and Officers Flagg and Henderson were present before Judge McGhee. Witnesses at the habeas corpus proceeding differed in their recollections of Gerald's testimony at the June 15 hearing. Mr. and Mrs. Gault recalled that Gerald again testified that he had only dialed the number and that the other boy had made the remarks. Officer Flagg agreed that at this hearing Gerald did not admit making the

---

1.   There is a conflict between the recollection of Mrs. Gault and that of Officer Flagg. Mrs. Gault testified that Gerald was released on Friday, June 12, Officer Flagg that it had been on Thursday, June 11. This was from memory; he had no record, and the note hereafter referred to was undated.

lewd remarks.[2] But Judge McGhee recalled that "there was some admission again of some of the lewd statements. He—he didn't admit any of the more serious lewd statements."[3] Again, the complainant, Mrs. Cook, was not present. Mrs. Gault asked that Mrs. Cook be present "so she could see which boy that done the talking, the dirty talking over the phone." The Juvenile Judge said "she didn't have to be present at that hearing." The judge did not speak to Mrs. Cook or communicate with her at any time. Probation Officer Flagg had talked to her once—over the telephone on June 9.

At this June 15 hearing a "referral report" made by the probation officers was filed with the court, although not disclosed to Gerald or his parents. This listed the charge as "Lewd Phone Calls." At the conclusion of the hearing, the judge committed Gerald as a juvenile delinquent to the State Industrial School "for the period of his minority [that is, until 21], unless sooner discharged by due process of law." An order to that effect was entered. It recites that "after a full hearing and due deliberation the Court finds that said minor is a delinquent child, and that said minor is of the age of 15 years."

No appeal is permitted by Arizona law in juvenile cases. On August 3, 1964, a petition for a writ of habeas corpus was filed with the Supreme Court of Arizona and referred by it to the Superior Court for hearing.

At the habeas corpus hearing on August 17, Judge McGhee was vigorously cross-examined as to the basis for his actions. He testified that he had taken into account the fact that Gerald was on probation. He was asked "under what section of . . . the code you found the boy delinquent?"

His answer is set forth in the margin.[4] In substance, he concluded that

2.   Officer Flagg also testified that Gerald had not, when questioned at the Detention Home, admitted having made any of the lewd statements, but that each boy had sought to put the blame on the other. There was conflicting testimony as to whether Ronald had accused Gerald of making the lewd statements during the June 15 hearing.

3.   Judge McGhee also testified that Gerald had not denied "certain statements" made to him at the hearing by Officer Henderson.

4.   "Q. All right. Now, Judge, would you tell me under what section of the law or tell me under what section of—of the code you found the boy delinquent?

"A. Well, there is a—I think it amounts to disturbing the peace. I can't give you the section, but I can tell you the law, that when one person uses lewd language in the presence of another person, that it can amount to—and I consider that when a person makes it over the phone, that it is considered in the presence, I might be wrong, that is one section. The other section upon which I consider the boy delinquent is Section 8-201, Subsection (d), habitually involved in immoral matters."

Gerald came within ARS § 8-201-6(a), which specifies that a "delinquent child" includes one "who has violated a law of the state or an ordinance or regulation of a political subdivision thereof." The law which Gerald was found to have violated is ARS § 13-377. This section of the Arizona Criminal Code provides that a person who "in the presence or hearing of any woman or child . . . uses vulgar, abusive or obscene language, is guilty of a misdemeanor. . . ." The penalty specified in the Criminal Code, which would apply to an adult, is $5 to $50, or imprisonment for not more than two months. The judge also testified that he acted under ARS § 8-201-6(d) which includes in the definition of a "delinquent child" one who, as the judge phrased it, is "habitually involved in immoral matters."

Asked about the basis for his conclusion that Gerald was "habitually involved in immoral matters," the judge testified, somewhat vaguely, that two years earlier, on July 2, 1962, a "referral" was made concerning Gerald, "where the boy had stolen a baseball glove from another boy and lied to the Police Department about it." The judge said there was "no hearing," and "no accusation" relating to this incident, "because of lack of material foundation." But it seems to have remained in his mind as a relevant factor. The judge also testified that Gerald had admitted making other nuisance phone calls in the past which, as the judge recalled the boy's testimony, were "silly calls, or funny calls, or something like that."

The Superior Court dismissed the writ, and appellants sought review in the Arizona Supreme Court. That court handed down an elaborate and wide-ranging opinion affirming dismissal of the writ. In their brief appellants urge that we hold the Juvenile Code of Arizona invalid on its face or as applied in this case because, contrary to the Due Process Clause of the Fourteenth Amendment, the juvenile is taken from the custody of his parents and committed to a state institution pursuant to proceedings in which the Juvenile Court has virtually unlimited discretion, and in which the following basic rights are denied:

1. Notice of the charges;
2. Right to counsel;
3. Right to confrontation and cross-examination;
4. Privilege against self-incrimination;
5. Right to transcript of the proceedings; and
6. Right to appellate review.

II.

The Supreme Court of Arizona held that due process of law is requisite to the constitutional validity of proceedings in which a court reaches the conclusion that a juvenile has been at fault, has engaged in conduct prohibited by law, or has otherwise misbehaved with the consequence that he is committed to an institution in which his freedom is curtailed. This conclusion is in accord with the decisions of a number of courts under both federal and state constitutions.

We do not in this opinion consider the impact of these constitutional provisions upon the totality of the relationship of the juvenile and the state. We do not even consider the entire process relating to juvenile "delinquents." For example, we are not here concerned with the procedures or constitutional rights applicable to the pre-judicial stages of the juvenile process, nor do we direct our attention to the post-adjudicative or dispositional process. We consider only the problems presented to us by this case. These relate to the proceedings by which a determination is made as to whether a juvenile is a "delinquent" as a result of alleged misconduct on his part, with the consequence that he may be committed to a state institution. As to these proceedings, there appears to be little current dissent from the proposition that the Due Process Clause has a role to play. The problem is to ascertain the precise impact of the due process requirement upon such proceedings.

[T]he features of the juvenile system which its proponents have asserted are of unique benefit will not be impaired by constitutional domestication. For example, the commendable principles relating to the processing and treatment of juveniles separately from adults are in no way involved or affected by the procedural issues under discussion. Further, we are told that one of the important benefits of the special juvenile court procedures is that they avoid classifying the juvenile as a "criminal." The juvenile offender is now classed as a "delinquent." There is, of course, no reason why this should not continue. It is disconcerting, however, that this term has come to involve only slightly less stigma than the term "criminal" applied to adults. It is also emphasized that in practically all jurisdictions, statutes provide that an adjudication of the child as a delinquent shall not operate as a civil disability or disqualify him for civil service appointment. There is no reason why the application of due process requirements should interfere with such provisions.

Beyond this, it is frequently said that juveniles are protected by the process from disclosure of their deviational behavior.

[T]here is no reason why, consistently with due process, a State cannot continue, if it deems it appropriate, to provide and to improve provision for the confidentiality of records of police contacts and court action relating to juveniles.

Further, it is urged that the juvenile benefits from informal proceedings in the court. The early conception of the Juvenile Court proceeding was one in which a fatherly judge touched the heart and conscience of the erring youth by talking over his problems, by paternal advice and admonition, and in which, in extreme situations, benevolent and wise institutions of the State provided guidance and help "to save him from a downward career." While due process requirements will, in some instances, introduce a degree of order and regularity to Juvenile Court proceedings to determine delinquency, and in contested cases will introduce some elements of the adversary system, nothing will require that the conception of the kindly juvenile judge be replaced by its opposite, nor do we here rule upon the question whether ordinary due process requirements must be observed with respect to hearings to determine the disposition of the delinquent child.

Ultimately, however, we confront the reality of that portion of the Juvenile Court process with which we deal in this case. A boy is charged with misconduct. The boy is committed to an institution where he may be restrained of liberty for years. It is of no constitutional consequence—and of limited practical meaning—that the institution to which he is committed is called an Industrial School. The fact of the matter is that, however euphemistic the title, a "receiving home" or an "industrial school" for juveniles is an institution of confinement in which the child is incarcerated for a greater or lesser time. His world becomes "a building with whitewashed walls, regimented routine and institutional hours. . . ." Instead of mother and father and sisters and brothers and friends and classmates, his world is peopled by guards, custodians, state employees, and "delinquents" confined with him for anything from waywardness to rape and homicide.

In view of this, it would be extraordinary if our Constitution did not require the procedural regularity and the exercise of care implied in the phrase "due process." Under our Constitution, the condition of being a boy does not justify a kangaroo court.

The essential difference between Gerald's case and a normal criminal case is that safeguards available to adults were discarded in Gerald's case. The summary procedure as well as the long commitment was possible because Gerald was 15 years of age instead of over 18.

If Gerald had been over 18, he would not have been subject to Juvenile Court proceedings. For the particular offense immediately involved, the maximum punishment would have been a fine of $5 to $50, or imprisonment in jail for not more than two months. Instead, he was committed to custody for a maximum of six years.

In Kent v. United States [383 U.S. 541 (1966)], we stated that the Juvenile Court Judge's exercise of the power of the state as *parens patriae* was not unlimited. We said that "the admonition to function in a 'parental' relationship is not an invitation to procedural arbitrariness." We announced with respect to such waiver proceedings that while "We do not mean . . . to indicate that the hearing to be held must conform with all of the requirements of a criminal trial or even of the usual administrative hearing; but we do hold that the hearing must measure up to the essentials of due process and fair treatment." We reiterate this view, here in connection with a juvenile court adjudication of "delinquency," as a requirement which is part of the Due Process Clause of the Fourteenth Amendment of our Constitution.

III.

Notice of Charges

Appellants allege that the Arizona Juvenile Code is unconstitutional or alternatively that the proceedings before the Juvenile Court were constitutionally defective because of failure to provide adequate notice of the hearings. No notice was given to Gerald's parents when he was taken into custody on Monday, June 8. On that night, when Mrs. Gault went to the Detention Home, she was orally informed that there would be a hearing the next afternoon and was told the reason why Gerald was in custody. The only written notice Gerald's parents received at any time was a note on plain paper from Officer Flagg delivered on Thursday or Friday, June 11 or 12, to the effect that the judge had set Monday, June 15, "for further Hearings on Gerald's delinquency."

A "petition" was filed with the court on June 9 by Officer Flagg, reciting only that he was informed and believed that "said minor is a delinquent minor and that it is necessary that some order be made by the Honorable Court for said minor's welfare." The applicable Arizona statute provides for a petition to be filed in Juvenile Court, alleging in general terms that the child is "neglected, dependent or delinquent." The statute explicitly states that such a general allegation is sufficient, "without alleging the facts." There is no requirement that the petition be served and it was not served upon, given to, or shown to Gerald or his parents.

We cannot agree that adequate notice was given in this case. Notice, to comply with due process requirements, must be given sufficiently in advance of scheduled court proceedings so that reasonable opportunity to prepare will be afforded, and it must "set forth the alleged misconduct with particularity." The "initial hearing" in the present case was a hearing on the merits. Notice at that time is not timely. Due process of law requires notice which would be deemed constitutionally adequate in a civil or criminal proceeding. It does not allow a hearing to be held in which a youth's freedom and his parents' right to his custody are at stake without giving them timely notice, in advance of the hearing, of the specific issues that they must meet.

IV.

Right to Counsel

Appellants charge that the Juvenile Court proceedings were fatally defective because the court did not advise Gerald or his parents of their right to counsel, and proceeded with the hearing, the adjudication of delinquency and the order of commitment in the absence of counsel for the child and his parents or an express waiver of the right thereto. The Supreme Court of Arizona referred to a provision of the Juvenile Code which it characterized as requiring "that the probation officer shall look after the interests of neglected, delinquent and dependent children," including representing their interests in court. We do not agree. Probation officers, in the Arizona scheme, are also arresting officers. They initiate proceedings and file petitions which they verify, as here, alleging the delinquency of the child; and they testify, as here, against the child. And here the probation officer was also superintendent of the Detention Home. The probation officer cannot act as counsel for the child. His role in the adjudicatory hearing, by statute and in fact, is as arresting officer and witness against the child. Nor can the judge represent the child. There is no material difference in this respect between adult and juvenile proceedings of the sort here involved. In adult proceedings, this contention has been foreclosed by decisions of this Court. A proceeding where the issue is whether the child will be found to be "delinquent" and subjected to the loss of his liberty for years is comparable in seriousness to a felony prosecution. The juvenile needs the assistance of counsel to cope with problems of law, to make skilled inquiry into the facts, to insist upon regularity of the proceedings, and to ascertain whether he has a defense and to prepare and submit it. The child "requires the guiding hand of counsel at every step in the proceedings against him."

We conclude that the Due Process Clause of the Fourteenth Amendment requires that in respect of proceedings to determine delinquency which may result in commitment to an institution in which the juvenile's freedom is curtailed, the child and his parents must be notified of the child's right to be represented by counsel retained by them, or if they are unable to afford counsel, that counsel will be appointed to represent the child.

At the habeas corpus proceeding, Mrs. Gault testified that she knew that she could have appeared with counsel at the juvenile hearing. This knowledge is not a waiver of the right to counsel which she and her juvenile son had, as we have defined it. They had a right expressly to be advised that they might retain counsel and to be confronted with the need for specific consideration of whether they did or did not choose to waive the right. If they were unable to afford to employ counsel, they were entitled in view of the seriousness of the charge and the potential commitment, to appointed counsel, unless they chose waiver. Mrs. Gault's knowledge that she could employ counsel was not an "intentional relinquishment or abandonment" of a fully known right.

V.

Confrontation, Self-Incrimination, Cross-Examination

Appellants urge that the writ of habeas corpus should have been granted because of the denial of the rights of confrontation and cross-examination in the Juvenile Court hearings, and because the privilege against self-incrimination was not observed. The Juvenile Court Judge testified at the habeas corpus hearing that he had proceeded on the basis of Gerald's admissions at the two hearings. Appellants attack this on the ground that the admissions were obtained in disregard of the privilege against self-incrimination. If the confession is disregarded, appellants argue that the delinquency conclusion, since it was fundamentally based on a finding that Gerald had made lewd remarks during the phone call to Mrs. Cook, is fatally defective for failure to accord the rights of confrontation and cross-examination which the Due Process Clause of the Fourteenth Amendment of the Federal Constitution guarantees in state proceedings generally.

Our first question, then, is whether Gerald's admission was improperly obtained and relied on as the basis of decision, in conflict with the Federal Constitution.

Neither Gerald nor his parents were advised that he did not have to testify or make a statement, or that an incriminating statement might result in his commitment as a "delinquent."

The Arizona Supreme Court rejected appellants' contention that Gerald had a right to be advised that he need not incriminate himself. It said: "We think the necessary flexibility for individualized treatment will be enhanced by a rule which does not require the judge to advise the infant of a privilege against self-incrimination."

In reviewing this conclusion of Arizona's Supreme Court, we emphasize again that we are here concerned only with a proceeding to determine whether a minor is a "delinquent" and which may result in commitment to a state institution. Specifically, the question is whether, in such a proceeding, an admission by the juvenile may be used against him in the absence of clear and unequivocal evidence that the admission was made with knowledge that he was not obliged to speak and would not be penalized for remaining silent. In light of Miranda v. Arizona, 384 U.S. 436 (1966), we must also consider whether, if the privilege against self-incrimination is available, it can effectively be waived unless counsel is present or the right to counsel has been waived.

It has long been recognized that the eliciting and use of confessions or admissions require careful scrutiny.

This Court has emphasized that admissions and confessions of juveniles require special caution.

The privilege against self-incrimination is, of course, related to the question of the safeguards necessary to assure that admissions or confessions are reasonably trustworthy, that they are not the mere fruits of fear or coercion, but are reliable expressions of the truth. The roots of the privilege are, however, far deeper. They tap the basic stream of religious and political principle because the privilege reflects the limits of the individual's attornment to the state and—in a philosophical sense—insists upon the equality of the individual and the state. In other words, the privilege has a broader and deeper thrust than the rule which prevents the use of confessions which are the product of coercion because coercion is thought to carry with it the danger of unreliability. One of its purposes is to prevent the state, whether by force or by psychological domination, from overcoming the mind and will of the person under investigation and depriving him of the freedom to decide whether to assist the state in securing his conviction.

It would indeed be surprising if the privilege against self-incrimination were available to hardened criminals but not to children. The language of the Fifth Amendment, applicable to the States by operation of the Fourteenth Amendment, is unequivocal and without exception.

It would be entirely unrealistic to carve out of the Fifth Amendment all statements by juveniles on the ground that these cannot lead to "criminal" involvement. In the first place juvenile proceedings to determine "delinquency," which may lead to commitment to a state institution, must be regarded as "criminal" for purposes of the privilege against self-incrimination. To hold otherwise would be to disregard substance because of the feeble enticement of the "civil" label-of-convenience which has been attached to juvenile proceedings. Indeed, in over half of the States, there is not even assurance that the juvenile will be kept in separate institutions, apart from adult "criminals." In those States juveniles may be placed in or transferred to adult penal institutions after having been found "delinquent" by a juvenile court. For this purpose, at least, commitment is a deprivation of liberty. It is incarceration against one's will, whether it is called "criminal" or "civil." And our Constitution guarantees that no person shall be "compelled" to be a witness against himself when he is threatened with deprivation of his liberty—a command which this Court has broadly applied and generously implemented in accordance with the teaching of the history of the privilege and its great office in mankind's battle for freedom.

It is also urged that the juvenile and presumably his parents should not be advised of the juvenile's right to silence because confession is good for the child as the commencement of the assumed therapy of the juvenile court process, and he should be encouraged to assume an attitude of trust and confidence toward the officials of the juvenile process. This proposition has been subjected to widespread challenge on the basis of current reappraisals of the rhetoric and realities of the handling of juvenile offenders.

In fact, evidence is accumulating that confessions by juveniles do not aid in "individualized treatment," as the court below put it, and that compelling the child to answer questions, without warning or advice as to his right to remain silent, does not serve this or any other good purpose. [I]t seems probable that where children are induced to confess by "paternal" urgings on the part of officials and the confession is then followed by disciplinary action, the child's reaction is likely to be hostile and adverse—the child may well feel that he has been led or tricked into confession and that despite his confession, he is being punished.

We conclude that the constitutional privilege against self-incrimination is applicable in the case of juveniles as it is with respect to adults. We appreciate that special problems may arise with respect to waiver of the privilege by or on behalf of children, and that there may well be some differences in technique—but not in principle—depending upon the age of the child and the presence and competence of parents. The participation of counsel will, of course, assist the police, Juvenile Courts and appellate tribunals in administering the privilege. If counsel was not present for some permissible reason when an admission was obtained, the greatest care must be taken to assure that the admission was voluntary, in the sense not only that it was not coerced or suggested, but also that it was not the product of ignorance of rights or of adolescent fantasy, fright or despair.

The "confession" of Gerald Gault was first obtained by Officer Flagg, out of the presence of Gerald's parents, without counsel and without advising him of his right to silence, as far as appears. The judgment of the Juvenile Court was stated by the judge to be based on Gerald's admissions in court. Neither "admission" was reduced to writing, and, to say the least, the process by which the "admissions" were obtained and received must be characterized as lacking the certainty and order which are required of proceedings of such formidable consequences. Apart from the "admissions," there was nothing upon which a judgment or finding might be based. There was no sworn testimony. Mrs. Cook, the complainant, was not present. The Arizona Supreme Court held that "sworn testimony must be required of all witnesses including police officers, probation officers and others who are part of or officially related to the juvenile court structure." We hold that this is not enough. No reason is suggested or appears for a different rule in respect of sworn testimony in juvenile courts than in adult tribunals. Absent a valid confession adequate to support the determination of the Juvenile Court, confrontation and sworn testimony by witnesses available for cross-examination were essential for a finding of "delinquency" and an order committing Gerald to a state institution for a maximum of six years.

The recommendations in the Children's Bureau's "Standards for Juvenile and Family Courts" are in general accord with our conclusions. They state that testimony should be under oath and that only competent, material and relevant evidence under rules applicable to civil cases should be admitted in evidence. The New York Family Court Act contains a similar provision.

VI.
Appellate Review and Transcript of Proceedings

Appellants urge that the Arizona statute is unconstitutional under the Due Process Clause because, as construed by its Supreme Court, "there is no right of appeal from a juvenile court order. . . ." The court held that there is no right to a transcript because there is no right to appeal and because the proceedings are confidential and any record must be destroyed after a prescribed period of time. Whether a transcript or other recording is made, it held, is a matter for the discretion of the juvenile court.

This Court has not held that a State is required by the Federal Constitution "to provide appellate courts or a right to appellate review at all." In view of the fact that we must reverse the Supreme Court of Arizona's affirmance of the dismissal of the writ of habeas corpus for other reasons, we need not rule on this question in the present case or upon the failure to provide a transcript or recording of the hearings—or, indeed, the failure of the Juvenile Judge to state the grounds for his conclusion. As the present case illustrates, the consequences of failure to provide an appeal, to record the proceedings, or to make findings or state the grounds for the juvenile court's conclusion may be to throw a burden upon the machinery for habeas corpus, to saddle the reviewing process with the burden of attempting to reconstruct a record, and to impose upon the Juvenile Judge the unseemly duty of testifying under cross-examination as to the events that transpired in the hearings before him.

For the reasons stated, the judgment of the Supreme Court of Arizona is reversed and the cause remanded for further proceedings not inconsistent with this opinion.

It is so ordered.

MR. JUSTICE HARLAN, concurring in part and dissenting in part. It can scarcely be doubted that it is within the State's competence to adopt measures reasonably calculated to meet more effectively the persistent problems of juvenile delinquency; as the opinion for the Court makes abundantly plain, these are among the most vexing and ominous of the concerns which now face communities throughout the country.

The proper issue here is, however, not whether the State may constitutionally treat juvenile offenders through a system of specialized courts, but whether the proceedings in Arizona's juvenile courts include procedural guarantees which satisfy the requirements of the Fourteenth Amendment.

[There are] three criteria by which the procedural requirements of due process should be measured here: first, no more restrictions should be imposed than are imperative to assure the proceedings' fundamental fairness; second, the restrictions which are imposed should be those which preserve, so far as possible, the essential elements of the State's purpose; and finally, restrictions should be chosen which will later permit the orderly selection of any additional protections which may ultimately prove necessary. In this way, the Court may guarantee the fundamental fairness of the proceeding, and yet permit the State to continue development of an effective response to the problems of juvenile crime.

Measured by these criteria, only three procedural requirements should, in my opinion, now be deemed required of state juvenile courts by the Due Process Clause of the Fourteenth Amendment: first, timely notice must be provided to parents and children of the nature and terms of any juvenile court proceeding in which a determination affecting their rights or interests may be made; second, unequivocal and timely notice must be given that counsel may appear in any such proceeding in behalf of the child and its parents, and that in cases in which the child may be confined in an institution, counsel may, in circumstances of indigency, be appointed for them; and third, the court must maintain a written record, or its equivalent, adequate to permit effective review on appeal or in collateral proceedings. These requirements would guarantee to juveniles the tools with which their rights could be fully vindicated, and yet permit the States to pursue without unnecessary hindrance the purposes which they believe imperative in this field. Further, their imposition now would later permit more intelligent assessment of the necessity under the Fourteenth Amendment of additional requirements, by creating suitable records from which the character and deficiencies of juvenile proceedings could be accurately judged. At the same time, these requirements should not cause any substantial modification in the character of juvenile court proceedings: counsel, although now present in only a small percentage of juvenile cases, have apparently already appeared without incident in virtually all juvenile courts; and the maintenance of a record should not appreciably alter the conduct of these proceedings.

The question remains whether certain additional requirements, among them the privilege against self-incrimination, confrontation, and cross-examination, must now, as the Court holds, also be imposed.

Initially, I must vouchsafe that I cannot determine with certainty the reasoning by which the Court concludes that these further requirements are now imperative. The Court begins from the premise, to which it gives force at several points, that juvenile courts need not satisfy "all of the requirements of a criminal trial." It therefore scarcely suffices to explain the selection of these particular procedural requirements for the Court to declare that juvenile court proceedings are essentially criminal, and thereupon to recall that these are requisites for a criminal trial.

The Court has, even under its own premises, asked the wrong questions: the problem here is to determine what forms of procedural protection are necessary to guarantee the fundamental fairness of juvenile proceedings, and not which of the procedures now employed in criminal trials should be transplanted intact to proceedings in these specialized courts.

[U]nlike notice, counsel, and a record, these requirements might radically alter the character of juvenile court proceedings. The evidence from which the Court reasons that they would not is inconclusive, and other available evidence suggests that they very likely would. At the least, it is plain that these additional requirements would contribute materially to the creation in these proceedings of the atmosphere of an ordinary criminal trial, and would, even if they do no more, thereby largely frustrate a central purpose of these specialized courts. Further, these are restrictions intended to conform to the demands of an intensely adversary system of criminal justice; the broad purposes which they represent might be served in juvenile courts with equal effectiveness by procedural devices more consistent with the premises of proceedings in those courts. As the Court apparently acknowledges, the hazards of self-accusation, for example, might be avoided in juvenile proceedings without the imposition of all the requirements and limitations which surround the privilege against self-incrimination. The guarantee of adequate notice, counsel, and a record would create conditions in which suitable alternative procedures could be devised; but, unfortunately, the Court's haste to impose restrictions taken intact from criminal procedure may well seriously hamper the development of such alternatives.

[Justice Black concurred, favoring an across-the-board incorporation of the criminal law protections in the Bill of Rights into the juvenile system where deprivation of liberty might occur.

Justice White concurred, agreeing with the majority, except on the self-incrimination issue, which he felt was not clearly presented because of lack of evidence as to whether Gault was compelled to be a witness against himself. Because there were other grounds for reversal, he felt this and the questions of confrontation and cross-examination should have been deferred.

Justice Stewart dissented.]

index